Grammatical Metaphor in Chinese

Grammatical Metaphor in Chinese

Yang Yanning

SHEFFIELD UK BRISTOL CT

Published by Equinox Publishing Ltd.

UK: Office 415, The Workstation, 15 Paternoster Row, Sheffield S1 2BX
USA: ISD, 70 Enterprise Drive, Bristol, CT 06010

www.equinoxpub.com

First published 2015

ISBN-13 978 1 78179 102 8 (hardback)

British Library Cataloguing-in-Publication Data

A catalogue record for this book is available from the British Library.

Library of Congress Cataloging-in-Publication Data

Yanning, Yang.
Grammatical metaphor in Chinese / Yang Yanning.
pages cm
Includes bibliographical references and index.
ISBN 978-1-78179-102-8 (hb)
1. Chinese language--Figures of speech. 2. Metaphor. 3. Chinese language--Spoken Chinese. 4. Chinese language--Terms and phrases. 5. Chinese language--Semantics. 6. Chinese language--Grammar, Comparative--English. 7. English language--Grammar, Comparative--Chinese. I. Title.
PL1279.Y367 2014
495.101'4--dc23
2014011970

Typeset by ISB Typesetting, Sheffield, UK

Printed and bound by Lightning Source Inc. (La Vergne, TN), Lighting Source UK Ltd. (Milton Keynes), Lightning Source AU Pty. (Scoresby, Victoria)

Contents

1 Introduction

1.1 The concept of grammatical metaphor and its usefulness

The relationship between meaning and wording has always been a central concern of language studies, although it is understood differently in various schools of linguistic thought. System Functional Linguistics (SFL), based on the work of M. A. K Halliday (1978, 1985), deals with this relationship by developing the concept of Grammatical Metaphor (GM). This book presents a systematic study of GM in Chinese from the perspectives of theoretical discussion, corpus analysis and typological interpretation. In this section, I provide a brief introduction to the concept of GM and explain the usefulness of GM research.

GM is a phenomenon arising from the stratification of the content plane in a language. In SFL tradition, a language is regarded as a complex semiotic system organized into various strata (Halliday and Matthiessen, 1999; 2004). The content plane of a language is stratified into two strata: semantics and lexicogrammar. The stratum of semantics is concerned with the transformation of the human experience of the world and interpersonal relationships into meanings. The stratum of lexicogrammar, which unifies the lexical and grammatical regions of language, is concerned with the further transformation of meanings into wordings. Halliday and Matthiessen (1999) claim that the semantic and lexicogrammatical strata in a language are related by the means of realization. In the development of human languages, this realizational relationship evolves first as the patterns in which semantic units are congruently mapped onto lexicogrammatical ones. For example, the semantic unit of sequence is congruently realized by the grammatical category of clause complex. The congruent patterns are not the only form of realization because the stratified content plane has the potential for a realignment of the mapping between semantic and lexicogrammatical units. For instance, the semantic unit of sequence can be realized grammatically as a clause or even a group instead of a clause complex. This realignment of the relationship between semantics and lexicogrammar, as defined by Halliday and Matthiessen (1999), is the phenomenon of GM.

The identification of GM within the framework of SFL is an important development in language research. The concept enhances the understanding of the nature of language, the semogenic processes of language and the relationship between language and context. As a phenomenon engendered by the interaction of semantics and lexicogrammar, GM contributes to the understanding of the nature of language at both semantic and lexicogrammatical levels. It extends the canonical sense of metaphor from lexical region to grammatical region at lexicogrammatical level. The term of metaphor is traditionally applied to the lexical transformation which can be described as 'variation in the use of words' (Halliday, 1985: 320). However, metaphor is also 'variation in the expression of meaning' (Halliday, 1985: 320) if it is described from the end of how a meaning is expressed. The variation in the expression of meaning thus involves both lexical and grammatical selections rather than simply the lexical transformation. That is, lexical metaphor and GM involves the same metaphorical principle although their transformed items differ in generality.

The notion of GM also demonstrates how the resource of lexicogrammar is expanded by the means of rewording. Apart from the congruent realization of a semantic unit, GM provides an additional resource in lexicogrammatical systems to express the same meaning. For this reason, GM is initially defined as 'an alternative lexicogrammatical realization of a semantic choice' (Ravelli, 1985: 55). GM is also a form of remeaning engendered by the semantic junction across ranks and categories, rather than a simple rewording which occurs at the level of lexicogrammar. Halliday and Matthiessen (1999) argue that GM opens up a new dimension of the semantic system in a language. In addition, there is a value-token relation between the metaphorical dimension opened up through GM and the congruent plane of meaning within the semantic system. In this sense, the concept of GM also increases our understanding of the nature of language at the semantic level.

Through the theoretical lens of GM, previous research within SFL (for example, Ravelli, 1985; Halliday, 1989; Martin, 1993) provides a better understanding of language from contextual and semogenic perspectives. It is observed that GM is interrelated with the three metafunctions of language, and thus with the register variables of mode, field and tenor. GM is a critical resource for managing Theme and information systems by which the textual metafunction of a text is realized. This managing power of GM gives rise to the variation of complexity in text which indicates the change of mode. In addition, GM is an important linguistic feature of writing for scientific and academic purposes because it has the power of reconstruing ideational meaning along the lines from sequence to figure and from figure to participant. Finally, the deployment of GM also changes the interpersonal meaning of a text and creates a language of power and technocratic control. As a phenomenon impacting on metafunctions and oriented to specific mode, field and tenor, GM has become a significant consideration with regards to the contextual analysis of language in use. GM is also a lexicogrammatical resource closely related to the three processes of semogenesis, namely, the evolution of human language (phylogenesis), the development of an individual speaker (ontogenesis), and the unfolding of a text (logogenesis). According to Halliday and Matthiessen (1999), the congruent and metaphorical expressions of a meaning are respectively the two poles of a continuum. To be more specific, the congruent expression evolves earlier in a language, emerges earlier in language development and comes earlier in a text. This connection between GM and the three axes of semohistory determines that GM is a useful tool in describing and comparing language use in temporal sense.

1.2 Research objectives

In the past three decades, many studies of GM have been carried out within the field of SFL (see Chapter 2 for detailed review). While these studies provide a wealth of information about different aspects of GM, the majority of them discuss GM with the focus on the most thoroughly investigated language of English. There has been very little research describing and analysing in depth the phenomenon of GM in other languages. As a phenomenon arising from the realignment of semantics and lexicogrammar, GM exists theoretically in all human languages. Any account of the characteristics of GM that aspires to a claim of universality should take the language other than English into consideration. Moreover, the cross-linguistic variations of semantic and lexicogrammatical systems determine that there are GM features which differ from language to language. The study of GM in the language other than English thus merits more attention because it provides a window into differences between languages.

The purpose of this book is to fill the gaps of previous GM studies by undertaking a comprehensive study of the phenomenon in Chinese and comparing GM in Chinese and English. The book first aims to show how the phenomenon of GM is identified, classified and deployed in Chinese. Given that all previous discussions of GM are linked to English, it is possible that the framework developed for GM description is not applicable to Chinese. I thus develop a theoretical framework for the identification and categorization of GM in Chinese. Based on the framework, the deployment of GM in Chinese is explored by analysing a corpus consisting of both written texts and spoken discourses. This book also aims to compare the identification, categorization and deployment of GM in Chinese and English.

If there are differences between the two languages in GM, it is necessary to understand the inherent reasons to which these differences can be attributed. I attempt to interpret the GM differences between Chinese and English from a typological perspective. In addition to the goals of investigating GM in Chinese and comparing GM in Chinese and English, one further goal of this book is to provide new insights into the theory of GM. Because of the substantial differences between Chinese and English in terms of language typology, using Chinese to address the GM questions is bound to increase our understanding of the universal features of GM in different languages. In sum, this book has three major objectives:

1. to explore how the phenomenon of GM is identified, classified and deployed in Chinese;
2. to show the differences between English and Chinese in GM and the inherent reasons for these differences:
3. to provide new insights into GM theory by analysing the phenomenon in a language other than English.

In order to achieve these objectives, the main issues of GM study must be sought to enable the detailed examination and characterization of GM in Chinese. These issues are outlined in this book through a critical review and a differentiation of the previous studies of GM. The relevant literature reviewed in Chapter 2 makes it clear that all the GM studies are generally concerned with four issues: (1) the exploration of the nature of GM; (2) the categorization of GM; (3) the semogenic research of GM; and (4) the contextual research of GM. The exploration of GM in Chinese in this book is thus undertaken by focusing on these issues. I first discuss the identification of GM in Chinese on the basis of the previous explorations of the nature of GM. I then provide a categorization of GM in Chinese by referring to the framework developed for classifying GM in English. The semogenic and contextual studies of GM in Chinese are combined under the topic of GM deployment in the language. Depending on the discussion of GM identification, categorization and deployment, I comparatively analyse the differences between Chinese and English in GM.

The identification of GM in Chinese has two purposes: (1) to define the phenomenon of GM within the semantic and lexicogrammatical system networks of Chinese,; and (2) to present the method of recognizing the phenomenon in Chinese. The need for identifying GM in the linguistic environment of Chinese arises from the distinction between general theory and particular description in language study. Halliday (1984) argues that GM is a universal feature present in all human languages. However, there is always the danger of imposing particular GM features in English on Chinese if the methods of GM identification developed for English are applied directly to the identification of GM in Chinese. In this case, the phenomenon of GM must be defined and explained within the systems of Chinese semantics and lexicogrammar. To achieve this purpose, this book presents the semantic and grammatical frameworks for the analysis of Chinese on the basis of Systemic Functional Grammar (SFG). The remapping relationship of semantic and lexicogrammar categories is examined to identify GM in Chinese. The detailed methods of recognizing GM instances in Chinese are described by distinguishing the congruent and metaphorical realizations of a semantic meaning in the language.

Several models of GM categorization have been developed in relation to the different features of the phenomenon (see Chapter 2 for details). This book classifies GM in Chinese into various categories on the basis of these models. However, using the GM categories in English as a guide for GM classification in Chinese gives rise to the possibility of adding GM categories only present in English to Chinese, or missing GM categories absent from English but inherent to Chinese. The GM categorization in Chinese is, therefore, conducted by examining the semantic shifts and grammatical movements really occurred in the remapping of meaning and wording. In other words, the models developed for categorizing GM in English are refined in the linguistic environment of Chinese.

In order to provide further insights into the features of GM in Chinese, this book conducts an empirical research on GM deployment by analysing a data set formed by written texts drawn from scientific textbooks and spoken discourses extracted from a large Chinese corpus. I first explore the distribution of different categories and subcategories of GM in Chinese, using the framework developed for the GM identification and categorization in this study. The analysis of GM deployment in 'real' texts enables the examination of interdependency between different categories of GM. The clusters of GM instances occurred in the texts are examined to define the GM 'syndromes' in Chinese. In addition, I investigate the impacts of contextual and developmental factors on the deployment of GM in Chinese. The correlation between GM deployment and the context of culture and situation is revealed by comparing the extent of GM use in texts drawn from different genres and registers. The effect of language development on GM deployment is detected by comparing the extent of GM use in texts representing different levels of writing.

This book finally compares the metaphorical expressions in Chinese and English. The comparison focuses on the identification, categorization and deployment of GM in the two languages provided that they are the central concerns of GM research. The detailed analysis is carried out in three aspects: (1) formal distance between congruent and metaphorical expressions; (2) subdivision of certain GM categories; and (3) the extent of using GM. Furthermore, this study interprets the GM differences between Chinese and English from the perspective of typology. In particular, the differences are explained by linking them to the typological variables of the order of grammatical constituents, the degree of grammatical specificity and the location of grammatical realizations.

GM is a phenomenon observed in both the ideational and the interpersonal dimensions of a language. In this book, the identification, categorization and deployment of GM covers both ideational GM and interpersonal GM to provide a comprehensive profile of GM in Chinese and set up a framework for further analysis of the interaction between two types of GM. The comparison of GM in English and Chinese, on the other hand, is restricted in this book to ideational GM due to the lack of previous research on interpersonal GM in English.

1.3 Research methodology

The methodology of this study has two characteristics: (1) the corpus-based investigation of GM; and (2) the combination of theoretical discussion and empirical research. If a linguistic phenomenon is prominently deployed in a variety of language, a specialized corpus can be used to explore the features of the phenomenon. Given the fact that ideational GM and interpersonal GM are mainly used in the registers of science and conversation (Halliday, 1998; Halliday and Matthiessen, 2004), I choose the scientific writing and casual conversation in Chinese as the specialized corpus for this study. In order to analyse the use of GM in Chinese, I employ a two-step method of data collection. First, the latest edition of scientific textbooks in Chinese is selected as the large corpus for the analysis of ideational GM. Second, a small corpus for the examination of GM deployment is collected from the textbooks in terms of genre distribution. Similarly, a large spoken corpus of 100 million Chinese characters is used for the purpose of analysing the use of interpersonal GM. The small corpus of spoken Chinese is formed by the discourses extracted from the large corpus with respect to register variables of Field and Tenor.

The large and the small corpora play different roles in this study. The large corpora are used not only as the language material from which the small corpora are drawn but as the source of examples to illustrate different categories of GM in Chinese. In other words, the description of different types of GM in Chinese is based on actual usage rather than invented examples. Throughout this book, the authentic examples of ideational GM from the large corpus indicate their provenance through a code in square brackets. The modified examples of GM are indicated with the words of 'modified' in square brackets. The scientific textbooks involved in this study are labelled in Table 1.1.

Level		*Secondary school*	*University*
Subject			
Physics	Volume 1	SP1	UP1
	Volume 2	SP2	UP2
Chemistry	Volume 1	SC1	UC1
	Volume 2	SC2	UC2

Table 1.1 Labels of scientific textbooks

The small corpus drawn from the textbooks, which is formed by 37 texts, is analysed to reveal the distribution of various types of ideational GM and examine the GM 'syndromes' in Chinese. The small corpus formed by conversation discourses extracted from the spoken Chinese corpus is mainly used for a qualitative analysis of interpersonal GM.

There have been many calls for studies of language phenomena that bring together theoretical explanation and corpus analysis (for example, Leech, 1991; Halliday and Matthiessen, 2004), and this is the approach taken in this book. The major concerns in this book are respectively treated with theoretical discussion and empirical research. The identification and categorization of GM in Chinese are conducted from a theoretical perspective, while the exploration of GM deployment in Chinese is based on an empirical study of 'real' texts. In addition, the comparison of GM in Chinese and English is achieved through a combination of theoretical and empirical approaches. I combine theoretical discussion with empirical research because they can mutually benefit from their interaction. The theoretical framework developed in this book allows for a quantitative analysis of the distribution of different types of GM. Likewise, the examples of GM drawn from the authentic texts can rectify flawed intuitions in the relevant theoretical discussion.

In this book, lexicogrammar functions in Chinese are capitalized in accordance with the conventions of SFG. On the contrary, semantic units in Chinese are spelt with lower case. For example, 'thing' refers to a semantic element, while 'Thing' indicates a grammatical function in the structure of a clause. The transcription system I use in this book for Chinese language is *pinyin*, the official romanization system of the People's Republic of China. The *pinyin* system is widely used in scholarly writings on Chinese in the West. Chinese characters are used only as an optional aid when there is any ambiguity in the *pinyin* system. It is worth noting that the Chinese syllables are represented with no tone although Chinese is a tone language. This is because GM is a phenomenon completely irrelevant to the pronunciation of Chinese words. In addition, the following abbreviations are used to represent some frequently used grammatical classes in Chinese clauses:

Asp.: Aspect markers (*le, zhe, guo*)
Partic.: Particles (e.g. *a/ya, ne, ma, ba*)
Meas.: Measurer for nouns (e.g. *ge, zhong*)
Sub.: Subordinating particle *de*

1.4 Outline of chapters

This book consists of nine chapters. Chapter 2 reviews previous studies of GM which provide a ready vocabulary for understanding the remapping of semantics and lexicogrammar in language. The review illustrates that the relevant literature can be divided into four parts, namely exploration of the nature of GM, categorization of GM, semogenic research of GM and contextual research of GM. This survey of literature creates a theoretical background for the study and, more importantly, clarifies the main issues to be explored in the following chapters.

Chapter 3 develops a framework for the functional analysis of Chinese in order to discuss how semantic meanings are realized by lexicogrammatical categories in Chinese. The framework is set up in the theoretical background provided by SFG and previous studies of Chinese. Given that the grammatical terms originally created for English analysis are used in the framework, all the descriptive categories involved are identified by examining their functions in the semantic system of Chinese. The framework consists of the systematic descriptions of Chinese clauses in experiential, interpersonal, and textual dimensions. The descriptions in these dimensions end up with realization statements for the Transitivity, Theme, Mood systems in Chinese. The framework also includes the descriptions of grammatical categories above and below clause in Chinese. The grammatical structures of clause complex and various types of group/phrase are examined for this purpose.

Chapter 4 discusses the identification of GM in Chinese on the basis of the grammatical framework developed in Chapter 3. It first defines the motifs of GM identification by reexamining the nature of the phenomenon. Transgrammatical semantic domains are then investigated to describe how semantic units and grammatical categories are remapped in Chinese. Following this, the chapter identifies the congruent and metaphorical realizations of semantic units in ideational and interpersonal domains in Chinese. In order to facilitate the identification of GM instances in Chinese, the chapter also introduces three linguistic phenomena which are critical for the construction of metaphorical expressions in the language.

Chapter 5 is dedicated to the categorization of ideational and interpersonal GM in Chinese. The metaphorical expressions within the ideational metafunction are categorized according to the 13 types of shift from one semantic element to another. Each category of ideational GM is further specified by describing the grammatical movements involved. Interpersonal GM in Chinese is classified respectively in terms of metaphor of mood and metaphor of modality. Metaphor of mood is divided by identifying the metaphorical realizations of various speech functions of command, statement and question. Metaphor of modality is differentiated by examining the metaphorical realizations of four types of modality, namely probability, usuality, obligation and inclination in Chinese.

Chapter 6 discusses the distribution and deployment of ideational GM in Chinese by analysing a corpus collected from scientific textbooks. Based on the categorization of GM in Chapter 5, this chapter explores how the various categories and subcategories of ideational GM and the GM syndromes in Chinese are distributed. The discussion in this chapter shows that the distribution of ideational GM instances in Chinese is not random, but rather it is motivated by the inherent features of the language. This chapter also investigates how the deployment of GM in Chinese is affected by the context of genre and language development.

Chapter 7 is concerned with the use of interpersonal GM in spoken Chinese. It reveals the distribution of differet types of interpersonal GM through an analysis of a large spoken Chinese corpus. This chapter establishes a framework for the description of social factors involved in the creation of spoken Chinese discourses by making reference to register theory in SFL. Based on the framework, the chapter investigates the way Chinese speakers choose different types of interpersonal GM in their conversations with respect to the topic of a discourse and the social relations between speakers and hearers.

Chapter 8 provides a comparison of ideational GM in Chinese and English and explains the GM differences concerned from the perspective of typology. This chapter first describes the typological variation between Chinese and English in terms of three variables most relevant to the lexicogrammatical realization of semantic meaning. The metaphorical expressions in the two languages are then compared to show how they differ in terms of GM structure, GM categorization and GM deployment. The differences defined are explained by attributing to the distinctions between Chinese and English in the typological variables involved.

Chapter 9 summarizes the conclusions reached in this book and gives a theoretical discussion about the application of the findings of this study.

2 Research background

2.1 Introduction

The purpose of this chapter is to provide a research background for the discussion in following chapters by reviewing the major literature on the study of GM. Moreover, the chapter aims to collect together often fragmented pieces of evidence to reconstruct a coherent view of GM. To achieve these purposes, I discuss the previous GM studies by differentiating them into four areas, namely, the exploration of the nature of GM, the categorization of GM, the semogenic research of GM and the contextual research of GM. The GM studies involved in each area are arranged chronologically in the detailed dissussion.

Corresponding to the four areas of GM studies, the main content of this chapter is organized into four sections. Section 2.2 reviews the explorations of the nature of GM which fall into three phrases in terms of the motif of GM identification. Section 2.3 describes how ideational GM and interpersonal GM are categorized from different perspectives. Section 2.4 examines the studies of the relationship between GM and three kinds of semogenesis. Section 2.5 summarizes how the use of GM is concerned with metafunctions, register variables and broader contexts of culture and society.

2.2 Exploring the nature of GM

As a relatively new concept within the theoretical framework of SFL, GM has always been discussed in previous research with a special attention to its nature. I examine all the explorations of the nature of GM and divide them into three phases from a historical perspective. GM is interpreted in the three phases of explorations respectively as the counterpart of lexical metaphor, the stratal realignment between semantics and lexicogrammar and the consequence of transgrammatical semantic domains. It is worth noting that the explorations of the nature of GM are divided into three phases for explanatory purposes. The following review shows that the discussions of the nature of GM at later stages in fact follow the main ideas of preceding studies.

2.2.1 Phase I: Interpretation of GM as the counterpart of lexical metaphor

The nature of GM is initially explored in the work of Halliday (1984a, 1985a, 1994) and Ravelli (1985) which provides a foundation for further study of the phenomenon. The notion of GM is first proposed by Halliday (1984a) in a short paper to name a phenomenon related to metaphor in the normal sense. It is claimed that the phenomenon is a kind of metaphor which is grammatical rather than lexical. In addition, this metaphor in grammatical sense can be recognized by a competent speaker of a language and compared with its non-metaphorical agnate. In other words, Halliday (1984a) makes an attempt to extend the boundary of metaphor, which is usually understood as a lexical phenomenon, to the grammatical field. While this introduction to the concept of GM is insufficient as an explanation of the nature of GM, it provides a starting point for further discussion of GM. It is also worth noting that Halliday (1984a) makes an assumption in this paper that GM is a phenomenon arising in every language.

The relationship between lexical metaphor and GM is further explored by Halliday (1985a) in the last chapter of *An Introduction to Functional Grammar*. In order to create a theoretical background for integrating lexical metaphor and GM, Halliday (1985a) interprets metaphor, metonymy and synecdoche from a grammatical perspective. The interpretation shows that these three types of rhetorical transference are based on three semantic relationships of elaboration, extension and enhancement. From this perspective, metaphor in a traditional sense can be understood as a lexical variation which realizes particular meaning. This change of perspective also indicates that lexical metaphor is just part of the general lexicogrammatical realization of meaning. In other words, 'there is also such a thing as grammatical metaphor, where the variation is essentially in the grammatical forms' (Halliday, 1985a: 320).

Halliday (1994) demonstrates the relationship between lexical metaphor and GM more explicitly in terms of the 'from above' and 'from below' perspectives in SFL. According to Halliday (1994: 342), lexical metaphor is viewed as 'variation in the meaning of a given expression'. This view is in effect the 'from below' perspective in SFL, which focuses on the form of a particular expression. On the other hand, metaphor can be viewed 'from above', as 'variation in the expression of a given meaning' (Halliday, 1994: 342). The explanation of metaphor from this angle takes meaning as the starting point in comparing different expressions. The two perspectives are contrasted in the following figure reprinted from the study of Halliday (1994).

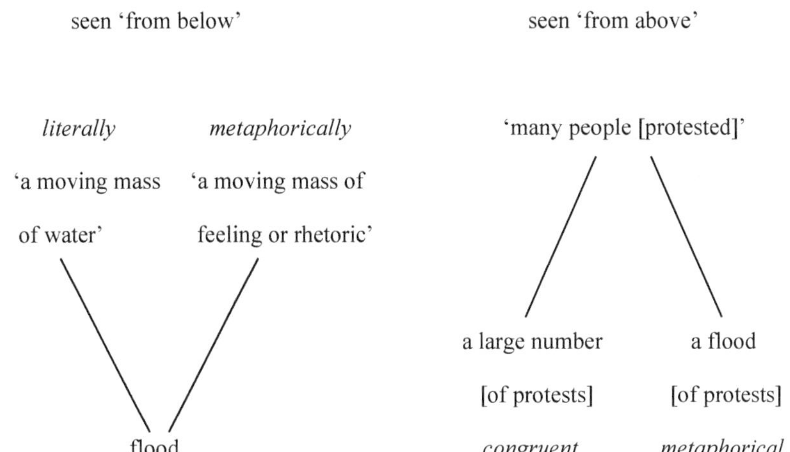

Figure 2.1: Two perspectives on metaphor (Halliday, 1994: 342)

Figure 2.1 shows that the critical motif in the earlier explorations of the nature of GM is the integration of metaphor in the lexical and grammatical poles of the lexicogrammatical continuum. Figure 2.1 also shows that Halliday (1994) uses 'congruent' instead of 'literal' to refer to the less metaphorical expression in grammatical metaphor. This is because the traditional concepts of 'literal' and 'metaphorical' are not appropriate for different expressions of a given meaning. This distinction of 'congruent' and 'metaphorical' realizations of a given semantic configuration is another focus in the first phase of explorations of the nature of GM.

The ideas of 'congruence' and 'metaphor' are initially used together to discuss varieties of language which are engendered in different social contexts. Halliday (2003/1956: 218) first refers to 'a grammatical structure which reflects a contextual structure (by matching it with maximum probability)' as 'congruent'. It is emphasized that this description of grammatical form does not have a universal sense and is valid with reference to particular formal criteria. Halliday (1978) also claims that the text expressed through the most typical form of representation is 'congruent'. The antilanguage engendered in antisociety, which is set up within another society as a form of resistance, is considered as a 'metaphor' of standard language. In sum, the initial distinction of 'congruent' and 'metaphorical' expressions is motivated by the theme of studying language in certain social contexts.

In the explorations of the nature of GM, the concepts of 'congruence' and 'metaphor' are employed to differentiate different realizations of a given semantic configuration. Halliday (1985a) argues that there is a typical way of saying things in the process of getting from meaning to wording. The lexicogrammatical realization arising from this typical way is the 'congruent' mode of representation. On the other hand, the realization developed along the way other than this typical way of saying things is recognized as a 'metaphorical' expression. Halliday (1985a) discusses the typical way of realizing meaning in relation to the 'unmarked' form of expression in the first edition of *An Introduction to Functional Grammar*. In the second edition of the book, Halliday (1994) takes the 'typical' way of saying things as the sole criterion of recognizing 'congruent' realizations. This change of criteria is determined by the fact that some instances of GM are in effect the 'unmarked' form of expression. For example, the expressions like 'do a dance' and 'make a mistake' are incongruent because the meaning of process in these expressions is coded as a nominal group. These metaphorical expressions, however, have become the 'unmarked' form of encoding for this type of process. As Ravelli (2003: 41) writes, 'it is possible for a metaphorical choice to be the unmarked one – in a particular register, for instance'.

It is worth noting that the 'congruent' and 'metaphorical' realizations are not totally synonymous (Halliday, 1985a; 1994). According to Halliday (1994: 342), 'the selection of metaphor is itself a meaningful choice, and the particular metaphor selected adds further semantic features'. This understanding of GM is demonstrated more explicitly in one of the two models of GM established by Ravelli (1985). On the basis of the understanding that 'congruent' and 'metaphorical' realizations are potentially co-representional, Ravelli (1985: 55) puts forward a model of GM in which GM is interpreted as 'an alternative lexicogrammatical realization of a semantic choice'. Ravelli (1985) also establishes an alternative model of GM interpretation to reflect the view that GM is the result of a compound semantic choice. These two models are illustrated in Figure 2.2, taken from Ravelli's (1985) thesis.

Figure 2.2 shows that the 'congruent' and 'metaphorical' realizations in Model A are semantically equivalent. According to Ravelli (1985: 103), this interpretation 'arises from the current understanding of GM, close to that of its rhetorical counterpart of lexical metaphor'. In contrast, GM in Model B is considered as a combination of semantic features. The meaning to be realized by GM is the result of compounding two semantic choices, while the congruent form is the realization of a simple semantic choice (Ravelli, 1985). These two models clearly reflect the different understandings of the nature of GM in the early studies of GM.

Ravelli (1985) claims that Model B is theoretically more adequate than Model A for the explanation of GM in the networks of SFL. In particular, 'grammatical metaphor may be easily described in a semantic network as two (or more) simple meaning choices forming a combined entry condition

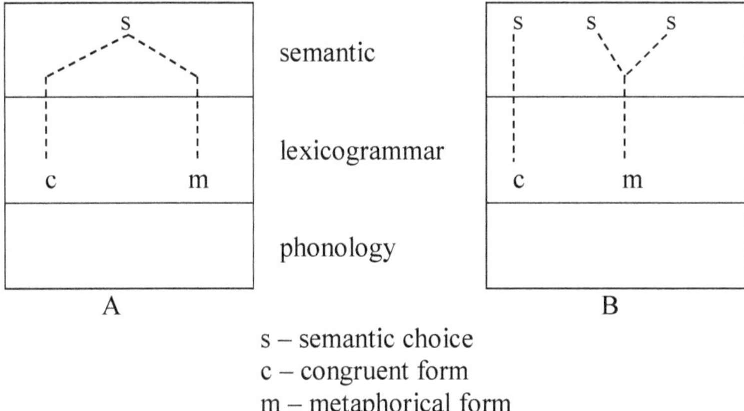

Figure 2.2: GM interpreted as realization choice and semantic compound (Ravelli, 1985: 104)

for another, which is then defined as metaphorical' (Ravelli, 1985: 105). Despite this theoretical advantage of Model B, Ravelli (1985) adopts Model A in the practical analysis of GM. This choice is mainly determined by the fact that the semantic system networks in SFL were not developed at this stage of GM study. Additionally, the adoption of Model A does not 'jeopardize the quantification of metaphor, or the established relations between metaphor, mode and complexity' (Ravelli, 1985: 106).

The earlier GM research also makes an attempt to locate GM in the system networks of semantics and lexicogrammar though the phenomenon is introduced as the complementation of lexical metaphor. As shown in Ravelli's (1985) modelling of GM, the phenomenon can be represented within the system networks from two perspectives. On the one hand, a metaphorical realization is treated as the choice at lexicogrammatical stratum. Ravelli (1985) claims that this method of locating GM is limited by two problems: (1) Various categories of GM are described as different phenomena; (2) recursion of GM cannot be explained in the network. On the other hand, the distinction of congruent and metaphorical realizations is accounted for in semantic system. The disadvantage of this method is that it does not allow for making meaningful distinctions at the level of lexicogrammar (Ravelli, 1985). These two methods, as Taverniers (2003: 29) summarizes, reflect the contrast between the two thinking lines of 'same meaning, different forms' and 'semantic variation as well as lexicogrammatical variation' in the early studies of GM.

The initial studies of Halliday (1985a, 1994) and Ravelli (1985) are fundamental to the further explorations of the nature of GM. However, their studies leave a number of issues to be clarified, for example, the position of GM in the system networks of semantics and lexicogrammar and the inherent reason for the emergence of GM. These issues mainly arise from the 'intuitive' explanation of GM and the premature stage of description of semantic systems in SFL. In the second-phase research of the nature of GM, these issues are explored by discussing them in a theoretical framework which is more systematic and powerful.

2.2.2 Phase II: Interpretation of GM as stratal realignment

The strata realignment between the semantic and lexicogrammatical levels of content plane in a language is the key motif in the second-phase studies of the nature of GM (Halliday, 1998; Halliday and Matthiessen, 1999). The relationship between different levels of language is noticed as early as in Halliday's (1978) study of antilanguage. It is pointed out that the variations from the standard language are observed at every level in an antilanguage. Each of these variations is interpreted by Halliday (1978: 173) as 'an alternative realization of an element on the next, or on some higher stratum'. In other words, there is the possibility that an element on a higher stratum has different realizations on a lower stratum. Interestingly, Halliday (1978) calls all these variations 'metaphorical variations' to show that an antilanguage is a metaphor for an everyday language. In this case, the term 'grammatical metaphor' is used to represent the variations occurring at the level of grammar. Although the connotation of the term 'grammatical metaphor' here is different from that of GM, this preliminary understanding of stratal tension provides a clue for further studies.

The first-phase research of the nature of GM throws some light on the relationship between GM and the stratal relationship between semantics and lexicogrammar. For example, Ravelli's (1985) models reveal that GM is linked to the realization relationship between semantics and lexicogrammar. Halliday (1998) discusses this relationship at greater length in a study of how human experience is construed by the language of science. As mentioned in Chapter 1, a language is understood within SFL as a semiotic system having various strata. Halliday (1998) explains the emergence of GM with reference to this feature of stratification in a language. It is pointed out that a language creates meaning with a relation of realization between the strata of semantics and lexicogrammar. In the ideational dimension, lexicogrammar construes experience into meaning in the pattern shown in Figure 2.3, as represented by Halliday (1998).

This pattern, however, is not always followed in construing experience into meaning. Frequently, the relations between semantic and lexicogrammatical units are different from those illustrated above. This is because

	Semantic		Lexicogrammatical
Ranks	sequence	realized by	clause complex
	figure	"	clause
	element	"	roup/phrase
Types of	Process	realized by	verbal group
Element	participant	"	nominal group
	circumstance	"	adverbial group/prepositional phrase
	relator	"	conjunction

Figure 2.3: Congruent realization pattern of semantic units

'the grammar has the power of construing, by the same token (that is, by virtue of being stratified), it can also deconstrue, and reconstrue along different lines' (Halliday, 1998: 190). When this reconstrual occurs, as claimed by Halliday (1998), the representation of experience is retransformed and undergoes a process of metaphor. The metaphor here is discussed in a grammatical sense since it is grammatical categories which vary in the process of transformation. In this case, the reconstrual of experience into new meaning gives rise to the phenomenon of GM. Halliday's (1998) study indicates that the phenomenon of GM is made possible by the stratified structure of human languages. To be more specific, 'there could be no metaphor without stratification – and once the content plane has become stratified, such transformation automatically becomes possible' (Halliday, 1998: 192). GM is thus defined by Halliday (1998: 192) as 'a realignment between a pair of strata: a remapping of the semantics on to the lexicogrammar'.

Halliday and Matthiessen (1999) explore the nature of GM in more depth by locating it in a broader theoretical environment of the meaning base in languages. In order to interpret experience not as knowledge but as meaning, Halliday and Matthiessen (1999) develop an ideational semantic system on the basis of SFL. They claim that one essential task of developing this semantic system is to model GM which is a particular phenomenon of the content plane in a language. According to Halliday and Matthiessen (1999), the emergence of GM is related to the natural development of the content plane in a language. Initially, the content plane is formed by semantics and lexicogrammar coupling in a congruent pattern. The content system of language evolves by extending the congruent pattern between semantic and lexicogrammatical strata. This dissociation of the congruent pattern between two levels of the content plane opens up the possibility of metaphorical expression. Therefore, Halliday and Matthiessen (1999: 7) define GM as 'the phenomenon whereby a set of agnate forms is present in the language having different mappings between the semantic and the grammatical categories'.

The explanation of GM as the realignment between semantics and lexicogrammar is a significant shift of motif in the explorations of the nature of GM. Compared with the 'intuitive' explanation of GM as the counterpart of lexical metaphor, the interpretation of GM in Halliday (1998) and Halliday and Matthiessen (1999) is more powerful because it depends on a systematic account of semantic networks in languages. Halliday and Matthiessen's (1999) semantic framework is, therefore, a crucial contribution to the understanding of the nature of GM. By using their semantic system and the lexicogrammatical system developed earlier in SFL, it is possible to analyse in detail the problems unsolved in the first-phase research of the nature of GM.

As mentioned, Ravelli's (1985) Model B in Figure 2.2 is more powerful in the understanding of GM because the model treats GM as the result of the compounding of semantic choice. However, the semantic compounding is not explored in detail for the lack of an explicit description of the semantic system. Halliday (1998: 227) discusses this feature of GM by introducing the concept of 'semantic junction' which is a phenomenon occurring across categories and ranks. In terms of category, the metaphorical expressions of *shakiness* and *development* do not lose their original meaning of quality and process although they are treated as if they are things. According to Halliday and Matthiessen (1999: 243), 'they are just a fusion or "junction", of two semantic elemental categories: *shakiness* is a "quality thing", *development* is a "process thing"'. Semantic junction also occurs in the sense of rank: *engine failure* 'is both a figure consisting of participant ("engine") and process ("fail") and an element (participant) consisting of thing ("failure") + classifier ("engine")' (Halliday and Matthiessen, 1999: 286). The discussion of semantic junction shows that GM 'is not just a variation form, identical in meaning with its congruent agnate – it also incorporates semantic features from the categories that its own form would congruently construe' (Halliday and Matthiessen, 1999: 286). In the light of semantic junction, it is possible to describe how two semantic choices are compounded to form an entry point for a metaphorical realization.

This shift of motif also enables the incorporation of GM in the semantic and lexicogrammatical system networks in SFL. This purpose is achieved by construing GM as a new dimension of the semantic system which elaborates the whole system in terms of a token-value relation. Halliday and Matthiessen (1999) argue that there is an elaborating relationship between metaphorical and congruent meanings. Particularly, the metaphorical meaning is the token and the congruent meaning is the value in the relation of identity. It is noted that this token-value type of relation is intra-stratal:

'the identity holds between different meanings, not between meanings and wordings' (Halliday and Matthiessen, 1999: 288). On the basis of this relationship between metaphorical and congruent meanings, Halliday and Matthiessen (1999) set up a semantic model in which GM is recognized as a dimension internal to the semantic system. This model is shown in Figure 2.4 reprinted from the study of Halliday and Matthiessen (1999).

Halliday and Matthiessen's (1999) model clearly illustrates the mapping between different domains of ideational meaning. The semantic domain of sequence may be construed as the domain of figure which is in turn mapped on the domain of participant. In this model, as indicated by Halliday and Matthiessen (1999: 294), 'each plane also has the same realizational potential in the lexicogrammar'. Thus, the realization domain in lexicogrammar is that of the metaphorical meaning. For example, if a sequence is construed metaphorically as a figure, the realization domain is clause rather than clause complex. This explanation in effect clarifies the issue of determining the rank at which GM is an option of lexicogrammar.

Apart from the more powerful explanation of the nature of GM, the explorations of the nature of GM in the second phase also provide new insights into the important concepts related to GM. First, the 'congruent' realization

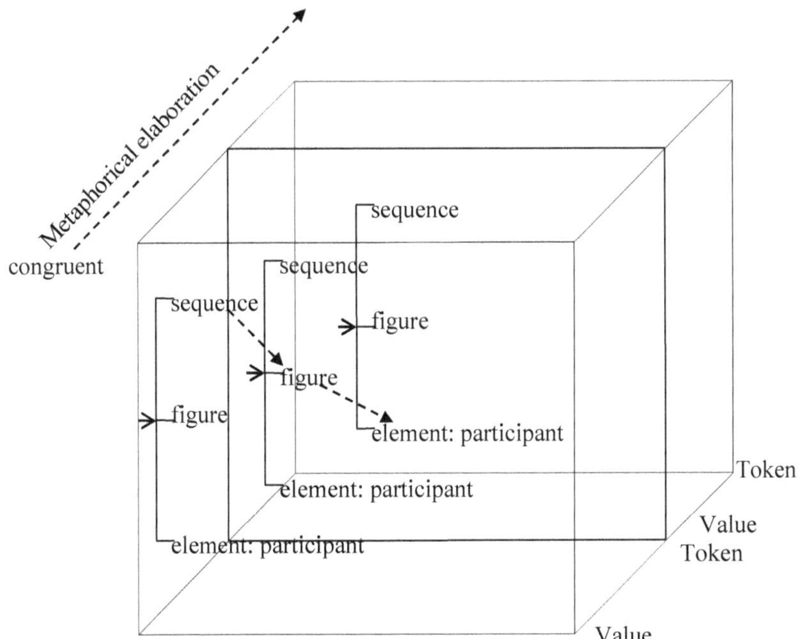

Figure 2.4: Metaphorical elaboration of the semantic system (Halliday and Matthiessen, 1999: 294)

is defined more explicitly adhering to the principle of stratal realignment. In the first phase of GM studies, 'congruent' realization is linked to the typical mode of expression which 'is selected in the absence of any good reason for selecting another one' (Halliday, 1984b: 14). The explanation of GM in terms of stratal realignment regards the 'congruent' as 'the pattern of relationships between the semantics and the grammar in which the two strata initially co-evolved' (Halliday, 1998: 208). The congruent mode of expressions is described more explicitly by pointing out its semogenic priority. That is, 'it evolved earlier in the language (phylogenesis); it is learnt earlier by children (ontogenesis); and it typically comes earlier in the text (logogenesis)' (Halliday and Matthiessen, 1999: 235). It is noted that all the agnate expressions form a continuum whose two ends are metaphorical and congruent. In this sense, an expression is only congruent by reference to the other more metaphorical wordings. The relationship between 'congruent' realization and language evolution is revisited in section 2.4.

Second, the integration of lexical metaphor and GM is interpreted more clearly with reference to the stratal organization of a language. Halliday (1998) points out that metaphor is canonically regarded as a transformation within the semiotic mode. This traditional sense of metaphor, however, is limited to the lexical end of the lexicogrammatical continuum. Halliday (1998) argues that the transformation also occurs in the domain of grammar. Thus, lexical metaphor and GM are similar in terms of metaphoric principle; they just differ in the sense of generality (Halliday and Matthiessen, 1999). In addition, Halliday (1998) theorizes lexical metaphor and GM respectively as 'same signifier, different signified' and 'same signified, different signifier'.

The final point to be emphasized in the second-phase studies of the nature of GM is the concept of 'fractal pattern', which is considered by Halliday and Matthiessen (1999) as part of the key to represent GM in semantic system networks. They believe that the establishment of token-value relation between metaphorical and congruent meanings lies in the fact that the token and value domains are similar enough. The principle behind this similarity is the fractal types of projection/expansion which penetrate throughout different semantic ranks. Halliday and Matthiessen (1999) state that the extending sequence 'he added and smiled' and the figure 'he added with smile' with an extending meaning are metaphorically agnate in the fractal pattern of extension. In other words, the domain of extension remains constant in the sequence and the figure. As Halliday and Matthiessen (1999: 294) suggested, 'the whole metaphorical elaboration is made possible by a fractal pattern that runs through the whole system'. This concept of 'fractal pattern' is redefined as transgrammatical semantic domains in the third phase of the research on the nature of GM.

2.2.3 Phase III: Approaching GM from transgrammatical semantic domains

The most recent exploration of the nature of GM is carried out in Chapter 10 of the third edition of *An Introduction to Functional Grammar* (Halliday and Matthiessen, 2004). The exploration is characterized by its investigation of the nature of GM with reference to 'transgrammatical semantic domains'. The phenomenon, as reviewed in the previous section, is briefly discussed as fractal patterns of meaning in the second-phase studies of the nature of GM. Halliday and Matthiessen (2004) provide a detailed description of the phenomenon to reveal how it is related to GM in the most recent exploration of the nature of GM. Based on the discussion of transgrammatical semantic domains, Halliday and Matthiessen (2004) highlight the two motifs of GM: (1) the remapping of semantics and lexicogrammar; and (2) the expansion of meaning potential. They follow previous GM studies by taking stratal remapping as the criteria for identifying metaphorical expressions. Additionally, it is emphasized that metaphorical modes of meaning are motivated by the need to expand meaning potential.

Halliday and Matthiessen (2004) first provide a model of the congruent mode of realizational relationship between semantics and lexicogrammar. This model is more comprehensive than the models developed in previous GM studies since it describes the realization patterns within each metafunction. Moreover, the intermediate semantic units between text and the region realized by the grammatical unit of clause are defined in Halliday and Matthiessen's (2004) model. This model is illustrated in Table 2.1 which is taken from Halliday and Matthiessen's (2004) study.

Halliday and Matthiessen (2004) view transgrammatical semantic domains and metaphor as two phenomena which enrich the fundamental principle of relationship between semantics and lexicogrammar. They suggest that the mapping of one semantic unit onto one grammatical unit is the foundation on which the relationship between semantics and lexicogrammar is based. In addition to the one-to-one correspondence of semantic and grammatical units, 'there are semantic domains that range over more than a single grammatical unit' (Halliday and Matthiessen, 2004: 592). It is noted that those grammatical units which realize the same semantic domain are semantically agnate, although they are not synonymous.

Halliday and Matthiessen (2004) recognize two fundamental domains spanning more than one grammatical unit: expansion and projection. They also describe in detail how these two semantic domains are manifested in different grammatical domains on the basis of the overall framework of SFL. First, they present a summary of the different grammatical environments in

	Logical	Experiential	Interpersonal	Textual
Semantics	Text			
	(Episodic patterns)		(Exchange patterns)	(Information flow patterns)
	Sequence ↘	Figure ↘	Proposition or proposal ↘	Message ↘
Lexicogrammar	Complex of ...	Clause		
	Taxis and Logico-Semantic type	Transitivity	Mood	Theme; Information
	Complex of ...	Group or phrase		

Table 2.1: Some semantic and lexicogrammatical units (Halliday and Matthiessen, 2004: 592)

which three types of expansion, namely elaboration, extension and enhancement are manifested. It is observed that the meaning of expansion is realized across metafunctions and grammatical ranks. Particularly, expansion is manifested by textual (Conjunction), logical (Interdependency; Modification) and experiential (Circumstantiation; Process type: relational) metafunctions. In addition, the manifestation occurs at the ranks of clause and group/phrase (see Halliday and Matthiessen, 2004: 598–600 for detailed description). Halliday and Matthiessen (2004) also notice that the grammatical manifestations are in effect different in meaning although they are semantically agnate patterns. This difference can be illustrated by examining their meanings in terms of ideational, interpersonal and textual metafunctions.

The semantic domain of projection is also manifested within different metafunctions, namely, the logical, the experiential and the interpersonal. Projection is distinguished from expansion in that it is manifested interpersonally rather than textually. Particularly, conjunctions are limited to the realization of expansion while interpersonal Adjuncts are only used for the purpose of manifesting projection (Halliday and Matthiessen, 2004). The difference between the manifestations of expansion and projection is illustrated in Table 2.2.

Table 2.2 shows that the manifestations of projection range over different grammatical domains. Logically, projection is realized by a clause nexus which reports facts or quotes ideas. The experiential realization of projection is concerned with mental and verbal clauses. Furthermore, projection is manifested interpersonally as modal assessment. According to Halliday and

		Expansion	Projection
Textual	Conjunction	Types of conjunction	–
Logical	Interdependency	Expansion nexuses	Projection nexuses (quoting and reporting)
Experiential	Process type	Relational	Mental/verbal
	Circumstance	Role, accompaniment, location, extent, cause, etc.	Angle, matter
Interpersonal	Modal assessment		Modality, polarity; comment

Table 2.2: Manifestation of expansion and projection at clause rank (Halliday and Matthiessen, 2004: 604).

Matthiessen (2004), the manifestations of projection are not synonymous. The logical manifestation is explicitly subjective in terms of orientation of assessment, while the experiential manifestation is explicitly objective. The interpersonal manifestation, in contrast, represents the orientation implicitly.

Modal assessment is taken as the main focus in Halliday and Matthiessen's (2004) investigation of projection. This is because 'there is thus a fundamental relationship between modal assessment, including modality, and projection' (Halliday and Matthiessen, 2004: 626). Modal assessment as a semantic domain disperses across different grammatical environments. In order to provide a full picture of modal assessment concerned with projection and appraisal, Halliday and Matthiessen (2004) tabulate all types of modal assessment (for detailed description see Halliday and Matthiessen, 2004: 608 - 612). Following this, Halliday and Matthiessen (2004) use modality, one type of modal assessment, as the way into GM in the interpersonal zone.

It is noted that a projecting clause is frequently used to express the modality which is congruently realized by a modal Adjunct. In this case, 'there has been a realignment in the realizational relationship between semantics and grammar' (Halliday and Matthiessen, 2004: 614). That is, a modalized figure congruently corresponding to the grammatical form of clause is realized by a clause nexus of projection. In this clause nexus, the modality and modalized propositions are separately realized by the projecting clause and the projected clause. In other words, the projecting clause is the metaphorical realization of the meaning of modality. This metaphor of modality is obviously based on the semantic relationship of projection.

The semantic domain of modality has many means of expression because it is in nature a very complicated system. In more detail, the realization of modality is determined by the systems of orientation, value and negation. Taking all these variables into consideration, Halliday and Matthiessen (2004) identify as many as 144 possible realizations of modality. They refer to the systems of orientation in order to recognize which choice in these realizations is a metaphorical representation of a modality. It is claimed that 'the explicit subjective and explicit objective forms of modality are all strictly speaking metaphorical, since all of them represent the modality as being the substantive proposition' (Halliday and Matthiessen, 2004: 624).

Speech function, like modality, can be represented as a substantive proposition which projects the original proposal or proposition (Halliday and Matthiessen, 2004). This realization of speech function in the form of a mental or verbal clause is regarded as one type of metaphor of mood by Halliday and Matthiessen (2004). They propose that there are two consequences for the expansion of meaning potential of speech function in the form of projecting clause nexus. First, it adds the option of making the subjective orientation of the speech functional selection explicit to the system. Second, it further elaborates the speech functional system in delicacy by using the lexicogrammatical resources of verbal and mental clauses. The shift between different moods for the purpose of realizing speech function is another form of metaphor of mood. The detailed classification of these metaphors of mood is discussed further in section 2.3. The preceding discussion shows that there are two subtypes of interpersonal GM, namely metaphor of modality and metaphor of mood.

Halliday and Matthiessen (2004) follow previous GM studies (Halliday, 1998; Halliday and Matthiessen, 1999) in discussing ideational GM. That is, ideational GM arises from the remapping between the semantic units of sequence, figure and element and the grammatical units of clause nexus, clause and group. However, it is indicated that the remapping is possible because semantic motifs such as expansion can be manifested repeatedly in the different environments of grammar (Halliday and Matthiessen, 2004). In other words, ideational GM is based on the existence of transgrammatical semantic domains.

Compared to previous GM studies, Halliday and Matthiessen (2004) approach GM from a different angle. That is, the exploration of the nature of GM is based on the analysis of transgrammatical semantic domains. The recognition of transgrammatical semantic domains enriches the descriptive framework of the interaction between semantics and lexicogrammar in a language. This enriched framework in turn makes the concept of GM more theoretically grounded. Furthermore, the understanding of interpersonal GM is improved by approaching the GM from the perspective of transgrammatical semantic domains. Ideational GM is well documented and discussed in the first two phases of studies of the nature of GM, while interpersonal GM is less explored. Halliday and Matthiessen (2004) first identify the metaphorical expressions in the interpersonal zone by examining how the semantic domain of projection is realized transgrammatically. Following this, they identify ideational GM through the same method of examining transgrammatical semantic domains. Ideational GM and interpersonal GM are thus successfully integrated by developing a universal criterion for GM identification.

Halliday and Matthiessen (2004) also reveal that GM gives rise to the expansion of meaning potential. More importantly, 'it is the pressure to expand the meaning potential that in fact lies behind the development of metaphorical modes of meaning' (Halliday and Matthiessen, 2004: 626). This interpretation of the inherent motivation of GM is a crucial contribution of the third-phase research of the nature of GM. It is found that ideational GM and interpersonal GM show different tendencies with respect to forming grammatical realizations to expand meaning potential. Ideational GM intends to downgrade the grammatical realization of certain semantic units, such as the realization of sequence in the form of clause. Interpersonal GM has the tendency of upgrading the grammatical domain of a metaphorical realization. For example, the meaning of modality is realized by a clause instead of a modal adjunct.

2.3 Categorization of GM

There are two basic types of GM occurring respectively within ideational and interpersonal metafunctions. Ideational GM and interpersonal GM are further classified into subcategories for the purpose of investigating the detailed properties of GM instances. This section reviews the major literature on GM categorization, comparing different approaches to the classification.

2.3.1 Ideational GM

The metaphorical expression in ideational zone involves two kinds of grammatical movement: 'one in rank, the other in structural configuration' (Halliday, 1998: 192). The first movement is 'down' in rank: sequences are alternatively realized by clauses and groups, figures are realized by groups. The second is 'across' in function: an individual element is reconstrued by the other types of element. In keeping with these grammatical movements, ideational GM has been classified from two perspectives. First, they are classified on the basis of the downranking grammatical movement. There are three groups of ideational GM which metaphorically realize the meaning of sequence, figure and element (Halliday and Matthiessen, 2004). Second, ideational GM is classified in terms of the metaphorical shifts from one semantic element to another. The categorization from this perspective is represented by two models respectively proposed by Ravelli (1985) and Halliday (1998). I first review the models of categorizing ideational GM from the perspective of semantic shift because they are developed earlier.

2.3.1.1 Categorization from the perspective of elemental shift

The first attempt of categorizing ideational GM is made by Ravelli (1985) in a study of correlations between GM, mode and complexity. The detailed GM categories are defined through a transitivity analysis of the clauses in eight English texts. In particular, the participant, process and circumstances of a clause are examined to see if the meanings of these elements are realized congruently or metaphorically. This method of determining metaphorical expression is based on Halliday's (1985a: 322) claim that 'part of knowing a language is to know what is the most typical "unmarked" way of saying a thing'. Ravelli (1985) recognizes nine types of GM, some of which have further subcategories. All these types of GM are summarized by Ravelli (1985) as shown in Table 2.3.

No.	*Semantic Choice*	*Metaphorical Realization Function/Class*	*Congruent Realization Class*
1a	material process	Thing/nominal group	verbal group
1b	mental process	Thing/nominal group	verbal group
1c	relational process	Thing/nominal group	verbal group
1d	verbal process	Thing/nominal group	verbal group
1e	behavioural process	Thing/nominal group	verbal group
2	process	Epithet, Classifier/adjective	verbal group
3a	quality of a Thing	Thing/ nominal group	adjective
3b	quality of a process	Epithet, Classifier/adjective	adverb
3c	quality of a process	Thing/nominal group	adverb
4a	modality	Epithet/adjective	(modal) adverb
4b	modality, modulation	Thing/nominal group	adjective, passive verb
5a	logical connection	Thing/nominal group	conjunction
5b	logical connection	Process/ verbal group	conjunction
6	circumstance	Process/verbal group	prepositional phrase
7a	participant	Classifier/adjective	nominal group
7b	participant	Thing/nominal group	nominal group
8a	expansion	Act/embedded clause	ranking clause
8b	projection	Fact/embedded clause	ranking clause
9	circumstance	Epithet, Classifier/ adjective	propositional phrase

Table 2.3: Ravelli's (1985: 58) categories of ideational GM

Ravelli (1985) clarifies that all the labels for the semantic choices in Table 2.3 are in effect grammatical terms. This is because the semantic systems network in SFL is not developed when Ravelli's (1985) exploration of GM is carried out. In this case, Ravelli (1985) interprets grammatical terms as names of semantic choices. It is also pointed out that 'the function of the congruent realization has not been given, as the name of the congruent functions is the same as that of the semantic choice' (Ravelli, 1985: 57). Furthermore, Ravelli (1985) notices that not every possible GM subcategory is included in Table 2.3, since the table only presents GM types found in the eight English texts.

Ravelli (1985) explains the features of certain types of ideational GM in Table 2.3. Three features are of particular significance for the further research of GM. First, Ravelli (1985: 59) states that category 1 (process meaning metaphorically realized as Thing) is 'by far the most frequent example of metaphor, averaging about 35% of all instances in each text'. She claims that the high frequency of category 1 explains why nominalization is the instance of metaphor of which there is the greatest cultural awareness. Second, Ravelli (1985) observes the metaphorical dependence between certain types of GM. For example, the metaphorical realization of process meaning as Thing (category 1) is accompanied by the grammatical movement from adverb to adjective (category 3b). The metaphorical dependence is defined by Ravelli (1985) as the 'syntagmatic plurality' of GM, which means GM instances in different categories are syntagmatically interdependent on each other. Third, Ravelli (1985) considers the phenomenon of 'paradigmatic plurality' or 'recursion' observed within categories 3c, 4b and 7b as an extremely important aspect of GM. In these categories, one metaphorical realization passes through the semantic network a second time and is realized metaphorically again. It is argued that the recursion of GM is 'a re-wiring mechanism to bring a realization of the network back into the system at a less delicate point' (Ravelli, 1985: 62).

Ravelli's (1985) model of GM categorization is slightly modified by Jones (1991) in a study of the relationship between GM and technicality. According to Jones (1991), Ravelli's (1985) table is not fixed as it only presents the types of GM found in eight texts. Thus, the table 'has the potential to add and remove categories and subcategories depending on the texts under analysis' (Jones, 1991: 183). Jones (1991) modifies Ravelli's (1985) table by adding some subcategories of GM. As mentioned above, Ravelli's (1985) categorization of GM is attempted before the semantic systems network in SFL is developed. Some types of ideational GM are not included in her model due to the limited range of GM used in the eight texts. However, Ravelli's (1985) classification of ideational GM is important in that it provides a practical method of discussing individual GM instances in detail.

Halliday (1998) proposes the second model of categorizing ideational GM from the perspective of elemental shift. He first describes the congruent pattern of relationship between semantics and lexicogrammar at word rank. The semantic functions of relator, minor process, process, quality and entity are respectively realized by the grammatical classes of conjunction, preposition, verb, adjective and noun in English. In a metaphorical expression, the realignment of congruent pattern gives rise to metaphoric moves in both semantic and grammatical strata. Halliday (1998: 208) claims that 'not all possible metaphoric moves actually occur'. He summarizes all the moves that do occur in terms of 'semantic shift', as shown in Figure 2.5.

Figure 2.5 shows that the semantic functions only move from left to right and not the other way round. Halliday (1998) simplifies these moves as the following ordering:

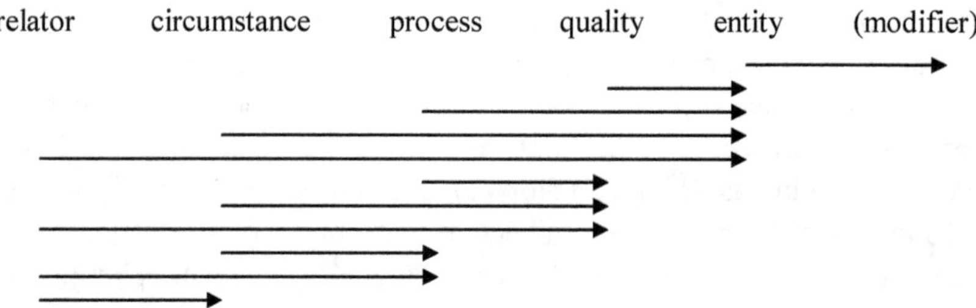

Figure2.5: All metaphoric moves that do occur

relator ⟶ circumstance ⟶ process ⟶ quality ⟶ entity

With respect to the meaning of this ordering, Halliday (1998: 211) writes:

> (1) any semantic element can be construed as if it was an entity (i.e., grammaticised as a noun); (2) a relator, a circumstance or a process can be construed as if it was a quality (i.e., grammaticised as an adjective); (3) a relator or a circumstance can be construed as if it was a process (i.e., grammaticised as a verb); (4) a relator can be construed as if it was a (minor process within a) circumstance (i.e., grammaticised as a preposition, in a prepositional phrase).

Halliday (1998) argues that there is a general drift towards 'thinginess' in ideational GM. The metaphoric moves take the semantic element of participant as the terminal point. Rather, 'the noun is the most metaphorically attractive category: everything else can end up as a noun' (Halliday, 1998: 211). Depending on this description of metaphoric moves, Halliday (1998) identifies 13 types of ideational GM and their subcategories. All these types of GM are presented in Table 2.4 reprinted from Halliday (1998).

Halliday's (1998) model of GM categorization is specified by Halliday and Matthiessen (1999) in their more systemic and semantics-oriented study of GM. Halliday and Matthiessen's (1999) discussion of GM is based on a detailed description of ideational semantics within the framework of SFL. In fact, one essential task for their ideational semantics is that of modelling GM (Halliday and Matthiessen, 1999). The metaphoric moves between various semantic elements are described more systematically as mappings

#	*semantic type*			*class shift*
	congruent	*metaphorical*		
1	quality		entity	adjective – noun
2i	process	event of process	entity	verb – noun
2ii		aspect or phase of process		tense/phase verb (adverb) – noun
2iii		modality of process		modality verb (adverb) - noun
3	circ.	[minor process]	entity	proposition – noun
4	relator		entity	conjunction – noun
5i	process	event of process	quality	verb – adjective
5ii		aspect or phase of process		tense/phase verb (adverb) – adjective
5iii		modality of process		modality of verb (adverb) – adjective
6i	circ.	Manner	quality	adverb – adjective
6ii		time, place etc.		prepositional phase – adjective
6iii		,,	(class)	prepositional phase – noun modifier
7	relator		quality	conjunction – adj.
8	circ.		process	*be/go* + proposition – verb
9	relator		process	conjunction – verb
10	relator		circ.	conjunction – prepositional (phase)
11	0		entity	0 – noun
12	0		process	0 – verb
13	entity		modifier (of entity)	noun - [various]

Table 2.4: Halliday's (1998: 209–210) types of GM

from a congruent category domain to a metaphorical one. The domains of elemental metaphors are represented by Halliday and Matthiessen (1999) in a table, repeated here as Table 2.5.

It is worth noting that Halliday and Matthiessen (1999) add the symbol 'Ø' to congruent domains to describe the GM categories of 11 and 12 which in fact have no corresponding congruent form. The GM instances in these two categories only occur as the accompaniment of other types of metaphorical expression.

Halliday and Matthiessen (1999) propose that there are two predominant motifs in ideational GM: one major and one minor. The major or primary motif is the drift towards 'thing', while the minor or secondary is the move

congruent:	metaphorical:			
	→ circumstance	→ process	→ quality	→ thing
quality → *unstable*				1 *instability*
process → *absorb*			3 *absorptive*	2 *absorption*
circumstance → *instead of;* *on the surface*		6 *replaces*	5 *alternative;* *superficial*	4 *replacement;* *surface*
relator → *for/because [b,* *for/because a]* *so [a, so, b]*	10 *because of;* *as a result*	9 *causes; proves;* *ensures, follows* *from*	8 *causal;* *consequent*	7 *cause, proof;* *result*
Ø →		12 *occurs; imposes* *does; has*		11 *phenomenon,* *fact*
thing, circumstance *driver [be safe]* *decided [today]*	13 expansion of thing (in environment of 1 or 2) *driver [safety], driver's [safety], [safety] of the driver* *today's [decision], [decision] of today*			

Table 2.5: Domains of elemental metaphors (Halliday and Matthiessen, 1999: 245)

from 'thing' to 'quality'. Halliday and Matthiessen (1999) explore the implication of the major motif, i.e., the drift towards thinginess, by examining the potential embodied by different semantic elements for construing experience. It is summarized that 'things are more easily taxonomized than qualities, qualities than processes, and processes more easily than circumstances or relations' (Halliday and Matthiessen, 1999: 264). These characteristics of semantic elements determine that the drift to thinginess is the major motif of ideational GM. With respect to the move from thing to quality, it only accompanies a metaphor of either type 1 or type 2. According to Halliday and Matthiessen (1999: 269), 'it is still within the compass of a participant in the figure; grammatically, it is within the nominal group'. That is, ideational GM is predominantly a 'nominalizing' tendency and semantically a shift from the logical towards the experiential (Halliday and Matthiessen, 1999). This means ideational GM makes maximum use of the potential for classifying experience, 'by turning all phenomena into the most classifiable form – or at least into a form that is more classifiable than that in which they have been congruently construed' (Halliday and Matthiessen, 1999: 269).

Halliday and Matthiessen (1999) stress that the individual types of ideational GM are treated as isolates for analytical purposes. It is necessary to add a dimension of complexity to ideational GM on both syntagmatic and paradigmatic axes. Syntagmatically, 'instances of grammatical metaphor typically occur not in isolation but in organic clusters or "syndromes"' (Halliday and Matthiessen, 1999: 249). In terms of the rank where metaphoric reconstrual takes place, Halliday and Matthiessen (1999) recognize three general types of ideational GM syndrome: (1) from figure to element; (2) from sequence to figure; and (3) from figure with process to figure with process as thing. It is also found that some of the GM categories such as categories 1 and 2 in these syndromes can occur independently. Other metaphoric shifts like category 13 occur only under the driving force of independent GM categories.

In terms of paradigmatic complexity, Halliday and Matthiessen (1999) claim that there are other wordings intermediate between an instance of ideational GM and its most congruent agnate variation. This feature of ideational GM means that metaphoricity is just a relative matter. Halliday and Matthiessen (1999) provide a practical way of unpacking metaphorical expressions. In particular, a metaphorical sentence would be reworded to make it intelligible to a child at different ages, say, 15, 12, 9 and 6. This method of unpacking GM creates a series of expressions with different degrees of metaphoricity. It is summarized that 'the semantic relations between one element and another, and between one figure and another, become progressively less explicit as the degree of metaphoricity increases' (Halliday and Matthiessen,

1999: 258). The syntagmatic and paradigmatic complexities discussed by Halliday and Matthiessen (1999) are in nature similar to the syntagmatic and paradigmatic pluralities observed in Ravelli's (1985) study.

Another significant contribution of Halliday and Matthiessen's (1999) study is the detailed differentiation of various types of GM into subtypes. This differentiation is based on the fact that a semantic element may involve various grammatical functions at different ranks of grammatical categories. For example, the semantic element of quality is construed as the grammatical functions of Attribute and Epithet respectively in a clause and a group. In this case, the semantic shift from quality to thing is concerned with the grammatical shifts from Attribute to Thing and from Epithet to Thing. The subdivision of GM categories is also concerned with the experiential structure of semantic elements. For instance, the circumstance realized by a prepositional phrase in English has a structure of minor Process + Participant. The semantic shift from circumstance to thing, therefore, contains the subtypes of minor Process to Thing and minor Process + Participant to Thing. Halliday and Matthiessen's (1999) method for differentiating GM subcategories is used in this book for the categorization of ideational GM in Chinese (see details in Chapter 5).

2.3.1.2 Categorization from the perspective of downgrading movement

According to Halliday and Matthiessen (2004), ideational GM downgrades the domain of grammatical realization of semantic units from clause nexus to clause, from clause to group/phrase, and even from group/phrase to word. They classify ideational GM into three types in terms of the semantic units where the downgrading starts, namely sequence, figure and element.

Halliday and Matthiessen (2004) define four possibilities of the downgrading realization of a sequence. First, only one of the two figures of sequence is realized metaphorically. If the original sequence expresses a meaning of expansion, the figure involved is reconstrued as a circumstantial element within the metaphorical clause. The relator of sequence is simultaneously realized as the minor Process in the circumstantial element. With respect to a projection sequence, the figure in question is realized incongruently as the Range of a verbal or a mental clause. Second, both figures of the sequence are downgraded as the elements of a circumstantial relational clause. The relator of the sequence is realized metaphorically as the Process in a clause. Third, the figures concerned are realized as the elements of an intensive relational clause. The relator of an expanding sequence is nominalized as the Thing of the nominal group serving as Value. In the case of projection, the projected figure may be construed as the Token in the relational clause. Fourth, the two figures in a sequence are realized as the constituents of a nominal group. With expansion, the relator and figure(s) are respectively reconstrued as the Head and the Modifier of a nominal group. With projection, the projecting figure and projected figure are realized as the Head and the downranked Qualifier in a metaphorical clause.

There are two types of the metaphorical realization of a figure (Halliday and Matthiessen, 2004). The first type is the metaphorical expression of a figure which retains the clause as the domain of realization. On the one hand, the whole figure is downgraded as a nominal group and a new Process with the meaning of 'happen' being created. On the other hand, part of the figure is downgraded as a nominal group when the Process is involved in two metaphorical shifts. First, the phase of a Process is transferred into an isolated Process. Second, the Process is reconstrued as a combination of Range and a new Process. This change from congruent Process to metaphorical Process + Range is actually the ideational GM category 12 identified by Halliday and Matthiessen (1999). The second type of the metaphorical realization of a figure takes group/phrase as the domain of realization. The Process in question is realized as the Thing of a nominal group.

With respect to the downgrading realizations of elements in a figure, Halliday and Matthiessen (2004: 652) state that a process is generally nominalized and serves as Thing except in an attributive relational clause where it is the Attribute that is nominalized. The other elements of the figure are reconstrued either as Qualifier or Deictic in the form of groups/phrases or as Classifier, Epithet or post-Deictic in the form of words.

The categorization of ideational GM in terms of downgrading movements clearly demonstrates how different ranks of grammatical constituents change in the process of metaphorical reconstrual of semantic units. Compared to the GM categorization from the perspective of elemental shift, this method is more concerned with the general aspect of GM. The types of ideational GM identified by Halliday and Matthiessen (1999) reveal the more detailed variations of semantic and grammatical constituents. In sum, the two methods of categorizing ideational GM complement each other in the typological study of ideational GM.

2.3.2 Interpersonal GM

Interpersonal GM is not classified as systematically as ideational GM because the metaphorical expressions within interpersonal function cannot be decomposed into detailed grammatical movements or semantic shifts. Another area of difficulty with interpersonal GM categorization is the inherent complexity of interpersonal meaning itself. Generally speaking, interpersonal GM is categorized into metaphor of modality and metaphor of mood. The review here follows this tradition and examines how the two types of interpersonal GM are further categorized.

2.3.2.1 Metaphor of modality

As mentioned in Section 2.2, all the explicit expressions of modality are metaphorical. The categorization of metaphor of modality is thus based on the classification of modality. According to Halliday (1994), modality is the intermediate area of meaning lying between positive and negative polarities. The classification of modality is concerned with the underlying speech function of a clause. The clause used for the exchange of information is a proposition, while the clause used for the exchange of goods-&-service is a proposal. The modality in a proposition means 'either (i) "either yes or no", i.e. "maybe"; or (ii) "both yes and no", i.e. "sometimes"; in other words, some degree of probability or of usuality' (Halliday, 1994: 356). On the other hand, the modality in a proposal means 'either (i) "is wanted to", related to a command, or (ii) "wants to", related to an offer; in other words, some degree of obligation or of inclination' (Halliday, 1994: 356). The modalities in proposition and proposal are respectively referred to Modalization and Modulation by Halliday (1985a; 1994). The system formed by these types of modality is illustrated in Figure 2.6.

Halliday (1985a; 1994) points out that the realizations of modality are determined by the basic distinction of orientation, which refers to the distinction between subjective and objective modality and between explicit and implicit variations. The combination of orientation distinction and modality types is presented by Halliday (1994) as in Table 2.6.

Table 2.6 shows that metaphor of modality can be classified in terms of the four types of modality. The metaphorical expressions of each type of modality can be further differentiated by considering their grammatical methods of realization. In particular, they are divided into the metaphors realized through mental clauses or attributive clauses.

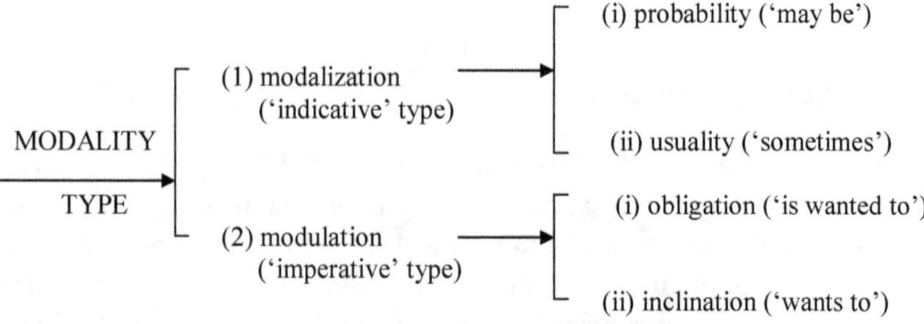

Figure 2.6: System of types of modality (Halliday, 1994: 357)

	Subjective: explicit	*Subjective: implicit*	*Objective: implicit*	*Objective: explicit*
Modalization: probability	I think [in my opinion] Mary knows	Mary'll know	Mary probably knows [in all probability]	it's likely that Mary knows [Mary is likely to]
Modalization: usuality		Fred'll sit quite quiet	Fred usually sits quite quiet	it is usual for Fred to sit quite quiet
Modulation: obligation	I want John to go	John should go	John's supposed to go	it's expected that John goes
Modulation: inclination		Jane'll help	Jane's keen to help	

Table 2.6: Modality types and orientation combined (Halliday, 1994: 358)

Table 2.6 also shows that there are systematic gaps in the combination of orientation and modality types, which represent 'semantic domains where the speaker cannot readily pose as an authority' (Halliday, 1994: 358). It is worth noting that the detailed description of these gaps is different in various GM studies. Halliday (1994) and Halliday and Matthiessen (2004) identify the gaps of the explicitly subjective realization of usuality and inclination and the explicitly objective realization of inclination. By contrast, only the explicitly subjective realization of usuality is defined as the gap in the studies of Halliday (1985a) and Martin *et al.* (1997). The inconsistent descriptions may be engendered by the different understandings of this problem and the inherent complexity of modality.

2.3.2.2 Metaphor of mood

The lexicogrammatical resource of mood expresses the four speech functions of statement, question, offer and command (Halliday, 1994). Statement, question and command, are congruently realized by the declarative, the interrogative and the imperative, while offer has no congruent form (Halliday, 1984b). However, Halliday (1994) notices that a particular speech function is frequently realized by mood system beyond the congruent pattern. Halliday and Matthiessen (2004) classify the metaphorical realizations of speech functions into two types according to their form of expression.

The first type of metaphor of mood is realized in the form of ideational projection. Halliday and Matthiessen (2004) demonstrate that speech function, just like modality, can be represented as a substantive proposition in its own right. The proposition involved is a sensing or saying figure projecting the original proposal or proposition. The possible patterns of metaphorical realizations of proposal and proposition in the form of projecting clause are summarized in Table 2.7 taken from Halliday and Matthiessen (2004).

The types of metaphor of mood in Table 2.7 realize the proposition and proposal by a clause nexus of projection rather than a clause. Halliday and Matthiessen (2004: 630) observe that 'the interpersonal projection embodied in speech function has thus been realized as if it was an ideational projection'. The metaphorical realizations other than ideational projections are defined by Halliday and Matthiessen (2004) as other kinds of mood metaphor. One major type is the realization of speech function of command by

	declarative		interrogative: yes/no		
speaker (speaker+)	I (we) implore you → to I (we) want you → to	I (we) would advise you → to I (we) would want → you to	may I (we) advise you → to		proposal: command
	I (we) assure you → that	I (we) can assure you → that	may I (we) assure you → that		proposition: statement
	I (we) ask you → whether I (we) wonder → whether	I (we) must ask you → whether I (we) must wonder → whether	may I (we) ask you → whether		proposition: question
addressee					proposal: command
		You must believe → that	Would you believe → that		proposition: statement
		You must tell me → whether	Would you say → that Could you tell me → whether	Do you mean → that	proposition: question
	temporal: present	modal: modulation		temporal: present	

Table 2.7: Metaphor of mood realized in the form of projecting nexus (Halliday and Matthiessen, 2004: 630)

declarative and interrogative clauses instead of imperative clauses. In particular, the mood domain in declarative and interrogative clauses is realized by adding Subject and Modal operators to imperative clauses. In addition to this type of metaphor of mood, some common speech-functional formulae are also treated as a kind of metaphor of mood by Halliday and Matthiessen (2004). These formulae are metaphorical in origin and have been extensively studied in speech act theory (Austin, 1975).

2.4 Semogenic research of GM

As an important kind of lexicogrammatical resource through which the meaning potential of language is expanded, GM is extensively investigated in relation to semogenic processes. Halliday and Matthiessen (1999) identify three time frames of semogenic processes: phylogenesis, ontogenesis and logogenesis. Phylogenesis refers to the evolution of language in human history, ontogenesis to the development of language in the individual, and logogenesis to the language change involved in the unfolding of a text (Halliday and Matthiessen, 2004). The semogenic research of GM is mainly conducted from the perspectives of phylogenesis and ontogenesis.

2.4.1 Phylogenetic research

Halliday (1988) provides the first investigation of GM from a phylogenetic perspective in his studies of scientific language. He examines the evolution of the linguistic features in modern scientific English through analysing the text samples from Chaucer's time to present day. The analysis shows that the lexicogrammatical resources deployed in scientific English undergo a series of changes within a period of about 400 years. Chaucer's writing contains the first two steps towards nominalized discourse: (i) technical nouns; and (ii) nominal groups with iterated phrase-and-group Qualifier. GM in the form of nominalization becomes an essential resource for constructing scientific discourse in Newton's (1704) writing of *Opticks*. Newton (1704) achieves two important discoursal effects by nominalizing processes or attributes. First, a complex phenomenon is packaged into a single semiotic entity by making it one element of clause structure. Second, the rhetorical functions of the nominalized phenomenon are rendered explicitly as Theme and New in the unfolding of argument. In addition, the pattern of process1 (nominal group) + relation (verbal group) + process 2 (nominal group) come into prominence in Newton's texts.

According to Halliday (1988), scientific English continues to develop after Newton's time (1642–1727) and displays many new features. Most of the features summarized by Halliday (1988) in terms of nominal and verbal elements are concerned with GM. On the one hand, nominal groups are used to package processes into information and distribute them by backgrounding and foregrounding. On the other hand, verbal groups are deployed for setting up logical relationship between nominalized processes. Both the reconstrual of experiential content as a nominal group and the presentation of relations between processes are realized by GM. Since the end of eighteenth century, all the features discussed above have emerged as the most highly valued model of scientific writing. The most recent development of scientific English in the twentieth century is the nominalization of causal relations. In sum, Halliday's (1988) research on the evolution of scientific English demonstrates that GM is an increasingly used grammatical resource since Newton's time (1642–1727) for the purpose of expanding the meaning potential of language.

Banks (2003) also conducts a phylogenetic research on GM by outlining the development of GM in the form of nominalized processes as a rhetorical recourse in scientific discourse. He examines the use of GM in the two extracts written in the period shortly before Newton's (1704) *Opticks*. The examination shows that there are precedents for Newton's (1704) adoption of GM as a rhetorical strategy. Banks (2003) thus claims that Newton's (1704) writing should not be treated as being the initiator of modern scientific discourse. Following this, Banks (2003) analyses the writing of Faraday (1838) and research articles in the early and late twentieth century in term of the deployment of GM. He concludes that 'there has been an increasing use of nominalized processes in scientific discourse over the last 250 years' (Banks, 2003: 142). Another important finding in Banks (2003) is that the deployment of GM is different in the early physical and biological sciences. As this finding is more concerned with the contextual research of GM, it is discussed at greater length in Section 2.5.

Despite the different opinions on the time of initial adoption of GM as a rhetorical strategy in scientific writing, Halliday (1988) and Banks (2003) illustrate that there is a correlation between GM and the development of language. Halliday (1993: 80) claims that GM is a natural process in the history of language and describes this process as follows:

> It is already beginning to appear in the writings of the ancient Greek scientists; from them it is carried over into classical Latin and then into medieval Latin; and it has continued to develop – but to a far greater extent – in Italian, English, French, German, Russian and the other languages of Europe from the Renaissance onwards.

2.4.2 Ontogenetic research

Halliday (1994: xviii) claims that 'grammatical metaphor is a dominant feature of adult language, and it is learned rather late'. It is proposed that a two-year-old can handle general concepts and a five or six-year-old can begin to handle abstract concepts. The ability to handle GM is not developed until around nine or ten years of age. According to Halliday (1998), the coupling of semantics to grammar is congruent in the meaning world of young children. The cross-coupling between semantics and grammar occurs as children are approaching adolescence. Halliday's (1994, 1998) argument is supported by relevant GM studies (for example, Derewianka, 1995; Painter, 2003; Torr and Simpson, 2003).

Derewianka (1995) undertakes a study of the language development in the transition from childhood to adolescence to investigate the evolution of GM in this period. Written texts and the surrounding oral interaction of these texts created by a child from the age of 5 to 13 are collected as data for GM analysis. All the GM instances in data are identified and categorized to show the ontological trends in the development of different types of GM. Derewianka's (1995) study shows that the development of GM is not a matter of a dramatic increase at puberty. Rather it is a relatively steady and uneven procession from the earliest texts through to the later. The unevenness of growth of GM is attributed to the expectations of teachers, the nature of writing tasks, and the exposure to texts containing GM. A more significant finding of Derewianka's (1995) study is the uneven development between different types of GM. It is found that the GM types such as 'quality: thing', 'process: thing', 'process: quality' and 'circumstance: quality' are used earlier and more frequently. The study also reveals that GM is first experimented in the spoken mode though it is a characteristic of written texts. Derewianka (1995) concludes that her study confirms Halliday's (1994) suggestion that GM is a significant dimension of language development in later childhood and distinguishes the children's language from that of adults. Derewianka (1995) argues that a dramatic increase in the amount of GM does not occur until 9 to 10 years of age. According to Derewianka (1995), this finding supports Halliday's (1994) claim that GM becomes a feature of older children's language at around this age.

Painter (2003) provides the evidence of the origins of the use of GM depending on an analysis of conversational data collected from two children from the age of 7 months to 2.5 years and from age 2.5 to 5 years. It is found that the possibility for using instances of GM arises after the grammatical systems are established at about age 2.5. The use of postmodifiers within the nominal group, which is defined as the earliest context for nominalization, appears from age 2 to 3 years. After age 4, both the metaphorical transformation of circumstance or process and the reconstrual of logical link as process are observed. Painter (2003) claims that these instances of language use are early examples of reconstruing experience using GM, although they are still far from the abstract form of written language. Thus, the first steps in the direction of ideational GM are taken from later preschool years.

Torr and Simpson's (2003) study is designed to survey the development of GM precursors in children's oral language in the home. For this purpose, the study collects data from extensive longitudinal diary studies of five children. By analysing the data, Torr and Simpson (2003) summarize the key developments which relate to children's subsequent ability to produce and interpret GM in the later years of primary schooling. The interpersonal GM involving the mismatch between speech function and grammatical form become fully established from 2 to 3 years of age. During the period from 3 to 4 years, the interpersonal GM in the form of projection like *I think* appears. It is from 4 to 5 years of age that children develop the ability to deal with abstract concepts and continue to elaborate interpersonal GM. Torr and Simpson (2003: 181) argue that 'GM does originate and flourish in interpersonal contexts during the preschool years'.

In addition to ontogenetic studies of GM in the language of native speakers, there has been research focusing on the use of GM by the adults who use English as second language and foreign language. Jones (1991) analyses the use of GM in the academic writing of overseas postgraduate students from different cultural and language backgrounds and suggests that the use of GM is more characteristic of native students' texts than that of second language learners' texts. Chen (2001) investigates the use of GM in the written English produced by Chinese university EFL learners. The study analyses 200 written texts in terms of the types of elemental GM, the impact of GM on the choice of process types and lexical density (LD) and compares some of these measures with those from other studies on native speakers and EFL learners. According to Chen (2001), the low measures for GM and LD in EFL learners' writing shows that their English is more characteristic of the language of native speakers in their early adolescence. In addition, Chen (2001) claims that EFL learners experience more of the frustration created by the stratal tension between semantics and lexicogrammar than native speakers of English in constructing the written English of expository types where the employment of GM is required.

This review of phylogenetic and ontogenetic research of GM shows that the use of grammatically metaphorical expressions is closely related to the evolution of language in human history and the development of language in the individual. With respect to logogenesis, it has not been systematically analysed in relation to GM. However, Halliday and Matthiessen (1999) point out that a congruent expression typically comes earlier than a metaphorical expression in a text. To sum up, the emergence of metaphorical realization of a semantic meaning is interrelated to all three major semogenic processes.

2.5 Contextual research of GM

Martin (1992: 490) argues that GM is 'the most important tool for understanding discourse semantics ... and for understanding the relationship between texture and context. It is thus the key to understanding text in context – to contextualizing the ineffable'. Ravelli (2003) also stresses that GM is central to an understanding of the relationship between language and context. The contextual research of GM falls into two areas in terms of the context involved. The first area of the research is concerned with the relationship between GM, metafunctions and register variables. The second area is the exploration of the motivation for using GM in centain contexts.

2.5.1 GM, register variables and metafunctions

Halliday (1978) suggests that there are three register variables: field, mode, and tenor, which respectively refer to the activity topic, rhetorical channel and role relationship of a text. In addition, these register variables tend to determine different areas of function in a language. The field of a text is associated with the ideational metafunction, mode with the textual and tenor with the interpersonal. Halliday (1985b) proposes that whether the text is spoken or written is the most important factor in determining the extent of GM. The earlier contextual research, therefore, focuses on the relationship between GM and the register variable of mode.

Ravelli (1985) analyzes a data set formed by four written and four spoken texts to investigate the relationship between mode, complexity and GM. In order to distinguish the variations in mode between texts, Ravelli (1985) presents the scale of mode with the complementary measures of lexical density and grammatical intricacy. A way of categorizing and measuring GM is also developed to define the scale of GM in the texts. The comparison of GM scale, complexity scale and mode variation shows that these three factors are correlated. More importantly, Ravelli's (1985: 109) study demonstrates that 'the extent of grammatical metaphor in a text varies in relation to variation in mode, primarily because metaphor contributes to complexity differences between texts of differing modes'.

Ravelli (1985) also notices that GM is the resource for the management of the Theme and Information systems. Similar meanings can be realized as different elements in a clause by using metaphorical expressions. This gives rise to the possibility of treating atypical parts of the message as Given or Theme. Ravelli (1985: 96) suggests that 'the textual metafunction, register variable of mode, and grammatical function of Theme are all interwoven.' Halliday and Matthiessen (1999) explain the relationship between GM and textual metafunction more explicitly. They argue that the only grammatical entity construing unmarked Theme without special effects is a nominal group, a nominalized clause or a nominalized clause complex. In order to map a meaning as the point of departure of message, it has to be constructed nominally. This nominalized Theme has a strong 'backgrounding' effect if it is located as Given, while the remainder of the clause is strongly 'foregrounded'. This kind of construction, as Halliday and Matthiessen (1999) comment, is powerful for reasoning and argument. Fan (1999) also investigates the cohesive function of GM in the form of nominalization and claims that the function is realized in the pattern of 'Rheme1–Theme2'. In other words, a clause can be connected to its preceding clause by a nominalized Theme which compresses the information in the Rheme of the preceding clause.

Another focus of GM contextual research is the influence of the register variable of field on the deployment of GM. Halliday (1993) describes GM as a phenomenon found particularly in scientific discourse and evolved first of all in that context. GM instances are extensively deployed in scientific discourse and observed in almost every sentence in this kind of writing. The inherent reason for adopting metaphorical expressions in the earliest scientific writing, as Halliday (1993) explains, lies in the need to create a new kind of knowledge. To be more specifc, the main impetus for GM seems to have continued to come from the language of science although GM is also used in the other varieties of language. All the metaphorical variations derive from the principle of organizing information into a form which suits scientific argumentation.

Previous studies (Martin, 1993a; Halliday and Matthiessen, 1999) reveal that metaphorical expressions are deployed differently in different fields of writing. Martin (1993a) examines the grammatical and semantic characteristics of science and history texts chosen from junior secondary school. Grammatically, scientific texts use identifying relational processes to define technical terms; historical texts use attributive relational processes to assign participants to familiar classes. Semantically, science tends to realize logical connections between clauses, while history prefers to bury reasoning inside the clause. According to Martin (1993a: 267), these differences between scientific and historical texts show that 'grammatical metaphor plays a different role in mediating between grammar and semantics in the two discourses'. To be more specific, GM in science discourse is used as a primary lexicogrammatical resource for building technical taxonomies. In history discourse, GM is used for realizing events as participants to carry forward reasoned argument. Martin (1993a) summarizes that GM respectively 'distills' and 'scaffolds' in science and history.

Halliday and Matthiessen's (1999) research on the language of weather forecasting and the language of recipes is also concerned with the GM deployment in different fields. One finding in their research is that the figure of being in weather forecasting texts is relevant to the deployment of GM. The weather processes and qualities are reconstrued as things which function as the participants of relational process. These metaphorical participants include weather phenomena like precipitation, weather systems, temperature, times, places and probabilities. By contrast, Halliday and Matthiessen's (1999) analysis of the recipe texts shows that those texts are free of GM since they highlight the figure of doing. This contrast between the languages of recipes and weather in GM deployment arises from the different topics in the two fields.

Halliday and Matthiessen (1999) also clarify the effect of GM on the ideational metafunction of language. They assert that GM in the ideational 'zone' is a resource for redeploying the lexicogrammatical categories evolved in the congruent mode of constructing experience. It is stressed that the metaphoric shifts does not destroy the natural relationship between meaning and wording. Rather, 'this relationship is extended further when new domains of realizations are opened up to semantic categories through metaphor' (Halliday and Matthiessen, 1999: 241).

The interaction of GM, tenor, and interpersonal metafunction has not been systematically explored in relevant GM studies. However, it is realized that the deployment of GM can change the tenor and interpersonal meaning of a text. Ravelli (2003: 53) argues that 'in connection with the change of interpersonal metafunction, there is a realignment of social relationships taking place'. Halliday (1998) points out that the use of ideational GM creates expert discourses which will become a language of power and technocratic control.

The review in this section indicates that GM is first a mode-oriented resource for organizing text and a field-oriented source for carrying reasoning and defining terms. Furthermore, the register variable of tenor is affected by the use of GM. In addition to the interaction between GM and register variables, the ideational, textual and interpersonal metafunctions of a language are all impacted by the use of GM. GM is thus a lexicogrammatical resource contextualized by the three register variables and their corresponding metafunctions.

2.5.2 Motivation for GM

The establishment of links between GM, register variables and metafunctions is not sufficient to explain the motivation for GM (Ravelli, 2003). Some researchers (Kress, 1989; Thibault, 1991; Melrose, 2003 and Hu, 2004) have attempted to reveal the motivation by analysing the use of GM in broader social and cultural contexts.

According to Kress (1989: 455), the concept of GM does not provide accounts of 'the whole complex of processes involved' and 'the social and political motivations which drive the metaphorical process'. Kress (1989) suggests that Halliday's (1978) categories of antilanguage and GM are united by the category of relexicalization. Rather, it is the social/cultural motivations that give rise to such relexicalization. Thibault (1991) argues that the inherent reason for the phenomenon can be accounted by referring to the theory of intertextuality. From the perspective of multiple intertextual criteria, there is a scale of more and less metaphorical/congruent expressions rather than a single grammatical encoding regarded as the congruent (Thibault, 1991). Social agents are trained to have access to their intertextual formations to understand the meaning expressed by different scales of GM. Melrose (2003) explores the motivation of GM by referring to the theory of ideology. The exploration shows that GM, especially nominalization, 'can be seen as a means of showing that you have gained mastery over a discipline, and you have therefore appropriated some power for yourself' (Melrose, 2003: 428). Hu (2004) claims that Halliday's (1985a, 1994) theory of GM is just one of five modes of *yufa yinyu* (grammatical metaphor). He attempts to explain the motivation of using all these types of *yufa yinyu* (grammatical metaphor) from a cognitive perspective.

2.6 Conclusions

This chapter reviews previous research of GM from four perspectives: theoretical exploration of the nature of GM, the categorization of GM, semogenic consideration of GM and the contextual consideration of GM. The literature review first shows that the understanding of the nature of GM has been continuously developed in the past 30 years. The earlier development of the understanding is represented by the shifts of the GM defining motif from alternative lexicogrammatical realization to the result of compound semantic choice. The more recent development is reflected by the incorporation of transgrammatical semantic domains into the explanation of GM. The review of GM categorization demonstrates that ideational GM is classified in terms of grammatical movement and interpersonal GM is differentiated by referring to its detailed methods of realization. The survey of semogenic and contextual research of GM makes it explicit that the deployment of GM is interrelated with language development and contextual configurations.

More generally, the review of literature reveals that GM identification, categorization and deployment are the three main concerns in the study of GM. The explorations of the nature of GM in three phases are in fact the attempts to clarify the issues of how to identify GM. The various classifying models reviewed in this chapter are concerned with the categorization of GM. The semogenic and contextual studies of GM investigate how the phenomenon is deployed in a language. In Chapters 4 to 8, the research of GM in Chinese and the comparison of GM in Chinese and English are conducted with a focus on these aspects.

This chapter shows that there is no comprehensive study of GM in the language other than English and very little comparison of GM in different languages. The aim of this book is thus to provide a study of GM in Chinese and demonstrates the similarities and differences between English and Chinese in GM. The study of GM in Chinese is undertaken within the theoretical approaches established by previous studies of GM.

3 A framework for the functional analysis of Chinese

3.1 Objective and approach

This chapter aims to provide a framework for the functional analysis of Chinese which serves as the basis for discussing GM in the language. There exist many studies of Chinese in the field of SFL (for example, Tam, 1979; Long, 1981; Tsung, 1986; Ouyang, 1986; McDonald, 1992; Fang *et al.*, 1995; Zhu, 1996; Shum, 2003; Halliday and McDonald, 2004). This chapter is not a collection of the findings in these studies although it draws heavily on them. Some conclusions of previous studies are adopted, while others are reconsidered to clarify the uncertainties involved. This chapter also makes reference to some well-known books of Chinese grammar, such as *Grammar of Spoken Chinese* (Chao, 1968) and *Mandarin Chinese: A Functional Reference Grammar* (Li and Thompson, 1981), to explicate some linguistic features in the language.

The framework in this chapter is established for the analysis of GM, which is essentially concerned with how semantic meanings are realized by lexicogrammatical categories. Thus, I do not examine the detailed features of each category in the lexicogrammatical system of Chinese. A functional account of lexicogrammatical categories involved in GM is sufficient for the following discussions in this book.

3.1.1 The principle of identifying descriptive categories in Chinese

According to Halliday (1994), SFG is developed for the functional analysis of any human language, although English is used as the language of illustration. Halliday (1994) remarks that there is a danger of assuming that the categories in English are valid in the description of any language. He suggests that any functional category in a language should be explained by reference to other categories in the language under description, as if no other language has been described before. Of course, this would not necessarily demand a new system of notation for the functional study of Chinese. The researchers mentioned above develop their functional models of Chinese description by referring to the linguistic systems initially set up for English.

Considering that it is unavoidable to use notions developed for English in Chinese analysis, I define grammatical categories involved on the basis of Halliday's (2003) 'from above' principle to ensure that the categories are not misinterpreted.

There are two kinds of categories in the analysis of languages: theoretical and descriptive. Theoretical categories in SFG refer to 'those such as metafunction, system, level, class, realization', while descriptive categories are 'those such as clause, preposition, Subject, material process, Theme' (Halliday, 2003: 201). Theoretical categories are general to all languages and necessary for the construction of a general linguistic theory. The descriptive categories, in contrast, are in principle language specific. In other words, they evolve in the description of a particular language. When the descriptive categories developed for English are to be used to describe, say, Chinese, they should be refined with respect to the language under study.

Halliday (2003) argues that all descriptive categories are identified from three perspectives: those of the higher level, the same level and the lower level. The higher level perspective involves the semantic meanings realized by descriptive categories; the same level perspective concerns how the categories are related to other parts of the lexicogrammatical system; and the lower level perspective focuses on the realization forms of descriptive categories in structure and in phonology. These perspectives are also referred to: (i) 'from above'; (ii) 'from around'; and (iii) 'from below'. Halliday (2003) notes that a formal grammar gives priority to perspective (iii). In a functional grammar, such as SFG, perspective (i) has priority, and perspective (iii) will typically be derived from it. That is, 'a functional grammar is one which explains the forms of the language by referring to the functions they express' (Halliday, 2003: 203).

Halliday (2003) claims that the 'from above' perspective should be adopted if the categories set up for one language are used as tools for exploring another. In particular, 'we look at the meaning of some category in the language of reference, and then ask if there is any category in the language under description that has a comparable function taken in the context of the whole' (Halliday, 2003: 204). Halliday's (2003) suggestion for identifying descriptive categories in a particular language is adopted in this chapter as a principle of constructing the framework of Chinese analysis. A descriptive category originally developed for English will be examined from perspective (i) to see whether it is applicable to Chinese. In other words, a descriptive category in Chinese is recognized by referring to its function in the Chinese expression. The identification of lexicogrammatical categories under this principle avoids the danger of carrying over the connotations of the original descriptive terms borrowed from English.

3.1.2 Paradigmatic and syntagmatic perspectives

Saussure (1959) points out that the meaning of a sign comes from relations which it enters into with other signs and there are two kinds of relationships between the units of linguistic system: syntagmatic and paradigmatic. Syntagmatic relations are 'those which a unit contracts by virtue of its combination with other units of the same level', while paradigmatic relations contracted by units are 'those which hold between a particular unit in a given syntagm and other units which are substitutable for it in the syntagm' (Lyons, 1977: 240).

According to Halliday (2003), SFG is characterized by its paradigmatic orientation. This means that the functional approach tends to prioritize the description of how grammatical choices stand in opposition to each other. However, it is also necessary to describe syntagmatic relations in order to set up a complete grammatical system network. Eggins (1994: 210) summarizes that 'a complete system network involves organizing the choices into systems, and specifying how those choices are realized as structures'. This indicates that a systemic functional network must capture both the paradigmatic and syntagmatic relations of a language.

The following discussion of each meaning system in Chinese first presents the grammatical choices of the system and then describes the structural realization of the system. The expressions of syntagmatic relations are referred to 'realization statements' in SFG. Eggins (1994: 210) suggests that the realization statements of various systems may involve specifying 'the presence of a functional constituent, the ordering of functional constituents, conflation of functional constituents, and specification of the sub-class of particular constituent'. In the following sections, I discuss the realizations of different systems in Chinese from these four points of view.

Using the metafunctions in a language as organizing principle, I first establish the framework for Chinese clause analysis from the perspective of experiential meaning, and then moves to the interpersonal and textual meanings. Following this, I discuss the logical relations between Chinese clauses and the structure of various groups or phrases in Chinese clauses. In relevant discussions, I compare the findings in previous research to show the contradictions between different models of Chinese description. The comparison reveals some grammatical categories which are critical for the functional description of Chinese. These categories are treated as the major focus in my discussions.

3.2 Analysing Chinese clause from experiential perspective

A language is analysed from an experiential perspective when we examine how it is used to talk about the external and internal worlds. According to

Halliday (1994: 106), 'our most powerful experience is that it consists of "goings-on" – happening, doing, sensing, meaning, and being and becoming'. It is claimed that the grammatical system by which these 'goings-on' are achieved is 'transitivity'. Rather, 'the transitivity system construes the world of experience into a manageable set of process types' (Halliday, 1994: 106). Halliday (1994) defines six types of process in the English transitivity system, namely material, mental, relational, behavioural, verbal and existential. In order to define the process types in Chinese, several models have been proposed in relevant research (Tam, 1979; Long 1981; McDonald, 1992; Zhou, 1997; Shum, 2003; Halliday and McDonald, 2004). This section briefly reviews these models to show the main uncertainties in the theoretical description of the transitivity system in Chinese. On the basis of the discussion of these uncertainties, I present the model of process type to be used in this book.

3.2.1 Various models of process types in Chinese

Based on a study of texts in translation, the transitivity system of Chinese is initially described by Tam (1979) with special reference to the correspondence between Chinese and English. It is asserted that a Chinese clause may embody one of four different types of process. These types of process are the relational, the verbal, the mental and the material. Tam (1979) also discusses in detail the justification for establishing one process type as different from another process type and the elements specific to each type of process.

Long (1981) recognizes five types of process in Chinese, namely material, ascription, mental, verbal and relational. The material type of process is further divided into subtypes of actor and patient, while the relational type includes the attribute and identifying subtypes of process. The particular point in Long's (1981) model is that the processes which involve no action but only assign a certain features to their participants in Chinese are named as ascription types of process.

McDonald's (1992) analysis of process types in Chinese is featured by drawing a broad three-way distinction between action, relation and state processes. Action processes in this system are distinguished from the other two types by 'being more susceptible to the different types of experience marking' and by 'their participants being more flexible in position, i.e. with a greater potential to be thematically marked' (McDonald, 1992: 441). The action process contains three subtypes: material, mental and verbal. Relation processes in McDonald's (1992) model cover largely the same range as relational processes in English. They are divided into identifying processes with the subtypes of 'equating' and 'attributing', and locating processes including the subtypes of 'existing' and 'locating'. The state process corresponds to the 'adjective sentence' in structuralist Chinese grammar (Liu and Pan, 2004). As mentioned above, this type of process is termed ascription process in Long's (1981) account of transitivity in Chinese.

Instead of providing a general survey on the processes in Chinese, Zhou (1997) focuses on the two types of process which are more salient in the study of Chinese transitivity, namely the material and the relational. Zhou's (1997) research is featured by its investigation on the range of relational processes in Chinese. In contrast to previous studies, the ascription process in Long (1981) or the state process in McDonald (1992) is not treated as an individual type of process in Zhou's (1997) analysis, but as a special part of relational process. Additionally, the relational process is defined by Zhou (1997) more extensively to contain certain clauses which belong to material process in other models.

The transitivity description of Halliday and McDonald (2004) is the most recent and comprehensive classification of process in Chinese. Halliday and McDonald (2004) recognize four process types of material, mental, verbal, and relational and provide detailed categorizations of each type of process. The processes with existential and behavioural meanings are not treated as individual types of process in this model. Instead, they are included in the relational and material processes respectively. More importantly, Halliday and McDonald (2004) claim that the differences between various models of Chinese transitivity system are attributable to two issues. First, the classification of process types in Chinese is concerned with the relationship between the system of transitivity and the systems of aspect and phase. The processes in Chinese are frequently realized by the combination of main verb and postverb. This linguistic feature determines that the process type may be classified in terms of main verb or postverb. Second, the different positions which are adopted with respect to the scope of relational type of process give rise to some uncertainties in the classification of processes in Chinese.

The need for a reliable categorization of Chinese processes cannot be overemphasized in order to analyse GM in depth. This study classifies processes in Chinese into six types by adhering to the principle of determining descriptive categories from the perspective of 'from above'. The reasons for this classification are explained in section 3.2.2.

3.2.2 Re-examination of process types

The debate over process types indicates that the following questions should be the main considerations on the classification of processes in Chinese:

(a) What is the scope of relational processes in Chinese?
(b) Are there existential processes in Chinese?
(c) Are there behavioural processes in Chinese?

Therefore, I focus the discussion of process classification in Chinese on relational, existential and behavioural processs.

3.2.2.1 Relational process

According to Halliday (1994: 119), 'every language accommodates, in its grammar, some systemic construction of relational processes'. However, the typological variations in Chinese and English determine that there are many differences in relational processes between the two languages. I first analyse whether the ascription or state process identified in relevant studies should be treated as a single type of process. Depending on the analysis, I describe the coverage and differentiation of relational processes in this study.

It is necessary to examine the feature of the 'adjective' in Chinese before any further discussion of the ascription/state processes in the language. There is a general recognition that 'adjectives' in Chinese share many characteristics of verbs across both traditional and functional research on Chinese. In the field of functional study of Chinese, Halliday (1956) refers to the 'adjective' in Chinese as the 'intensive verbal group'. The traditional research of Chinese adjectives is represented by the following statement of Chao (1968: 663):

> We are using the term 'verb' in the wide sense of any word which can be modified by the negative *bu* 'not' or *mei* (have not or did not) and which can serve as the predicate or the center of a predicative expression. Verbs in this wide sense will then by synonymous with predicatives, which will then include verbs in a narrow sense as well as adjectives, since Chinese adjectives can function as predicates or centers of predicates.

Li and Thompson (1981) also show that there are many similar characteristics shared by verbs and adjectives in Chinese. In their grammar book for Chinese, there is no class of 'adjective' at all.

When the predicate in a Chinese clause is an adjective, *shi* (be) is not necessary for the expression, as shown in Example 3.1.

(3.1)	*Zhongguo*	*hen da.*
	China	very big
	'China is very big.'	

This kind of expressions is defined as ascription and state types of process repectively by Long (1981) and McDonald (1992). Thus, the structure of state/ascription clause is determined by the special feature of adjectives in Chinese. As explained by Halliday and McDonald (2004: 358), 'in ascriptives, the Attribute is conflated with the Process'. Hence, Example 3.1 could be analysed in the framework of SFG as:

(3.2)	*Zhongguo*	*hen da.*
	China	very big
	Carrier	Process/Attribute

As already mentioned, this study follows Halliday's (2003) principle of 'from above' to determine whether a descriptive category is valid in Chinese. That is, the individual category is identified by examining its function in a language instead of its form. In the case of state/ascription process, this type of process is defined by referring to its structure. In other words, the state/ascription type of process has been identified by giving more attention to formal features than functional explanations.

Functionally, relational processes are concerned with expressions which set up a relation between two separate entities. Therefore, the grammatical form of this relation in individual languages should not be taken as the reason for creating new type of process. In this case, the state/ascription process in previous studies should be considered as the relational process with a specific form in Chinese. This type of process is named as 'ascriptive' subtype of relational process in this study, following the term developed by Halliday and McDonald (2004).

Furthermore, this is not saying that *shi* (be) cannot be used in the relational clauses including Attributes. In many cases, *shi* is used for the purpose of emphasis (Zhou, 1997), which is comparable to the use of 'do' in certain English statements. For example:

(3.3) *Tianqi* *<u>shi</u>* *hen leng.*

weather is very cold
'The weather is <u>really</u> very cold.'

When *shi* is purely used as a Process, the Attribute in a clause is generally realized by a noun or a nominal group ending with the lexical marker of *de*. This type of process is named as 'categorizing' subtype of process by Halliday and McDonald (2004), as shown in Examples 3.4 and 3.5:

(3.4) *Ta shi xuesheng*
he is student
'He is a student.'

(3.5) *Shu pi shi lüse de.*
book cover is green Sub.
'The book cover is green.'

Both the ascriptive and categorizing subtypes of relational process in Chinese construe the intensive relationship between Carrier and Attribute. In addition to this intensive relation, Carriers and Attributes are also linked by the relations of circumstantial and possessive. The circumstantial relational processes in English serve to establish between two entities a relationship of time, place, manner, cause, accompaniment, role, matter or angle (Halliday, 1994). Except for the locative (time and place) and causal-conditional relation, the circumstantial choices are generally realized by minor processes (prepositional phrases) in the grammatical network of Chinese. This can be shown by the comparison of Example 3.6a in English and Example 3.6b in Chinese:

(3.6a) The Earth's magnetic field concerns the inner structure of the Earth.

(3.6b) *Diqiu cichang gen diqiu nebu jiegou youguan.*
the Earth magnetic field and the Earth inner structure relevant

The comparison shows that the circumstantial relationship of matter realized as a process in English is expressed by a minor process in Chinese. The circumstantial type of relational processes in Chinese thus has a smaller scope than its counterpart in English. The possessive type of relational processes in Chinese, as Tam (1979) suggests, has the same range of choices as that in English.

In sum, the processes in Chinese which express the attributive relationship between Carrier and Attribute are divided into three subtypes: intensive, circumstantial and possessive. In addition to the attributive relationship, there is also the identifying relationship in Chinese processes by which the participants of Identified and Identifier are linked. The verbs involved in this subtype of process include *shi* (be), *biaoshi* (indicate), *daibiao* (represent) *zuowei* (act as), etc. In addition, each of the process subtypes of intensive, circumstantial and possessive is observed in the expression of identifying relationship (Halliday and McDonald, 2004). The differentiation of relational processes in this study is presented with their examples in Table 3.1:

3.2.2.2 Existential process

The expressions of existential meaning are viewed as a special form of relational processes in previous studies. This study upgrades existential processes as a single type of process by considering the distinctive feature of verb *you* (have/has; exist), which is the major verb for expressing existential meaning. In Chinese, different meanings are often expressed by the words with the same morphological form. These words should be identified as different expressions according to their meanings. According to Liu and Pan (2004), the verb *you* has as many as five meanings. These meanings, in

	Attributive		*Identifying*
Intensive	Ascriptive:	*Ta hen congming.* he very clever 'He is very clever.'	
	Categorizing:	*Ta shi xueshen.* He is student 'He is a student.'	*Ta shi nage laoshi.* He is that teacher 'He is that teacher.'
Circumstantial	*Huiyi zai xingqiyi.* meeting on Monday 'The meeting is on Monday.'		*Mingtian shi guoqing.* tomorrow is national day 'Tomorrow is the national day.'
Possessive	*Ta you yiliang che.* he has one car 'He has a car.'		*Na che shi wode.* that car is mine 'That car is mine.'

Table 3.1: Subtypes of relational process in Chinese

a functional sense, could be divided into three subtypes (Tam, 1979). The first type of them is concerned with possessive type of relational process, as shown in Example 3.7:

(3.7) *Nin you yitao gongyu*
you have an apartment
'You have an apartment.'

The second type of '*you*' has the meaning of 'exist'. The translation of clauses with this type of '*you*' is invariably certain form of 'there is'. See Example 3.8a and 3.8b:

(3.8a) *You che.*
exist car
'There is a car.'

(3.8b) *You yige nan da de wenti.*
exist one difficult answer Sub. question
'There is a question difficult to answer.'

This kind of *you* clauses is distinctive from the other types of clause in that they only invole one participant. Moreover, these *you* clauses cannot normally accept the aspect markers, *le* and *guo* (Aspect markers are indicated as 'Asp.' hereafter in this book). What remains to be discussed is the third type of *you*, such as Example 3.9:

(3.9) *You ren deng ni.*
has people wait you
'Somebody is waiting for you.'

In this clause, *you* constitutes the participant of this type of clause when the identity of the participant is unknown. It is comparable to the 'somebody' or 'someone' in English, representing the unknown element. Semantically, when the participant of a Chinese process is unidentified, it is formally realized as '*you* + noun'. More importantly, this type of clause can be found in all types of process except those with existential meanings. Tam (1979) argues that this structure is the marked form of the process in which the form is involved. This can be shown by Tam's (1979: 82) examples:

(3.10a) Unmarked
Baba shi ziran de laoban.
father is natural boss
'My father is a natural boss.'

(3.10b) Marked
You ren shi ziran de laoban.
has people is natural boss
'Somebody is of course the boss.'

The function of existential processes in a language is to show the existence of an Existent. In other words, there is always only one participating entity in this type of process. The relational processes, on the other hand, have the function of relating two participants. The examination of the verb *you* in Chinese shows that the second type of *you* is obviously not involved in the 'being' relationship between two entities. The 'one participant' feature of this type of *you* process and the special meaning of *you* in these processes show that there is an individual existential type of process in Chinese. It is worth noting that the existential process is also realized by other verbs such as *fasheng* (happen), *chuxian* (appear) and *cunzai* (exist). Existential processes realized by these verbs almost always have aspect marking. For example:

(3.11) *Chuxian le yi ge duihua kuang.*
appear Asp. one Meas. dialogue window
'There appears a dialogue window.'

3.2.2.3 Behavioural process

Behavioural processes in English, as Halliday (1994: 139) claims, 'are the least distinct of all the six process types because the processes have no clearly defined characteristics of their own'. It is possible that the similar consideration prevents some researchers from recognizing behavioural processes in Chinese. Tam (1979), McDonald (1992) and Halliday and McDonald (2004) do not recognize an individual type of process labelled as behavioural. This study sets up the category of behavioural process because this type of process can be semantically distinguished from other types of process in Chinese. It means there is a special type of process in Chinese which is used to express physiological and psychological behaviour. More importantly, this type of process has a specific form of lexicogrammatical realization which is worth giving a separate label. For instance, a number of verbs in Chinese are used to express human physiological and conscious behaviour: *ku* (cry), *xiao* (laugh), *kan* (look), *ting* (listen), etc. The participant who is behaving in this type of process in Chinese is labelled as Behaver in this study. A behavioural process may involve another participant which is named Behaviour, as we can observe in the following example:

(3.12) *Ta* (Behaver) *kan* *zhe* *tiankong* (Behaviour).
he look at Asp. sky
'He is looking at the sky.'

One difficulty in recognizing behavioural processes in Chinese is that the language does not have a formal distinction between the verbs for mental perception processes and those for the behavioural. English uses paired verbs to express these processes, such as 'see' and 'watch'. In contrast, there is only one verb of *kan* in Chinese for both the 'see' and 'watch' meanings in English. Chinese develops a special system of 'postverb' to express the result of the action or behaviour in different processes, as shown in the following clauses:

(3.13a) Behavioural: *Wo zixide kan le.*
I carefully watch Asp.
'I watched carefully.'

(3.13b) Mental: *Wo kan dao le he.*
I see arrive Asp. river
'I saw the river.'

In the mental process, the postverb *dao* is attached to the main verb *kan* to express the meaning of 'see' in English. The comparison of these two clauses indicates that one basic issue in the classification of process types in Chinese is whether a verbal group should be assigned to a process type in terms of main verb or postverb (Halliday and McDonald, 2004).

3.2.2.4 Other types of processes

So far I have discussed three types of process: the relational, the existential and the behavioural by making reference to previous models of functional description of transitivity system in Chinese. With respect to the other types of processes in Chinese, the discrepancy between these models is not so great. In this section, the processes of verbal, mental and material are examined by focusing on the participants in these processes and the subdivision of these processes.

A. Verbal process

This type of process expresses the meaning of 'saying'. Like the similar type of process in English, 'saying' here should be interpreted in a rather broad sense. As summarized by Halliday and McDonald (2004), this type of process also involves verbs such as *biaoshi* 'indicate', *zhenming* 'prove' and *fouding* 'deny' which can occur with a personalized participant or a 'fact'. Thus the participant involved in any instance of this type of process covers both human and inanimate elements. This kind of participant is named the Sayer. The other kinds of participant probably involved in the verbal process in Chinese are: Receiver, Verbiage and Target (Halliday and McDonald: 2004). Similar to those in English, these participants in Chinese respectively refer to whom the saying is directed, what is said and the entity that is targeted by the process:

(3.14a) *Ta gaosu wo* (Receiver) …
he told me
'He told me …'

(3.14b) *Ta jieshao le youxi de buzhou* (Verbiage).
he introduce Asp. game Sub. procedure
'He introduced the procedure of the game.'

(3.14c) *Ta piping le women* (Target).
he criticize Asp. us
'He criticized us.'

The expressions of Chinese verbal processes are often not a single clause but a clause complex, as can be seen from Example 3.15:

(3.15) *Ta shuo ni gai xiaoxin.*
he say you should careful
α β
'He says you should be careful.'

Example 3.15 shows that the first clause is a verbal clause with structure of 'Sayer + Process', while the second serves as the projected clause of the first. Like the same kind of clause complex in English, the projected clause does not enter into the structure of the verbal process and has the status of a wording.

B. Mental process

Mental processes are involved in the expression of 'sensing' both in Chinese and in English. The first characteristic of this type of process is the nature of the two participants in the process. Unlike any other types of processes, one of the participants in a mental process must be human. This human participant is obligatory in all mental process clauses and acts as the one who experiences the process in question. The nature of this kind of participant in the process is so distinctive that it deserves a particular label: Senser. The other participant of the process is the phenomenon that is 'sensed'. In the system of Chinese transitivity, it is simply named as Phenomenon after Halliday's (1994) label in English. Four subtypes of mental processes can be recognized in Chinese. According to Halliday and McDonald (2004), these subtypes of mental processes are named as: cognitive, affective, desiderative and perceptive.

Another point to be considered is whether the mental processes in Chinese could also be represented as two-way processes. Halliday (1994) indicates that the mental processes in English generally have semantic equivalents. In particular, the paired verbs of 'like' type (I like it) and 'please' type (It pleases me) are used in the language. Tam (1979) observes that some of the mental processes in Chinese can be viewed from two standpoints as well. For example, the clauses of *Wo haipa ta.* (I fear him.) and *Ta xia wo.* (He frightens me.) use a pair of verbs which are semantic equivalents to each other. Halliday and McDonald (2004) also note that the affective subtype of mental processes in Chinese include some pairs of 'like' type and 'please' type verbs. Although the Chinese verbs cannot be paired up so neatly as those in English, the fact that mental processes have the two-way feature is useful for the recognition of this type of process.

C. Material process

The material process is distinguished from all the other types of process in Chinese in that it takes full range of time and voice categories (Halliday and McDonald: 2004). The 'doer' of a material process is called the Actor because the process is involved in physical actions. Any material process in Chinese has an Actor, even though in many cases the Actor may be omitted in real expressions. The process is frequently directed at a second participant named as Goal. As the two nuclear participants in the material process, Actor and Goal may be either animate or inanimate. Halliday and McDonald (2004) divide material processes in Chinese into intransitive and transitive types according to the number of the nuclear participant involved. The intransitive subcategory has one nuclear participant of Actor, while transitive subcategory includes the nuclear participants of Actor and Goal.

In addition to Actor and Goal, there are other elements functioning as non-nuclear participant in the material process of Chinese: Range and Beneficiary. The two elements of Range and Beneficiary are deployed respectively in the intransitive and transitive types of material clause. Range in Chinese can be described as the 'cognate object' recognized by Chao (1968). In particular, a cognate object may consist of an expression for '(a) the number of times of an action, (b) its duration, (c) its extent, and (d) the course of locomotion' (Chao, 1968: 312). The Range of Chinese could be grouped according to this categorization of 'cognate objects'.

Like that in English, the Beneficiary in Chinese also has two subdivisions: Recipient, the one to whom something is given, and Client, the one for whom something is done. The important difference between English and Chinese in the use of Beneficiary is that only the Recipient in Chinese can be introduced without a preposition, never the Client (Tam, 1979). In English, either Recipient or Client 'may appear with or without a preposition, depending on its position in the clause' (Halliday, 1994: 145). Tam (1979) claims that there are certain verbs in Chinese that inherently presuppose Recipient: 送 *song* (give), 赏 *shang* (reward), 借 *jie* (loan), 留 *liu* (leave behind), etc. The Client, on the other hand, must be introduced by the prepositions such as 给 *gei* (on behalf of, for the benefit of), 为 *wei* (for the sake of, for the benefit of) and 替 *ti* (in place of, on behalf of).

To summarize the discussion of process types in Chinese, the types of process recognized in this section and the participants specific to each type of process are presented in Figure 3.1.

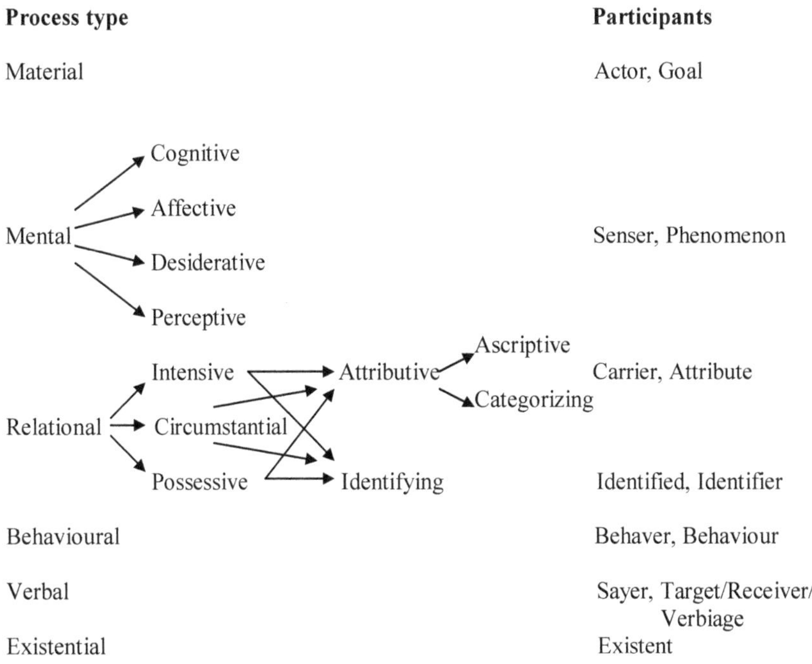

Figure 3.1: Summary of process types in Chinese

3.2.3 Circumstances in Chinese

I have delimited the scope of each type of process in Chinese, setting up a framework constructed by these processes and their participants. The framework shows that a Chinese clause consists of a single Process and one or two Participants. In addition to Participant and Process, there is probably another kind of element in Chinese clauses: the element of Circumstance. Similar to Process and Participant, Circumstance is recognized from the 'from above' perspective. Halliday (1994) defines Circumstances as the elements which function as the background against which the process takes place. The study adopts this notion and considers any minor process functioning as indirect participant in Chinese as a Circumstantance.

3.2.3.1 Structural features of Circumstances in Chinese

Circumstance in English is 'a kind of additional minor process, subsidiary to the main one' and introduces 'a further entity as an indirect participant in the clause' (Halliday, 1994: 152). Previous studies (Chao, 1968; Li and Thompson, 1981) show that this kind of minor processes is also valid in Chinese. More importantly, the minor processes in both languages are largely introduced by prepositions which are interpreted as a kind of 'mini-verb'. The characteristics of prepositions are thus critical for the description of Circumstance in Chinese.

Prepositions in Chinese have very different forms from those in English. In modern Chinese, as Li and Thompson (1981: 360) indicate, 'most of the prepositions used to be verbs at earlier stages of the language, and most of them still have characteristics of verbs and can be used as verbs that have similar meanings'. In other words, the prepositions in Chinese are evolved from the verbs with the same morphological form. The preposition in Chinese is traditionally termed as 'coverb' (Chao, 1968: 749). The reason for such a term is that this class of words is partly like verbs and partly like prepositions, therefore, the term 'coverb' is coined to avoid labelling them either verbs or prepositions (Li and Thompson, 1981). Prepositions are distinguished from verbs in that 'they do not, as a rule, have aspects and that they do not function as centers of predicates' (Chao, 1968: 749). This study recognizes Chinese prepositions according to these criteria proposed by Chao (1968).

The close relationship between verbs and prepositions determines that many prepositions in Chinese are less specific than those in English in terms of meaning (see Section 8.2.2). Certain types of Circumstance are therefore construed by the minor Process plus a 'facet' of the Participant in question (Halliday and Matthiessen, 1999). The 'facet' is realized by a postnoun and attached to a circumstantial element to indicate the precise location of participant, such as *zhong* in the following example:

[(3.16a) *Zai* *zhenkong* *zhong* (facet)
in vacuum inside
'in a vacuum'

The facet structure is also used to construe locations in abstract and temporal meanings:

(3.16b) *Zai* *zhe zhong* *qingkuang* *xia* (facet)
at this type situation below
'in this situation'

(3.16c) *Zai* *na duan* *shijian* *li* (facet)
in that period time inside
'in that period of time'

The use of facet in Chinese circumstance is an important point in the further discussion of GM categorization and the comparison of GM in Chinese and English.

In terms of whether or not a participant is involved, Circumstances in Chinese are divided into two groups with different structures (Halliday and McDonald, 2004). The Circumstance in group (1) can be further recognized as type (a) or type (b) in terms of whether or not a 'facet' is involved in it. In the following table, the eight types of Circumstance in Chinese recognized in this study and their realization statements are categorized according to Halliday and McDonald's (2004) principle.

The discussion of Circumstances in Chinese focuses on the minor processes introduced by prepositions. This is of course not saying that

Structure	*Circumstance*	*Example*	*Realization statement*
(1a) + Participant + Facet	Location	zai kongqi zhong (in air inside)	Prepositional phrase (preposition + noun + postnoun)
(1b) + Participant − Facet	Comparison Instrument Matter Accompaniment Source Cause Location	bi jiejie (with sister) yong shou (with hand) guanyu ta (about him) gen gege (with brother) an guding (according to rules) wei fumu (for parents) zai jia (at home)	Prepositional phrase (preposition + noun)
(2) − Participant	Manner Location	manman (slowly) mingtian (tomorrow)	Adverbial group

Table 3.2: Structural division of Circumstances

Circumstances in Chinese are limited to the prepositional phrases in the language. Table 3.2 shows that a Circumstance is also realized by an adverbial group in Chinese. The characteristics of each type of Circumstance in Chinese are described in Section 3.2.3.2.

3.2.3.2 Description of various types of Circumstance

On the basis of previous research on prepositions in Chinese (Chao, 1968; Li and Thompson, 1981), I briefly describe the circumstances listed in Table 3.2 as follows.

A. Location

The element of Location is used to refer to both the time and the place of Chinese clauses. In addition, Locations may be either static or directional. The contrast between static and directional intersects freely with the contrast between time and place. Prepositions frequently involved in various types of Location are illustrated in Table 3.3.

	Static	*Directional*
Time	'*zai*' (in/at)	'*cong*' (from) '*dao*' (by) '*dengdao*' (by, by the time of)
Place	'*zai*' (in/at)	'*cong*' (from) '*dao*' (to) '*shang*' (up) '*xia*' (down) '*xiang*' (towards) '*wang*' (towards)

Table 3.3: Propositions involved in various types of Location

(a) Time. When the time reference is static, *zai* is not used in relative time expressions. For example:

(3.17a) *Mingtian qu xili.*
tomorrow go to department
'I am going to my department tomorrow.'

Zai is, however, used for the expression of individual years, months and days:

(3.17b) *Wo zai 1974 nian chusheng.*
I in 1974 year born
'I was born in 1974.'

When the time is directional, prepositions are always required to introduce the circumstantial element. The element either traces back to a starting point in the past or projects into a stopping point in the future:

(3.17c) *Zhanlan cong xia xiqiyi kaishi.*
exhibition from next Monday start
'The exhibition will start from next Monday.'

(b) Place. When the place element in a Chinese clause is static, it is more likely that *zai* is deployed to indicate the exact location.

(3.18) *Ta zai bangongshi shuijiao*
he in office sleep
'He sleeps in his office.'

When the place is directional, the preposition is necessary for the expression. It does not indicate where the major process takes place, but rather clarifies whether the major process moves towards or from a place. There are plenty of Chinese clauses with directional place Circumstances. The following example represents them:

[(3.19) *Ta cong Beijing huilai.*
he from Beijing come back
'He came back from Beijing.'

B. Comparison

The circumstantial element of Comparison in Chinese clauses may be either similarity or difference.

(a) Similarity. Chao (1968) differentiates between the 'equal degree' and the 'equalling degree' in the expression of similarity. The former one is explicitly compared in the form of A *gen* (and/with) B *yiyang* (equally) + Adj., which could be translated into 'A is equally Adj. as B'. The formula in the later form of the similarity is A *you* (have/has) B + Adj., in which A equals B to a certain degree. The translation of this form is 'A is as Adj. as B'. The following two clauses are the examples of these two kinds of similarity:

(3.20a) *Ta gen jiejie yiyang gao.*
she with sister equally tall
'She is equally tall as her sister.'

(3.20b) *Ta you jiejie gao.*
she has sister tall
'She is as tall as her sister.'

(b) Difference. The difference is generally introduced by *bi* and *bijiao* (than, compare to) in different clauses of Chinese. Such clauses are represented by Example 3.21:

(3.21) *Waimian bi wuli re.*
outside than house hot
'The outside is hotter than the inside of house.'

The marker of negative similarity and difference are, in the majority of cases, *bu* and *mei* (not), which are used right before the prepositions mentioned above. For example:

(3.22a) *Ta bu gen jiejie yiyang gao.*
she not with sister equally tall
'She is not equally tall as her sister.'

(3.22b) *Ta mei you jiejie gao.*
she not has sister tall
'She is not as tall as her sister.'

C. Instrument

The term 'instrument' is self-explanatory. It describes the instrument which the actor uses to accomplish his mission. The prepositions involved are 用 *yong* (use) and 拿 *na* (hold), which are illustrated in the following example:

(3.23) *Ta yong kuaizi chi fan.*
he use chopsticks eat meal
'He eats his meal with chopsticks.'

D. Cause

This kind of Circumstance serves to indicate the cause for which the main process takes place and is introduced by either 为 *wei* (for) or 因为 *yinwei* (because of):

(3.24) *Wei fumu, ta zai xiao chengshi gongzuo.*
for parents he in small city work
'He works in a small city for his parents.'

E. Accompaniment

The circumstantial element is named as 'accompaniment' because the noun introduced by the minor process accompanies the actor of the main process in finishing the action. This type of circumstance is always introduced by one of the following prepositions: 跟 *gen*, 同 *tong* and 和 *he* (and/with). See Example 3.25:

(3.25) *Ta gen gege qu faguo.*
he with brother go to France
'He went to France with his elder brother.'

F. Manner

The circumstance of Manner in Chinese is usually introduced by *de* (adverbial particle) and realized by adverbial groups. It describes the manner in which the major process takes place. Comparatively speaking, the scope of Manner in Chinese is not as broad as that in English. It only contains the equivalent meaning of the subtype of Circumstance which is referred to Quality in English. The '*manman de* (slowly)' in the following expression is the example of circumstance of Manner:

(3.26) *Ta manman de zou.*
he slowly partic. walk
'He walks slowly.'

G. Matter

The prepositions 对 *dui*, 对于 *duiyu* and 关于 *guanyu* (about, concerning) are used most frequently to introduce Matter in Chinese, as shown in Exmaple 3.27.

(3.27) *Guanyu qizhong kaoshi, shijian hai meiyou ding.*
about final examination time yet not decide
'As far as the final examination is concerned, its time has not been decided.'

H. Source

A Source is deployed to show the dependency of the main process. The prepositions involved in this type of Circumstance are *an*, *anzhao* and *yizhao*. For example:

(3.28) *Anzhao guiding, women zhi neng zheyang zuo.*
according to rules and regulations we only can this do
'According to the rules and regulations, we can only do this.'

Halliday (1994: 150) states that 'the distinction between participant and circumstance is probably relevant in all languages; but in some it is drawn relatively sharply, while in others it is shaded and blurred'. As far as Circumstance and Participant in Chinese are concerned, the distinction between them is blurred by the special feature of prepositions in the language. For instance, the noun *kuaizi* (chopsticks) in example (3.23) can be explained either as the indirect participant in a Circumstance or a Participant because the preposition *yong* (use) can be used as a verb as well. The position of circumstance in Chinese clauses is another point to be emphasized. Unlike the Circumstance in English, which can be positioned either before or after the major Process of the clause in question, the same element in Chinese must precede the major Process, except for the circumstance of Manner which follows the main verb with *de*.

3.2.4 Realization statement of transitivity system

So far I have explored the grammatical choices which paradigmatically define the transitivity system of Chinese. In this section, the syntagmatic relations in experiential meaning are examined to show how the transitivity system is realized.

The differences between different types of process are in effect oppositional choices in the transitivity system of Chinese. Each type of process is associated with certain functional Participants and circumstantial elements. Thus, I focus my description on the structures of different types of process and their Participants and Circumstances. The functional labels in Chinese are written with an initial upper case letter, while the realization of each process type is indicated by a downward pointing arrow. To make the realization statement more manageable, the formal expressions typically used for the functional elements are listed as well.

3.2.5 The ergative perspective

The preceding sections sort the transitivity system in Chinese into six types of process and identify the Participants and Circumstances involved in these process types. This section explores the possibility of generalizing these different types of process from the ergative point of view. Many linguists (for example, Anderson, 1968; Fillmore, 1968) discuss the ergative systems in human languages with different working definitions. In the field of SFG, the ergative system contains one inherent Participant which is semantically the 'key figure' in any clause (Halliday, 1994). The Participant is 'the one through which the process actualized, and without which there would be no process at all' (Halliday, 1994: 163). From the ergative point of view, Halliday (1994) interprets the different types of process with one representational structure common to English clauses.

3.2.5.1 Ergative interpretation of Chinese clauses

Similar to those in English, Chinese clauses can also be generalized from the perspective of ergativity. The main reason for adopting this perspective is the recognition that a large number of verbs in Chinese show a systematic alternation between two patterns of use. Consider the following pairs of process for examples:

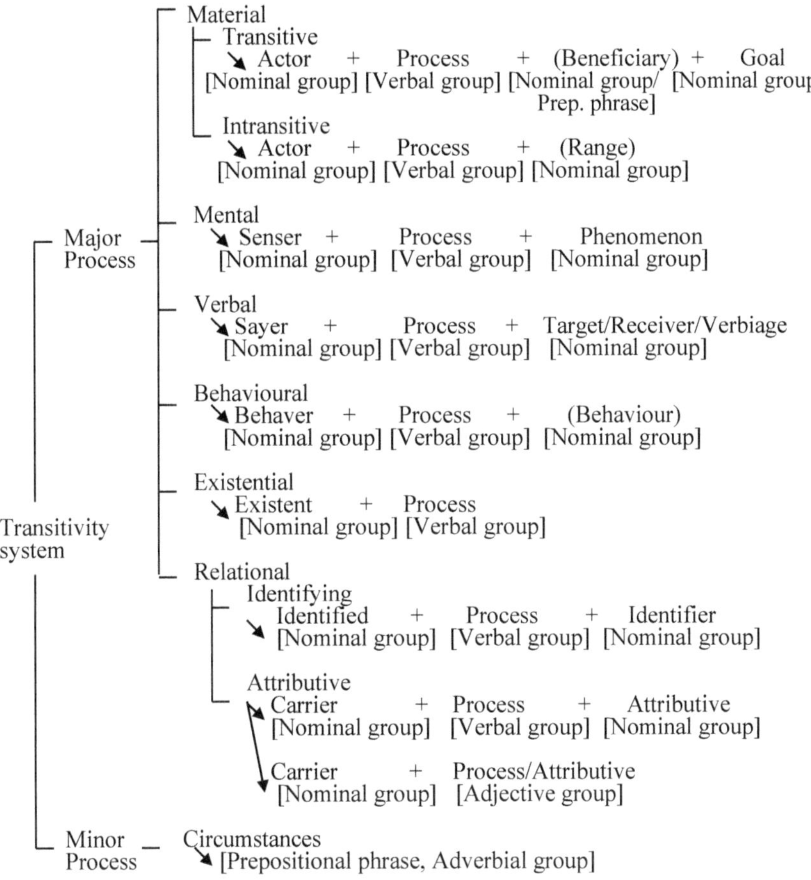

Figure 3.2: Realization statement of transitivity system in Chinese

(3.29)	*Jihua gaibian le.*	*Women gaibian le jihua.*
	plan change Asp.	we change Asp. plan
	'The plan changed.'	'We changed the plan.'
	Che kai zou le.	*Ta kai zou le che.*
	car drive away Asp.	he drive away Asp. car
	'The car drove away.'	'He drove away the car."

The transitivity analysis of these pairs of Chinese clauses recognizes the types of these processes and labels the Participants in these clauses according to whether processes extend to another participant or not. The ergative analysis, on the other hand, examines whether these processes are encoded as happening by themselves or as being caused to happen. As shown in Example 3.29, every pair of clauses is hosted by the same Participant in the processes. Halliday (1994: 163) suggests that the participant is termed as Medium for it is 'the entity through the medium of which the process comes into existence'. In addition, the 'participant functioning as an external cause' (Halliday, 1994: 164) is labelled as Agent. The same notions are also used in the ergative interpretation of Chinese clauses. The examples above are thus analysed as follows:

(3.30)	*Jihua*	*gaibian*	*le.*	*Women*	*gaibian*	*le*	*jihua.*
	plan	change	Asp.	we	change	Asp.	plan
	Medium	Process		Agent	Process		Medium
	'The plan changed.'			'We changed the plan.'			
	Che	*kai zou*	*le.*	*Ta*	*kai zou*	*le*	*che.*
	car	drive away	Asp.	he	drive away	Asp.	car
	Medium	Process		Agent	Process		Medium
	'The car drove away.'			'He drove away the car.'			

The ergative interpretation of Chinese clauses is useful for the generalization of certain particular constructions in Chinese which are treated as distinctive phenomena in transitivity analysis. This issue is discussed in detail below.

3.2.5.2 *Ba* and *Bei* constructions

There are two groups of constructions represented by the use of *ba* and *bei* in Chinese. Both *Ba* and *Bei* constructions are much discussed topics in the study of Chinese grammar. This section provides an explanation of these constructions from the ergative point of view.

Structurally, the forms of *Ba* and *Bei* constructions are straightforward. *Ba* in a material process is placed immediately before the Goal in the process.

(3.31)	*Ta*	*ba*	*che*	*kai zou*	*le.*
	he	Ba	car	drive away	Asp.
	Actor		Goal	Process	
	'He drove away the car.'				

In the *Bei* construction, the Goal in the above clause is followed by the passive coverb *bei*. The meaning of the clause could be expressed with a *Bei* construction as follows:

(3.32) *Che bei ta kai zou le.*
car Bei he drive away Asp.
Goal Actor Process
'The car is driven away by him.'

Ba and B*ei* constructions share some similarities. First, they select a similar class of verbs, which express the disposal of something in some way (Chao, 1968). Second, the verbs in both *Ba* and *Bei* clauses are placed in the final position of the clauses. Hence, the information focus in *Ba* and *Bei* clauses is on the final position of the process. The main difference between *Ba* and *Bei* constructions is that the clause containing *Bei* construction is used for the realization of passive meaning.

From the perspective of ergativity, both *ba* and *bei* are used to mark the participant affected by the process in question. In other words, they are deployed to indicate Medium in Chinese clauses. The ergative analysis of the above examples is as follows:

(3.33a) *Ta ba che kai zou le.*
he Ba car drive away Asp.
Agent Medium Process
'He drove away the car.'

(3.33b) *Che bei ta kai zou le.*
car Bei he drive away Asp.
Medium Agent Process
'The car is driven away by him.'

3.2.5.3 Pivotal construction

The pivotal construction is another topic which is frequently discussed by Chinese linguists (for example, Chao, 1968; Li and Thompson, 1981). Similar to *ba* and *bei* constructions, the pivotal construction in Chinese could also be explained ergatively. The defining characteristic of the pivotal construction is that 'it contains a noun phrase that is simultaneously the subject of the second verb and the direct object of the first verb' (Li and Thompson, 1981: 607). Tam (1979) suggests that the construction is divided into three groups according to semantic meaning of the first verb. The first group includes the verbs such as *zhun* (permit) and *jinzhi* (prohibit). The second group uses the verbs with a persuading meaning, like *quan* (persuade), *cui* (urge) and *qing* (request). The verbs involved in the last group are *ling* (lead), *dai* (take along), etc. The following clauses are the examples of pivotal construction in different groups.

(3.34) Group 1 *Jingli* *zhun* *ta* *xiuxi.*
manager permit he have a rest
'The manager permits him to have a rest.'
Group 2 *Muqin* *quan* *ta* *qu* *yiyuan.*
mother persuade he go to hospital
'His mother persuades him to see a doctor.'
Group 3 *Ta* *ling* *wo* *zou.*
he lead I go
'He leads me to go.'

All these clauses can be analysed with the introduction of Initiator which is defined as the function takes account of the executive role (Halliday, 1994). The analysis is shown in Example 3.35:

(3.35)

Jingli	*zhun*	*ta*	*xiuxi.*	
Muqi	*quan*	*ta*	*qu*	*yiyuan.*
Ta	*ling*	*wo*	*zou.*	
Initiator	Process	Actor	Process	

From the ergative point of view, the Participant acting as the 'subject' of the second verb and the direct 'object' of the first verb is the Medium of the clause. The other participant is the Agent of the clause. These clauses are interpreted ergatively as:

(3.36)

Jingli	*zhun*	*ta*	*xiuxi.*	
Muqi	*quan*	*ta*	*qu*	*yiyuan.*
Ta	*ling*	*wo*	*zou.*	
Agent	Process	Medium	Process	

The discussion of the ergative system in Chinese provides us with a new perspective for the analysis of various types of Chinese clause. The ergative examination of those long-debated Chinese constructions is very useful for the discussion of GM in the languge. The analyses of *Ba, Bei* and pivotal constructions show that these constructions involve only one clause because they centre around one participant of Medium. In addition, the logical meanings in Chinese can be realized by these constructions. In other words, the logical meanings in Chinese are frequently construed at the rank of clause. This point is critical for the understanding of the differences between Chinese and English in GM (see Chapter 8 for more details).

3.3 Analysing Chinese clause from textual perspective

According to Halliday (1994: 37), 'in all languages the clause has the character of a message: it has some form of organization giving it the status of a communicative event'. Halliday (1994: 37) defines 'the element which serves as the point of departure of the message' as the Theme in clause. Rather, there are different ways in which the point of departure for a message can be manifested in different languages. This section discusses how the message in a Chinese clause is organized and manifested with the focus on the element of Theme. The discussion is based on the traditional and functional studies of textual organization in Chinese.

3.3.1 Structuralist theories of textual organization in Chinese clause

There have been many structuralist studies of textual organization in Chinese (for example, Chao, 1968; Zhu, 1982; Li and Thompson, 1981, Tsao, 1979). These studies show that Chinese clauses ordinarily have an element which acts as the point of departure of the message. The element is put at the beginning position of a clause. These studies describe the element by using the terms 'subject' or 'topic'.

Chao (1968) claims that the full sentence in Chinese has two elements: 'subject' and 'predicate', which can be separated by a pause, a potential pause or a pause particle. The 'subject' is the subject matter to talk about, while the 'predicate' is the speaker's comment on the 'subject'. In addtion, what is expressed by the 'subject' need not be the performer of an action. Chao (1968: 69) also remarks that 'the grammatical meaning of subject and predicate in a Chinese sentence is topic and comment, rather than actor and action'.

Zhu (1982) describes the 'subject' in Chinese from the perspectives of structure, semantics and expression. Structurally, the 'subject' normally precedes the 'predicate' and is marked out by an optional pause or particle. Semantically, the 'subject' may be concerned with the action expressed by verb in different relations of agent, patient, recipient, time, etc. Expressively, the 'subject' is the content that the speaker is most interested, while 'predicate' is a statement about the topic chosen.

The descriptions of Chao (1968) and Zhu (1982) show that one part of a clause in Chinese serves as the content with which the whole clause is concerned. The 'subject' in their discussion is determined mainly by the 'surface structure' of the clause rather than its relations to the verb. In this sense, the notion of 'subject' in the studies of Chao (1968) and Zhu (1982) is very close to the concept of Theme in SFG. In addition, Chao (1968) and Zhu (1982) notice that a full clause in Chinese can serve as the 'predicate' in another clause and refer to this phenomenon as 'S-P Predicate' and 'subject-predicate' structure respectively. In this case, a clause in Chinese may contain two 'subjects', i.e., the 'subject' of the whole clause and the 'subject' of the 'predicate' part as illustrated in Example 3.37.

(3.37) *Zhege* *ren* *xinyan* *hao.*
this person heart good
Subject — Predicate
Subject — Predicate
'This person is kind-hearted.'

In contrast to the models of Chao (1968) and Zhu (1982) in which 'subject' and 'topic' are largely equivalent notions, other descriptive systems of Chinese consider them as entities of different kinds. Li and Thompson (1981) assert that 'topic' and 'subject' are semantically two concepts. They notice that the 'topic-prominent' nature of Chinese distinguishes the language typologically from many other languages. The 'topic' in Chinese is 'what the sentence is about' and 'sets a spatial, temporal, or individual framework within which the main predication holds' (Li and Thompson, 1981: 85). In addition to the semantic characteristic of topics, there are also two formal properties shared by all topics. First, a 'topic' in Chinese 'always occurs in sentence-initial position'. Second, 'a topic can be separated from the rest of the sentence by a pause or by one of the pause particles' (Li and Thompson, 1981: 86). The notion of 'topic' in Li and Thompson's (1981) system is to a certain extent equal to the Theme in SFG.

Li and Thompson (1981: 87) define the 'subject' in Chinese as 'the noun phrase that has a "doing" or "being" relationship with the verb in that sentence'. They stress that each verb requires a specific type of noun phrase to be its 'subject' in a Chinese clause. In this sense, the 'subject' is very similar to the notion of Participant in SFG.

Since 'topic' and 'subject' bear a distinct relationship to the rest of the clause, their occurrence is independent of each other. Li and Thompson (1981) recognize four possibilities: (a) both topic and subject discretely present; (b) a topic identical to the subject; (c) topic present but not subject; or (d) neither topic nor subject present. Their examples are adopted here as illustrations (Li and Thompson, 1981: 88–90).

(3.38a): + Topic, + Subject
Na zhi *gou,* *wo* *yijing* *kan-guo* *le.*
that dog, I already look Asp. Asp.
'That dog, I have seen already.'

(3.38b): Topic = Subject
Wo *xihuan* *chi* *pingguo.*
I like eat apple
'I like to eat apples.'

(3.38c): + Topic, – Subject
nei ben shu chuban le
that book publish Asp.
'That book, (someone) has published it.'

(3.38d): Topic, – Subject
(Ni jian -guo Lisi ma?)
you look Asp. Lisi question particle
'Have you seen Lisi?'
— *Mei kan-guo*
Neg. look Asp.
'(I) haven't.'

Similar to Li and Thompson (1981), Tsao (1979) also believes that the 'topic' and 'subject' in Chinese are different notions. But he argues that 'topic' and 'subject' belong to different levels of grammatical organization. While 'subject' is an element of sentence structure which 'bears some selectional relation to the main verb of a sentence' (Tsao, 1979: 84), 'topic' is a discourse element which 'may extend its semantic domain to more than one sentence' (Tsao, 1979: 88).

3.3.2 Systemic functional studies of the textual organization in Chinese clause

In the field of systemic functional studies of Chinese, the key research on clause structure is the study of Fang *et al.* (1995). The features of the message structure in Chinese clauses are summarized as follows (Fang *et al.*, 1995: 240):

(1) Structurally, the clause divides into two parts: the first part, the beginning of the message; the second, the continuation of the message;
(2) The different parts of the clause tend to have different information status: the first part known, definite; the second part new, indefinite; and
(3) The first part of the clause is significant in the creation of discourse.

On the basis of the summary, Fang *et al.* (1995) construct a framework for Chinese textual organization in terms of Theme-Rheme structure. A Chinese clause is made up of Theme (starting point of message), and Rheme (continuation of message) from the perspective of its textual function. The Theme normally comes first in the clause, and may be marked off from the Rheme by a pause and/or a textual particle such as *a, ba, me, ne.* The Rheme which follows the Theme may contain an experiential (aspectual) particle and/or an interpersonal (modal) particle.

The most significant contribution of Fang *et al.*'s (1995: 245) study is the finding that 'the elements of the thematic and transitivity structures which define the clause are not necessarily isomorphic'. In other words, a clause in Chinese may have a thematic element which has no experiential function. *Daxiang* (elephant) in the following example drawn from McDonald (1992: 439) does not function as an element of the experiential structure.

(3.39)	*Daxiang*	*bizi*	*hen chang.*
	elephant	nose	very long
	Theme	Rheme	
		Carrier (process)	Attribute

'Elephants, their trunks are very long.'

The word of *daxiang* would be introduced by a minor process in the form of *zuowei/guanyu/duiyu daxiang* (as an elephant) if it functions as a circumstance of Matter.

The finding is emphasized here for two reasons: first, it provides a method to solve the problem of 'subject' in Chinese; second, it provides an important criterion for delimiting the boundary of a clause in Chinese. The studies of 'subjects' in Chinese within the formal tradition show that the starting part of a Chinese clause is often isolated from the clause. Grammarians involved in these studies fail to explain the existence of both 'topic' and 'subject' in Chinese because the two elements are considered in the same dimension of language function. As already mentioned, the notions of 'subject' and 'topic' could be 'translated' into Actor and Theme in SFG. Fang *et al.* (1995) supply a possible resolution to the problem by denying the necessary connection between Theme and Actor. As for the second point, Themes in English are simultaneously the elements of transitivity system. The clause structure of Chinese, in contrast, is featured by the existence of element which only functions as the Theme in textual meaning. Fang *et al.* (1995: 245) thus define a clause in Chinese as 'the combination of a single thematic structure and a single transitivity structure'. This definition gives insight into the clause structure in Chinese and solves a major problem in recognizing a clause in the language.

Fang *et al.* (1995) further explore the relevance of thematic progression patterns to the clustering of clause complex in Chinese. They claim that two considerations appear important from the textual point of view. First, a Theme-Rheme structure could be recognized in a Chinese clause complex because the clause complex as a whole has a point of departure. In addition, 'it is the initial clause that is automatically treated as the Theme of the clause complex' (Fang *et al.*, 1995: 247). This is illustrated by the following example:

(3.40) *Ruguo ni bing le, women keyi xiuxi.*
if you illness Asp., we can rest
β α
Theme Rheme
'If you are sick, we can take a break.'

Second, 'the clauses in a clause complex may share a common Theme' (Fang *et al.*, 1995: 246). In this case, the shared Theme is typically omitted except in the first clause of the Chinese clause complex, as illustrated by the example adapted from Fang *et al.* (1995: 263).

(3.41) (Shared Theme) Rheme
Ta quchu kapian, saijin yidou, likai banggongshi.
s/he take out card stuff in pocket leave office
'He took out a card, stuffed into his pocket and left the office.'

3.3.3 Characteristic themes in Chinese

The systemic functional study of Chinese textual meaning by Fang *et al.* (1995) shows how it is possible to use SFG to define and explain the ordering of elements within Chinese clauses and clause complexes. The framework set up in their study is generally adopted in the practical analysis in this study. However, there are still some essential considerations of Theme in Chinese which are not covered in the study of Fang *et al.* (1995). In the following section, I examine characteristic Themes to reveal further the nature of textual function in Chinese.

3.3.3.1 Unmarked and marked theme

Halliday (1994) recognizes 'unmarked' and 'marked' Themes in English by examining how a Theme conflates with the various elements in Mood system. According to Fang *et al.* (1995), there is no Mood system at clause level in Chinese. This gives rise to the claim that it is impossible to define 'marked' and 'unmarked' Themes in the language. This study follows Halliday's (2003) point of view that the Mood system is recognizable in Chinese. Although the Mood system of Chinese has nothing like the clear interplay of Subject and Finite found in English (see Section 3.4.2), it is possible to identify the elements of Subject and Finite in Chinese. Halliday and McDonald (2004) point out that the most usual Theme in Chinese clauses is a nominal group which functions as Subject. This study defines the 'unmarked' Theme in a Chinese clause as the Theme conflated with Subject in the clause. When the element other than Subject occupies the initial position of the clause, it is named as 'marked' Theme in Chinese. The following clause from a Chinese novel is a typical example of the use of 'marked' theme.

(3.42) *Zai zhe youmei de yese zhong, wo tazhe ruanruan de shatan.*
at this beautiful Sub. night among I step soft Sub. beach
Marked Theme Rheme
'At this beautiful night, I walk along the soft beach.'

3.3.3.2 Multiple themes

There are often lexical elements preceding the normal Theme in Chinese clauses and clause complexes. These lexical elements express textual and interpersonal meanings, functioning to fit the content of a clause with the context around it. In English, these elements are separately defined as textual and interpersonal Themes, while the element expressing experiential meaning is named topical Theme. The same criteria are also adopted in this study for the analysis of multiple Themes in Chinese. For example, the following clause contains textual, interpersonal and topical Themes.

(3.43)	*Danshi,*	*buxingde,*	*ta*	*bing*	*le.*
	but	unfortunately	he	ill	Asp.
	Textual Theme	Interpersonal Theme	Topical Theme	Rheme	

'But, unfortunately, he is sick.'

3.3.3.3 Theme in interrogative clauses

The interrogative clauses in Chinese could be divided into three groups according to Li and Thompson (1981). The first group is the 'question-word' interrogative, in which the presence of a question word causes the construction to be an interrogative clause. Question words in Chinese are the semantic equivalent of *wh*-words in English such as who, what, where, which, and so forth. In general, the question words occur in the same position in the Chinese clause as do non-question words which have the same grammatical function. For example, the question word *shui* (who) could be replaced by any Chinese noun with the meaning of personal name. The identification of Theme in this kind of interrogative clause is similar to that of a declarative clause in Chinese. An example is analysed as follows:

(3.44)	*Laoshi*	*shi*	*shui?*
	teacher	is	who
	Theme	Rheme	

'Who is the teacher?'

The second group of interrogative clause is named as 'A-not-A question' by Li and Thompson (1981). This type of question clause is composed of a statement followed by an A-not-A form, such as *dui bu dui* (right not right), *hao bu hao* (good not good), *shi bu shi* (be not be). Obviously, this kind of clause is the semantic equivalence of the yes/no interrogative Mood in English. Similar to the question-word interrogative, the initial part of the message is regarded as the Theme of the 'tag-question' interrogative, as illustrated in Example 3.45.

(3.45)	*Ta*	*shibushi*	*laoshi?*
	She	be not be	teacher
	Theme	Rheme	
	'Is she a teacher?'		

The final group, called the 'particle question', is signalled by the presence of a question particle in sentence-final position, for example:

(3.46)	*Ni*	*hao*	*ma?*
	you	well	question particle
	Theme	Rheme	
	'How are you?'		

As the example illustrates, this kind of interrogative clause in Chinese has the same textual structure as a declarative clause. Its textual function is therefore analysed in the same way as that in a declarative clause.

This examination of the Theme-Rheme structure in Chinese interrogative clauses shows that the analysis of this kind of clauses in Chinese is relatively less complicated than in English. In other words, the identification of Theme and Rheme in interrogative clauses could follow the method developed for analyzing declarative clauses in Chinese.

3.3.3.4 Thematic bracketing

According to Halliday and McDonald (2004: 323), thematic bracketing refers to 'setting off a particular portion of the clause as thematic by structural means'. The Theme created by thematic bracketing is of particular importance to the study of GM because many Themes involved in thematic bracketing in Chinese are in effect the instances of GM. Halliday and McDonald (2004: 323–324) define two methods of achieving thematic bracketing, namely, 'nominalizing the verbal group, or some combination of elements that includes the verbal group, and adding the subordinating particle *de* at the end'. As reviewed in Chapter 2, nominalization of verbal group is one of the most frequently observed GM types. The attachment of *de* to grammatical constituents in Chinese often engenders a form of nominalization. Thus, GM is a significant structural means in changing a particular constitute in clause as the Theme.

The nominalized Theme and the Rheme are linked by the relational verb *shi* (be) and form an identifying type of relational process. This type of clause is shown in Example 3.47.

(3.47)	*Zui*	*zhongyao*	*de*	*shi*	*sudu*	*de*	*gaibian.*
	most	important	Sub.	is	speed	Sub.	change
	Theme			Rheme			

'The most important point is the change of speed.'

3.3.4 Realization Statement of Theme System

The paradigmatic examination of the Theme system in Chinese clauses shows that the system is initially realized through a structure of Theme + Rheme. The system also simultaneously contains the choices between different types of Theme. These choices and their realization are summarized in Figure 3.3 to capture the features of Theme system in Chinese.

As this network of realization statement shows, there are three main kinds of Theme choices in the Theme system of Chinese. Each choice of the system is realized by a structure or structures located in the particular positions of Chinese clauses. So far, I have examined the textual organization of

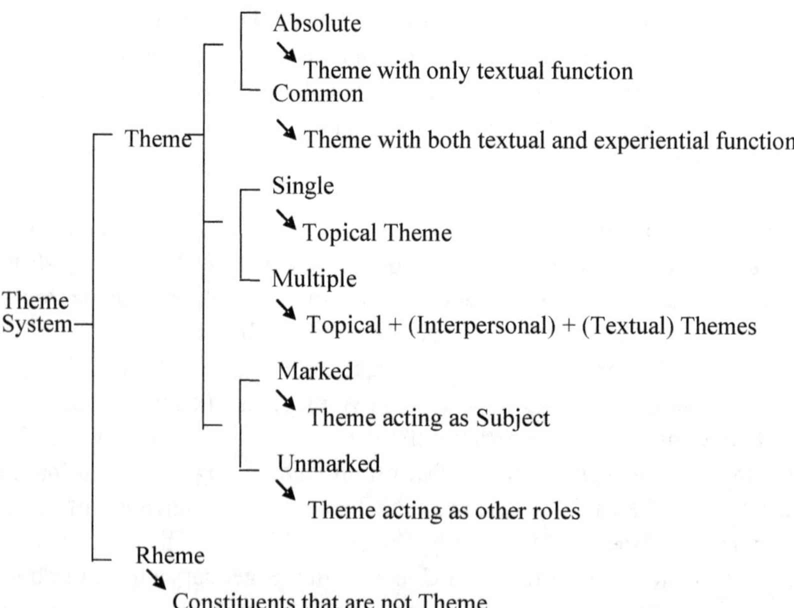

Figure 3.3: Realization statement of Theme system

Chinese clause and present a framework for its analysis. Section 3.4 is concerned with the interpersonal function in Chinese clauses.

3.4 Analysing Chinese clause from interpersonal perspective

One of the main purposes of communication with language is to establish and maintain interpersonal relationships among people. This section discusses how interpersonal meaning in Chinese is realized as lexicogrammatical systems. The discusson focuses Mood and Modality systems in Chinese because the realization of GM is mainly concerned with them. I first describe the components of interpersonal system in Chinese, providing a foundation for the discussion of Mood and Modality.

3.4.1 Components of interpersonal system

A. Subject

Halliday (2003: 205) claims that the Subject in English has two functions in the Mood system: 'it takes responsibility for the proposition, and it also plays a part in realizing the distinction between one category of mood and another'. As for the Subject in Chinese, Halliday (2003: 205) explains that 'there is a nominal element in Chinese which does the first job but not the second – and since it is not required for making the distinction between declarative and interrogative'. Halliday's (2003) explanation shows that the Subject in Chinese plays no part in signalling the mood of a clause. As mentioned in the preceding discussion of textual function, this feature is directly related to the similarity between the structures of interrogative and declarative clauses in Chinese.

B. Finite

Whether or not there is the element of Finite in Chinese has always been a topic of discussion in related studies (for example, McDonald, 1992; Halliday and McDonald, 2004). This study argues that there is the element of Finite in the interpersonal configuration of Chinese clauses. The Finite in English refers to the element which 'has the function of making the proposition finite' (Halliday, 1994: 75). In particular, an element of Finite functions to give a clause the time reference of speaking or the judgement of the speaker. According to Halliday (1994: 75), 'finiteness is thus expressed by means of a verbal operator which is either temporal or modal' and 'there is one further feature which is an essential concomitant of finiteness, and that is POLARITY'. There are verbal operators in Chinese which function to make a clause finite. However, these operators only involve the speaker's judgement and the expression of polarity because Chinese is a language without tense system. Seen against this background, the Finite in Chinese refers to the verbal operator which signals the modality and polarity of a clause. These verbal operators are examined in more detail in the following discussion of Modality system in Chinese.

C. Predicator

The Predicator in a Chinese clause refers to the rest of the verbal group apart from the Finite. In the sense of ideational meaning, a Predicator expresses the process in which the Subject is involved. The verbal group functioning as a Predicator contains a main verb as Event, which may be attached by a postverb realizing phase and a verbal particle indicating aspect. It is worth noting that a Chinese Predicator is also realized in the form of an adjective group. As discussed in Section 3.2.2, clauses with ascriptive meaning are the type of expression where a Predicator is realized by an adjective group. Another distinctive feature of Predicator in Chinese is that it is sometimes involved in the expression of interrogative Mood. This point is described at greater length in the discussion of Mood system.

D. Complement

A Chinese clause may include one or two Complements, which refer to both objects and complements in the traditional studies of Chinese grammar. Functionally, Complements are the elements which could have been chosen as Subjects, but were not. There is, however, one kind of clause in Chinese which has no complement. This is the ascriptive type of relational process which, as discussed above, only includes Subject and Predicator.

E. Adjuncts

The Adjunct in Chinese is typically realized by the adverbial group or prepositional phrase in a clause and is divided into three subtypes: Circumstantial, Conjunctive and Modal. Modal Adjuncts are of particular importance to the present study because they are frequently used to express metaphorical meanings. The role of Modal Adjunct is typically performed by an adverbial group.

F. Mood particles

A series of particles in Chinese occurs in the final position of clauses serving different functions. Among these functions, an important one is to indicate the Mood of the clause concerned. Traditional Chinese grammar refers to these particles as *yuqi ci* (Mood word) and suggests that the function of them is to relate the utterance involved to conversational context (Li and Thompson, 1981). There are four particles which are used most frequently to indicate different Moods, namely *ma*, *ne*, *ba* and *a/ya*. As already exemplified in Section 3.3.3.3, *ma* is the marker of one type of interrogative. The Mood particle *ne* can indicate the declarative and interrogative Mood. Finally, *ba* and *a/ya* are involved in the expressions of interrogative and imperative Mood. Section 4.6.2 discusses the use and categorization of these Mood particles in more detail.

All the interpersonal elements discussed above are illustrated in the following example:

(3.48)	*Ni*	*neng*	*zai*	*jichang*	*jie*	*wo*	*ma?*
	you	can	at	airport	pick up	me	
	Subject	Finite		Adjunct	Predicator	Complement	Mood particle

'Can you pick me up at the airport?'

As mentioned above, the Subject in Chinese is not a crucial component in the Mood system. It is also observed that the Subject and Finite in Chinese are arranged in the same order in clauses of different Mood types. As such, the ordering of Subject and Finite is not responsible for the construction of Mood system. Section 3.4.2 examines how the meaning of Mood is expressed by a different system in Chinese.

3.4.2 Mood system in Chinese

3.4.2.1 The existence of Mood system

There are different answers to the question whether there is a system of Mood in Chinese. On the one hand, some functional linguists (Fang *et al.*, 1995) regard Chinese as a language without a Mood system. On the other hand, Halliday (2003) argues that Chinese has a Mood system by considering the function of the system. Halliday (2003: 205) defines Mood as 'a system for exchanging information and goods-&-services, one through which speakers are enabled to argue'. According to this definition, there apparently is a Mood system in Chinese language, but it is not the same as in English (Halliday, 2003). This study follows the opinion of Halliday (2003) and explains how Mood system is realized in Chinese.

3.4.2.2 Realizations of different types of Mood

There are three primary types of Mood in Chinese: declarative, interrogative and imperative, which are realized mainly by specific grammatical structures and/or Mood elements. These elements and structures are examined in this section to show how they are used for different types of Mood.

A. Declarative

The declarative is the unmarked type of Mood in Chinese, in which the elements are typically ordered as Subject + Finite + Adjunct + Predicator + Complement. In certain environments, any of the above elements can be ellipsed since none of them is compulsory for the expression of Mood. The Mood particle *ne* is occasionally used in some declarative clauses with specific meaning. There is one subset of the declarative clause which is exclamative in function (Halliday and McDonald, 2004). These exclamative clauses are marked by a degree adverb *duo* (how), *tai* (too) or *zhen* (really), and/or by a Mood particle *a*. The following clause adapted from the study of Halliday and McDonald (2004: 332) is one example of exclamative clause.

(3.49)	*Yifu*	*zhen*	*piaoliang*	*a!*
	dress	really	pretty	
	Subject	Adjunct	Predicator	Mood particle
	'How pretty the dress is!'			

B. Interrogative

In Section 3.3.3.3, the interrogative clauses in Chinese are divided into three groups: question-word, A-not-A, and question particle. This classification of interrogative clause illustrates the different methods involved in the expression of interrogative Mood. First, the interrogative Mood can be expressed by a question-word, which is either a noun or an adverb. The question-word appears as functional elements of Subject, Complement or Adjunct in interpersonal system. Second, the interrogative Mood is realized by an A-not-A structure, which occurs in the position of Predicator or Finite. If the first element of A-not-A structure is a main verb, the structure functions as Predicator. In the case that the element to be repeated is a modal verb, the structure is located in the position of Finite. This situation is shown in the following examples:

(3.50a)	Subject	Predicator
	Ni	*qu bu qu?*
	you	go not go
	'Are you going or not?'	

(3.50b)	Subject	Finite	Predicator
	Ni	*neng bu neng*	*qu?*
	you	can not can	go
	'Can you go or not?'		

Finally, the interrogative Mood can be marked by adding a Mood particle at the end of a declarative clause. The Mood particle *ma* can solely express the Mood of interrogative, while other Mood particles are used together with question-word or A-not-A structure.

C. Imperative

The unmarked expression of an imperative clause has a Subject in the form of personal pronouns and a Predicator realized by a verb. The personal pronouns expressing Subject are concerned with first person like *wo*(I) and *women* (we) or second person including *ni* (you) and *nimen* (you). The Predicator in certain process types may be preceded by an Adjunct with the meaning of manner.

In addition to special structures and Mood elements, the Mood system of Chinese is occasionally realized by an isolated mental/verbal clause or an intonation, which generally co-occurs with the structures and elements discussed above. This examination of Mood systems in Chinese shows that there is no structure which is picked up and reused to keep the exchange of information going in the language, like the structure of 'Subject + Finite' in English. Thus, there is no need to recognize the constituents of Mood (the combination of Subject and Finite) and Residue (the rest part of a clause) in the analysis of Mood meaning in Chinese. In this study, a Chinese clause is directly divided into functional components which have been discussed above.

3.4.3 Modality in Chinese

Modality has been a topic of interest for a long time in the literature of Chinese linguistics. Many books and articles (for example, Wang, 1959; Chao, 1968; Lü, 1982) have been written on the subject but only a few of them adopt a systemic-functional approach. The traditional studies of modality in Chinese are confined to the use of modal verbs. The other realization forms such as adverbs, full verbs and mood particles are ignored in the majority of related studies. The most systematic research of Modality within systemic functional tradition is conducted by Zhu (1996). This description of Modality system draws heavily on Zhu's (1996) study though some conclusions of the study are not adopted. Considering the importance of modal verbs in realizing Modality in Chinese, it is necessary to take a brief look at the modal verbs in Chinese before the detailed discussion of Modality.

3.4.3.1 Modal verbs

In English, there is a distinction between modal and non-modal auxiliary verbs. Chinese, as already mentioned, has no such thing as non-modal auxiliaries corresponding to 'be' and 'have' in English. The terms of modal verb, auxiliary verb and *nengyuan* (ability–wish) verb are used interchangeably by Chinese linguists. Depending on the previous studies concerning the syntactic profiles of modal verbs, Zhu (1996: 186) suggests that they could be distinguished from the main verbs in that:

1. They, unlike full verbs, cannot take aspectual markers such as *zhe* and *le*;
2. They, unlike full verbs, cannot appear in one-word imperatives; and
3. They, unlike full verbs again, cannot form a Predicator by themselves in the transitivity system except in elliptical sentences.

In addition, Zhu (1996) provides a new classification of the modal verbs on the basis of the research of Wang (1959), Chao (1968) and Lü (1982). This classification is shown in Figure 3.4 drawn from Zhu (1996).

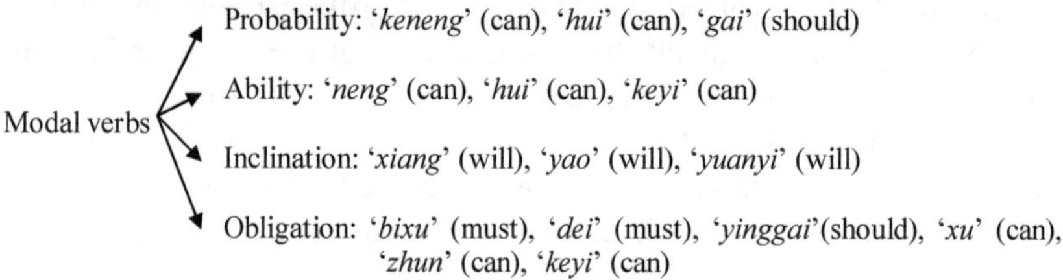

Figure 3.4: Classification of Modal verbs in Chinese (Zhu, 1996: 189)

With this classification, Zhu (1996) further argues that the modal verbs in the category of probability serve as the modal operators in Modalization, while those in the other three categories are the operators in Modulation. This study modifies the categorization in the following discussion of Modalization and Modulation.

3.4.3.2 Modalization

The term Modalization used by Halliday (1994: 89) refers to both probability and usuality. In this section, I describe separately these two interpersonal functions in Chinese.

A. Probability

Broadly speaking, the probability in Chinese is realized by modal verbs, other word classes or by modal verbs plus some other word classes (Zhu, 1996). As Figure 3.4 illustrates, the modal verbs that can express probability are *keneng* (can), *hui* (can) and *gai* (should). *Keneng* and *hui* indicate a low degree of probability, while *gai* expresses a high degree of probability. Adverbs also play an important role in the realization of probability. The four adverbs *yiding*, *kending*, *biding* and *zhun* with the meaning of 'certainly' all express a high degree of probability. In certain cases, adverbs and modal verbs co-occur to express the meaning of probability. *Zhun gai* (certainly should) and *yiding hui* (certainly can) are the examples of this kind of expression.

According to Zhu (1996), full verbs such as *xiangxin* (believe), *guji* (estimate), *kan* (think) and *xiang* (reckon) are also involved in the expression of probability. These verbs can combine with adverbs or modal verbs that indicate high degree of probability. In addition, the probability in Chinese could be realized by the Mood particle *ba*, which is located at the end of a clause. For example:

(3.51)	*Tamen*	*dao*	*jichang*	*le*	*ba?*
	they	arrive at	airport	Asp	Mood particle

'It is possible that they have arrived at the airport.'

B. Usuality

As far as the function of usuality in Chinese is concerned, Zhu (1996: 189) claims that 'frequency is not expressed by modal verbs or any other forms that indicate probability'. Hence, He believes that usuality is not part of Chinese Modality. This study recognizes that the usuality in Chinese can be realized through other forms than modal verbs. For example, the usuality is expressed by adverbs with different degrees of oftenness, such as *yizhi* (always), *jingchang* (usually) and *youshi* (sometimes). As it is not the aim of this discussion to offer a detailed description of all the possible forms concerned in usuality realization, the other forms expressing the usuality are not investigated here. Nevertheless, above examples show that modality system in Chinese includes the expression of usuality.

3.4.3.3 Modulation

Zhu (1996) argues that there are three subtypes of Modulation in Chinese, namely, inclination, obligation and ability. This description of Modulation in Chinese only covers two kinds of interpersonal meaning: inclination and obligation. Halliday (1994: 359) explains that the meaning of ability or potentiality is 'on the fringe of the modality system'. In English, 'can' is 'in any case untypical of the modal operators' (Halliday, 1994: 359). The modal verbs in Chinese to realize the meaning of ability are similar in function to those in English. Therefore, the expression of ability in Chinese is not regarded as one type of modulation in the framework of this study.

A. Inclination

Zhu (1996) recognizes three degrees of inclination: high, median and low, or insistence, intention and willingness. According to Zhu (1996), inclination can be realized by modal verbs and adverbs. The four modal verbs *yao* (will), *xiang* (wish), *yuanyi* (will) and *ken* (will) can be used for the indication of inclination in Chinese. The adverbs *yiding* (must), *pian* (must), *fei* (must) also express the meaning of inclination.

B. Obligation

The meaning of obligation also has different degrees of value: high, median and low, or compulsion, expectation and permission (Zhu, 1996). These degrees of obligation are typically realized by modal verbs. Compulsion is expressed by the modal verbs of *yao*, *bixu* and *dei*, which are semantically equal to 'must' in English. Expectation is realized by the modal verbs of *yinggai*, *yingdang* and *gai*, which have the same meaning of 'should' in English. Finally, permission is indicated by *keyi*, *xu* and *zhun*, which can be translated as 'may' in English. Occasionally, the obligation meaning is realized by other word classes. Full verbs of *yaoqiu* (require), *qiangpo* (compel), *rang* (let) and *yunxu* (permit) are sometimes deployed in Chinese as the alternative forms of obligation realization.

3.4.4 Subjective and objective modality in Chinese

The description of the subjective and objective Modality in Chinese is significant for this study because it is the basis for the discussion of interpersonal GM in the language. The expressions of Modality can be graded according to how far a speaker overtly accepts responsibility for the attitude being expressed. The speaker may express his attitude subjectively by making it clear that this is his own point of view; or the attitude could be expressed objectively 'by making it appear to be a quality of the event itself' (Thompson, 1996: 60). Both subjective and objective natures of assessment in English are typically highlighted by expressing Modality in a separate clause, as illustrated in the following examples (Thompson, 1996: 60):

(3.52) Objective: It's quite possible that he is ill.
Subjective: I expect he is ill.

There are intermediate ways of expressing Modality between the two extremes of emphasizing subjectivity and creating objectivity, for example:

(3.53) He is possibly ill.
He could be ill.

In Chinese, there are also the expressions of Modality in the form of separate clauses. The subjective Modality in Chinese is realized by the structure of *wo* (I) + verb, which appears to be a proposition about the speaker himself. The objective Modality is generally expressed by a relational process, which is featured by the use of verb *you* (see Section 4.6.3 for details). See Example 3.54:

(3.54)	Objective:	*You*	*keneng*	*ta*	*bing*	*le.*
		exist	possibility	he	ill	Asp.
		'It is possible that he is ill.'				
	Subjective:	*Wo*	*juede*	*ta*	*bing*	*le.*
		I	expect	he	ill	Asp.
		'I expect he is ill.'				

In addition to verbal, mental and relational clauses, the structure of '*shi ... de*' is also deployed for expressing Modality explicitly in Chinese. These expressions with different structures are discussed at greater length in the investigation of GM identification in Chinese (see Section 4.6.3).

3.4.5 Realization statement of Mood and modality systems

I present the structural statements of Mood and Modality in Chinese on the basis of the preceding discussion. As the interpersonal meaning of a Chinese clause is construed by both Mood and Modality systems, their realizations are summarized together in the network below.

As shown in Figure 3.5, the realizations of Mood and Modality in Chinese are quite different from those in English. Instead of being limited to the interaction between Subject and Finite, Mood system in Chinese is constituted by all the interpersonal elements in a clause. Similarly, the Modality system in Chinese is also made up of Finite, Adjunct and Predicator. The preceding discussion of the interpersonal system in Chinese focuses exclusively on the grammatical systems of Mood and Modality, without paying much attention to the rest of the clause in question. Although much of the interpersonal meaning of a Chinese clause is realized by Mood and Modality, it is necessary to point out that the recognition of other interpersonal systems is also useful in the functional analysis of Chinese.

3.5 Analysing grammatical units above and below the clause in Chinese

The preceding analyses of Chinese from the perspectives of experiential, textual and interpersonal meanings have been limited to the unit of clause. It is also necessary to describe the grammatical units above and below the clause in order to set up a complete framework for Chinese analysis. Two or more clauses in Chinese are combined into a clause complex. In addition, a Chinese

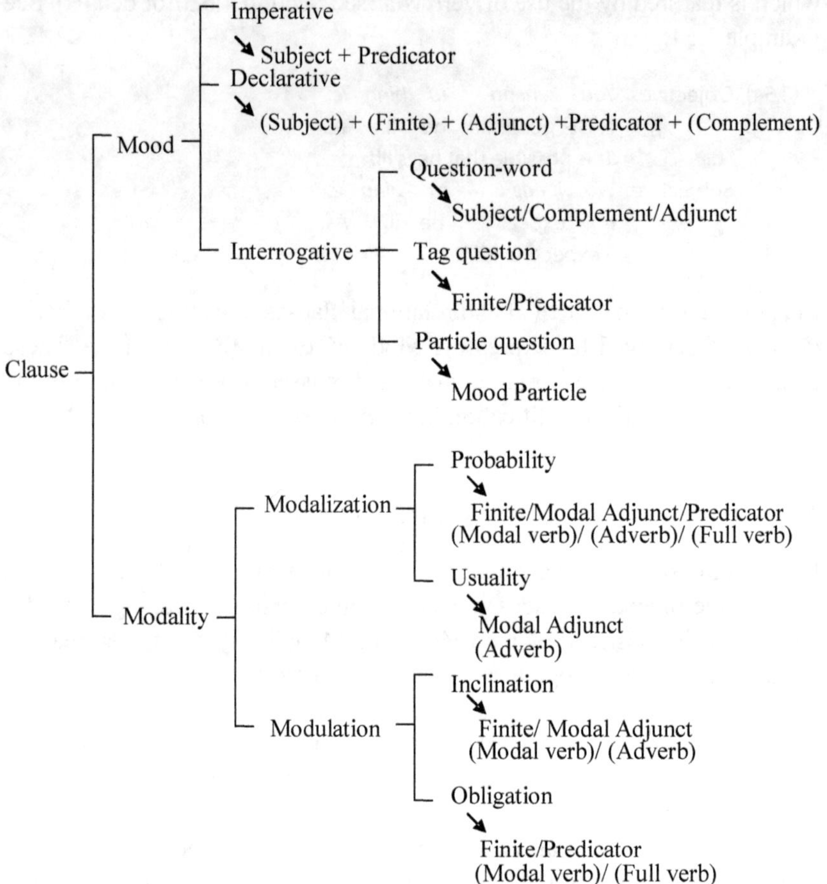

Figure 3.5: Realization statements of Mood and Modality systems

clause is constructed by various types of groups and phrases. I first examine the structure of clause complexes in Chinese to show how clauses relate to each other in terms of the logical component of grammatical systems. Following this, I discuss the structures of groups and phrases in Chinese.

3.5.1 Logical relations between Chinese clauses

According to Halliday (1994), the relations between English clauses are interpreted in two systemic dimensions: interdependency system of parataxis and hypotaxis and logico-semantic system of expansion and projection. Previous functional studies of Chinese clause complexes (Ouyang, 1986; Fang *et al.*, 1995; Halliday and Matthiessen, 1999) reveal that these

A. Interdependency relations

Parataxis:	1 (primary)	2 (secondary)
Hypotaxis:	α (primary)	β (secondary)

B. Logico-semantic relations

I: Expansion

Elaboration	= (primary equals secondary)
Extension	+ (primary is added to secondary)
Enhancement	x (primary is multiplied by secondary)

II: Projection

Locution	" (primary projects secondary as wording)
Idea	' (primary projects secondary as meaning)

Figure 3.6: Logical relations in the clause complex in Chinese (Fang *et al.*, 1995: 246)

categories are also applicable to the analysis of Chinese. Semantically, the clause complexes in English and Chinese cover the similar range of logical relations (Halliday and Matthiessen, 1999). In particular, the relationship within a Chinese clause complex may be one of expansion and projection, and may be either paratactic or hypotactic. The main categories of these relations with symbols used to represent them are shown in Figure 3.6.

It is worth noting that the clause complex in Chinese does not cover all the possible combinations of interdependency and logico-semantic relations (Ouyang, 1986). There is not the combination of hypotaxis and elaboration relations in a Chinese clause complex because of the absence of non-defining relative clauses in the language. In English, there are relative clauses which are introduced by a set of nouns and adverbs serving as relative. When these clauses are embedded and function as Epithet in either a nominal or an adverbial group, they are defining relative clauses. In contrast, those not embedded and functioning as Epithet are named as non-defining relative clauses. Halliday (1994: 226) proposes that 'the combination of elaboration with hypotaxis gives the category of non-defining relative clause'. There are no non-defining relative clauses in Chinese because of the lack of relatives. The comparison between the following Chinese and English expressions of the same meaning illustrates this point.

(3.55)	English:	John ran away, which surprised everyone.								
	Chinese:	*John*	*pao*	*le, mei*	*ge*	*ren*	*dou*	*zhenjing*	*le.*	
		John	run away	Asp.	every	Mea.	person	all	surprised	Asp.

Example 3.55 shows that the Chinese equivalent of the English clause complex is constructed as a paratactic clause complex. The combination of hypotactic and elaboration is thus not a type of logical relation in Chinese.

The difference between English and Chinese in the structure of a clause complex is also engendered by their distinctive grammatical systems. According to Halliday and Matthiessen (1999), the unmarked paratactic relation in a Chinese expansion is typically not marked by any conjunction. The hypotactic relations in Chinese are also unlike those in English in that the dependent clause almost always precedes the one on which it depends. Rather, the dependency relation is signalled obligatorily in the primary clause and optionally in the dependent one, instead of the other way round as in English (Halliday and Matthiessen, 1999). Despite all these differences, the categories listed in Figure 3.6 are still suitable for the analysis of clause complexes in Chinese. Example 3.56 shows how different kinds of interdependency and logico-semantic relations are represented in detailed analysis.

(3.56)						
	1	*Ta*	*xiang*	*kan*	*hui*	*shu,*
		he	want	read	a while	book
	+2 β	*yinwei*	*tai*	*lei,*		
		because	too	tired		
	2 x α	*kan*	*bu*	*cheng,*		
		Read	not	attain		
	+3	*zheshi*	*dianhua*	*xiang.*		
		at this time	phone	ring		

'He wants to read book for a while but fails as he is too tired. At this time, the phone rings.'

There are both paratactic and hypotactic relations in Example 3.56. The paratactic relation is realized by two clauses and one clause complex, the clause shown as '1' is the starting point of paratactic meaning, and the clause complex and the clause respectively shown as '2' and '3' continue the expression. The hypotactic relation occurs at the second level. The clause complex itself is made up of two parts respectively shown as 'α' and 'β'. Example 3.56 also illustrates the logico-semantic relations in Chinese. The clauses '1', '2' and '3' are connected by a relationship of extension, while clauses 'α' and 'β' are linked by a relationship of enhancement.

Categories	**Examples**
a. Conjunction proper	'*erqie*' (and, also); '*suoyi*' (so)
b. Adverbial conjunctions	'*budan*' (not only); '*yinwei*' (because)
c. Adverbial connectives	'*hai*'(still); '*que*' (on the contrary)
d. Repetitive connectives	'*...yue ... yue*' (the more … the more)

Figure 3.7: Tsao's (1990: 347) classification of 'clause conjunctives' in Chinese

3.5.2 Conjunctions and conjunctive adjuncts in Chinese

Tsao (1990) claims that 'clause conjunctives' in Chinese are classified into four categories in most traditional studies of Chinese (for example, Wang, 1956; Chao, 1968; Chu, 1983; Li and Thompson, 1981), as shown in Figure 3.7.

According to Tsao (1990), category (a) occurs only at the initial position of the second clause in a clause complex, while category (c) never occurs at the initial position of a clause no matter whether it appears in the first or the second clause. Category (b) is more variable in terms of its position in clauses. Category (d) is distinguished from the other categories by the fact that the same morpheme in used in two clauses.

Tsao's (1990) classification shows that linking elements, which occur in Chinese clauses to indicate logical relations, involve both conjunctions and adverbs. These elements are referred to as conjunction and conjunctive adjunct in SFG. The structural features of Chinese clause complexes are closely associated with the use of conjunctions and conjunctive adjuncts. Conjunctions and conjunctive adjuncts are often syntactically optional in Chinese clause complexes. They do not necessarily occur at the beginning position of a clause even when they are used. In fact, they can occur at various positions in a clause.

I classify Conjunctions and conjunctive Adjuncts in Chinese clause complexes in terms of the logical relations involved. Given the absence of linking elements in projecting clause complexes, Conjunctions and conjunctive adjuncts are only used to construct expansion relations. To be more specific, these linking elements in Chinese are concerned with the expressions of extension and enhancement meanings. The conjunctions and conjunctive adjuncts occurring most frequently in Chinese are listed in Table 3.4.

3.5.3 Groups and phrases in Chinese clause

Halliday and McDonald (2004) recognize three groups and one phrase in Chinese, namely verbal group, nominal group, adverbial group and prepositional phrase. Nominal groups and verbal groups are treated as the main focus in this section since they are more important in GM analysis.

3.5.3.1 Nominal group

A nominal group in Chinese is comprised of one Thing and series of elements categorizing the Thing. These categorizing elements include Deictic, Numerative, Measurer, Epithet, and Classifier. Halliday and Matthiessen (2004) define Deictic in a language as the element indicating whether some

	Paratactic	*Hypotactic*
Extension	erqie, bingqie (and) huo, huozhe (or) budan … erqie… (not only…but also) ye (and) tongshi (at the same time) dan, danshi, keshi (but)	ciwai, lingwai (besides) er (while) que (whereas,while) hai (still)
Enhancement	jiu, cai (then) yushi (so) ranhou (then) conger (thus) yue … yue… (the more…the more)	ruguo (if) yinwei (because) zhiyao (unless) suiran (although) wei (for) dang (when) ruguo … jiu … (if … then…) zhiyao …jiu … (unless…then…) … zhiqian (before) … zhihou (after)

Table 3.4: Classification of conjunctions and conjunctive adjuncts

specific subset of the Thing is intended or not. This definition means that there are both specific and non-specific types of Deictic in Chinese. There is not a specific Deictic in Chinese with the meaning of 'the' in English. Non-specific Deictics in Chinese have no item expressing the meaning of 'either' or 'neither'. The Numerative in Chinese also falls into two subtypes: the quantifying and the ordering. A quantifying Numerative in a nominal group must be used together with a Measurer which is a unique element in Chinese. The Measurer in Chinese is traditionally referred to as 'measure' or 'classifier' in relevant studies (Chao, 1968; Li and Thompson, 1981) and can be further divided into various kinds. The choice of measure word is largely determined by the nature of a noun. For example, the noun *shu* (book) is typically used together with the Measurer 本 *ben* (piece):

(3.57) *Wo mai le liang ben shu.*
I buy Asp. two piece book
'I bought two books.'

The Epithet in Chinese is used to indicate the quality of a Thing. It is expressed in the form of adjective, noun, nominal group or even embedded clause and linked to the Thing by subordinating participle *de*. In addition, all the Epithets in a Chinese nominal group must precede the Thing involved. This contrasts with English where the quality of a Thing can be indicated by both Epithet and Qualifier, the former being used before the

Thing and the latter following the Thing. In this sense, the Epithet in Chinese has a larger scope than its counterpart in English. The Classifier has the function of clarifying the subclass of the Thing in question. It can be realized by an adjective or a noun. In many cases, the adjective and the noun involved in realizing Classifier can also be used for the expression of Epithet. Similar to those in English, the words functioning as Classifier do not accept degrees of comparison or intensity. Finally, it is worth noting that all the categorizing elements discussed above must be located before the Thing in a nominal group. This typological property is of particular importance in this study because it gives rise to many features of GM in Chinese.

3.5.3.2 Verbal group

Different attempts have been made to describe the structure of verbal groups in Chinese within the framework of SFG. McDonald (2004) claims that the verbal group in Chinese is strictly an experiential phenomenon which realizes the Process in transitivity system. In addition, 'it may be simple, i.e. consist at group rank of only Event; compound, i.e. consist at group rank of Event plus Extension; or complex, i.e. consist of a number of verbs joined in some kind of logical relation' (McDonald, 2004: 242). Halliday and McDonald (2004) propose that the verbal group in Chinese expands both before and after its Head. The position preceding Head is reserved for interpersonal meaning of polarity and modality, while the position following Head is used for experiential meaning of aspect and phase. In other words, the verbal group in Chinese is constructed by interpersonal and experiential components of meaning.

The structure of verbal group is analyzed in this study by adopting the view proposed by Halliday and McDonald (2004). A verbal group in Chinese consists of three types of structural elements: Auxiliary, Event, and Extension. The Auxiliary covers the elements expressing the meanings of polarity, modality and aspect in a verbal group. These meanings are realized by affirmative and negative adverbs, auxiliary verbs and particles respectively. Event is realized by the main verb in a verbal group, while Extension is expressed by the class of postverb in Chinese. The postverb extends the meaning represented by the main verb in a direction or to a result and forms an elaborate system of phase in Chinese (Halliday and McDonald, 2004).

I adopt the terms of McDonald (2004) in dividing verbal groups into three types: the simple, the compound and the complex. However, these types of verbal groups have different structures from those in McDonald's (2004) model because they are constructed by elements with both interpersonal and experiential meanings. The detailed structure of various types of verbal group is summarized in Table 3.5.

Verbal group type	*Structure of functional components*
Simple verbal group	Auxiliary + Event; Event
Compound verbal group	Auxiliary + Event + Extension; Event + Extension
Complex verbal group	Auxiliary + Event + Event; Event + Event

Table 3.5: Structure of various types of verbal group in Chinese

Table 3.5 shows that the element of Auxiliary is not a compulsory component in Chinese verbal groups. Moreover, the complex verbal group is comprised of the 'serial verbal construction' which has the structure of 'Event + Event'.

3.5.3.3 Adverbial group and propositional phrase

I discuss the adverbial group and the propositional phrase in Chinese together because both of them are used for the realization of Circumstance in the transitivity system of a clause. Halliday and McDonald (2004: 316) recognize two kinds of adverbial group in Chinese: '(i) those with adverb as Head, with or without a Modifier of intensity; (ii) those with adjectival verb as Head, possibly reduplicated, and followed by the adverbial particle *de'*. The first type of adverbial group is further classified into clausal and verbal subtypes. The clausal ones express interpersonal and textual meanings or the experiential meaning of location, while the verbal ones only express the experiential meaning of time and modality. Another important difference between them is that only the clausal subtype can be thematized in a clause. The second type of adverbial group in Chinese is in effect transferred from the adjective by adding the adverbial particle *de*. This type of adverbial group is used to realize the experiential meaning of manner.

The discussion in Section 3.2.3.1 shows that the Circumstance in Chinese is mainly realized in the form of a prepositional phrase. When a Circumstance has the meaning of location or direction, the prepositional phrase involved often includes a postnoun. The preposition in the phrase expresses the general location, while the postnoun indicates the relative position or 'facet' (Halliday and McDonald, 2004). In terms of experiential structure, the prepositional phrases in Chinese fall into two groups: those with the form of 'minor Process + Participant + Facet' and those with the form of 'minor Process + Participant'.

3.6 Summary

This chapter provides a framework for the systemic functional analysis of Chinese. Because the terminology in SFG is developed in the linguistic environment of English, the key terms in the framework are defined under the principle of 'from above' to prevent any distortion of the linguistic characteristics in Chinese. There has been a substantial reliance on previous studies of Chinese throughout the discussion in this chapter. In fact, this chapter focuses its discussion on the controversial issues in the relevant studies and attempts to provide new insights into these uncertainties.

This chapter establishes a three-dimensional framework for the analysis of Chinese clause by discussing the experiential, textual and interpersonal systems operating in Chinese. Rather, the realization statements of various systems are also described to show how functional elements in Chinese are realized as grammatical structures. The chapter also investigates the systems of grammatical units above or below a clause in Chinese, namely clause complex and various groups and phrases. These descriptions of systems and their realization statements serve as the basis for further research of GM in Chinese

4 Identification of grammatical metaphor in Chinese

4.1 Introduction

Chapter 4 discusses the identification of GM in Chinese on the basis of the grammatical framework developed in Chapter 3. The purpose of this chapter is twofold – to define the phenomenon of GM in Chinese, and to describe how the instances of GM in Chinese are recognized. For these purposes, I first revisit previous research of GM to clarify the motifs of GM identification in Chinese. The semantic stratum in Chinese is then examined to outline its categories in terms of textual, interpersonal and ideational meanings. In order to identify GM in Chinese, I examine the transgrammatical semantic domains in the language which create a linguistic environment for the phenomenon of GM. The examination reveals the remapping relationship between semantics and lexicogrammar in Chinese. Following this, I differentiate congruent and metaphorical realizations of semantic categories in Chinese. The grammatical variations involved in metaphorical realizations are also clarified to provide practical method for recognizing individual GM instances. Finally, I discuss three lexicogrammatical phenomena which play critical roles in the identification of GM in Chinese.

4.2 Motifs of GM identification in Chinese

The literature review in Chapter 2 shows that the understanding of the nature of GM varies in different phases of GM studies, which in turn results in various working definitions of GM. In addition, the differences between ideational GM and interpersonal GM increase the difficulty of identifying GM in Chinese. I thus revisit the findings in different phases of GM research to specify the key motifs of GM identification in Chinese. These motifs serve as the common foundation for the ideatification of ideational GM and interpersonal GM.

4.2.1 Three motifs of GM

Previous research on GM falls into three successive phases in which the understanding of the nature of GM is consistently developed. The nature of GM is initially explored by Halliday (1984, 1985, 1994) and Ravelli (1985) whose work provides a starting point for further study of the phenomenon. The key motif in the earliest exploration of the nature of GM is the integration of metaphor in lexical and grammatical poles of lexicogrammatical continuum. The differentiation of 'congruent' and 'metaphorical' realizations of a given semantic unit is another focus in the early explorations of the nature of GM. The first phase studies of GM also throw some light on the relationship between GM and the stratal interaction between semantics and lexicogrammar.

The interaction between the semantic and lexicogrammatical levels of the content plane in a language is the key motif in the second phase of GM research (Halliday, 1998; Halliday and Matthiessen, 1999). According to Halliday and Matthiessen (1999), the emergence of GM is related to the natural development of the content plane in a language. Initially, the content plane is formed by semantic and lexicogrammatical strata coupling in congruent patterns. The content plane of a language evolves by extending the congruent patterns between semantic and lexicogrammatical strata. The disruption of the congruent patterns between the two levels of content plane opens up the possibility of metaphorical expression. GM is thus defined as the remapping of the semantics on to the lexicogrammar in this phase of GM exploration.

The third phase of GM research is mainly concerned with the discussion of the nature of GM undertaken by Halliday and Matthiessen (2004). It follows previous GM research by taking stratal remapping as the criteria for identifying metaphorical expressions. However, Halliday and Matthiessen (2004) carry out their identification of GM on the basis of the examination of transgrammatical semantic domains. Halliday and Matthiessen's (2004) method of GM identification is more reliable because it represents GM in the overall semantic system of a language. Additionally, Halliday and Matthiessen (2004) propose that GM systematically expands the meaning potential by creating new patterns of structural realization. In other words, metaphorical modes of meaning are motivated by the need to expand meaning potential. This interpretation of the inherent motivation of GM greatly enhances our understanding of the nature of GM.

This brief reexamination of previous GM research indicates that the realignment between semantics and lexicogrammar is the main motif of GM identification. In addition, the reliance of GM on transgrammatical semantic domains and the expansion of meaning potential are the other two motifs of GM identification.

4.2.2 Common foundation of ideational GM and interpersonal GM

The three motifs of GM identification serve as the common foundations for the identification of ideational GM and interpersonal GM. Chapter 2 shows that ideational GM and interpersonal GM are distinctive with respect to the direction of grammatical movement. Ideational GM first involves a grammatical movement 'down' in rank: sequences are alternatively realized by clauses and groups; figures are reconstrued by groups. Correspondingly, ideational GM is concerned with the grammatical movement from the elements in a clause to the components in a nominal group, as well as from the Conjunction in a clause complex to the Process in a clause. The general tendency for ideational GM is to 'downgrade' the grammatical category realizing a particular semantic unit (Halliday and Matthiessen, 2004). In contrast, interpersonal GM is characterized by its tendency to upgrade the categories of grammatical realization. Halliday and Matthiessen (2004) observe that both the metaphorical realizations of mood and modality systems are concerned with projection which upgrades the category of grammatical realization from clause to clause complex.

Although ideational GM and interpersonal GM have different directions in terms of grammatical movements, both of them arise from the remapping between semantics and lexicogrammar. Furthermore, they are similarly deployed for the underlying principle of expanding the meaning potential of a language (Halliday and Matthiessen, 2004). To be more specific, the metaphorical realizations of semantic units in ideational dimension increase the meaning potential of construing our experience of the world. The metaphorical realizations of the speech functional system provide new meaning potential for negotiation between speakers of a language. The metaphorical realizations of modality systems expand the methods of making interpersonal assessment. Additionally, the study of Halliday and Matthiessen (2004) indicates that ideational GM and interpersonal GM rely on the same linguistic phenomenon of transgrammatical semantic domains.

The discussion above shows that the three motifs of GM, namely the remapping of semantics and lexicogrammar, the expansion of meaning potential, and the reliance of GM on transgrammatical semantic domains, are the common foundations of ideational GM and interpersonal GM. Therefore, both ideational GM and interpersonal GM identified in this book refer to the remapping of semantic and lexicogrammatical systems in Chinese which relies on the transgrammatical semantic domains and gives rise to the expansion of the meaning potential in the language.

4.3 Semantic stratum in Chinese

The notion of GM is developed on the basis of the studies of semantics and lexicogrammar within the theoretical framework of SFL. Therefore, it is impossible to identify the phenomenon of GM in Chinese without the description of semantic and lexicogrammatical stratums in the language. Chapter 3 has presented a description of the lexicogrammatical stratum in Chinese by discussing the systems involved in clause, clause complex and group/phrase. This section describes the semantic stratum in Chinese, taking the grammatical systems established in Chapter 3 as the basis for further discussion.

4.3.1 Textual meaning

The basic semantic unit of textual meaning in Chinese is message, which is realized by the structure of 'Theme + Rheme' in grammatical stratum. In real expressions, messages combine to form a larger unit of textual system which is referred to as 'information flow pattern' by Halliday and Matthiessen (2004: 588). However, the information flow pattern in Chinese is not simply constructed by a sequence of 'Theme + Rheme' structures. As shown in Section 3.3.2, the clauses in a Chinese clause complex frequently share a common Theme which only appears in the first clause. In other words, the information flow pattern in Chinese can be realized by a group of clauses centred on a shared Theme, as illustrated in the following clause complex.

(4.1)	*Zhe tai dianji,*	*tiji xiao,*	*jiage di,*	*mali qiang.*
	this Meas. engine	size small	price low	power strong
	Shared Theme	Theme1+Rheme1	Theme2 + Rheme2	Theme3 + Rheme3

'This engine is small in size, low in price and strong in power.'

The clause complex demonstrates that an information flow pattern in Chinese is constructed by a sequence of messages with the same point of interest. Several information flow patterns with different points of interest then make up a text in Chinese. The semantic system in textual dimension of Chinese thus consists of three orders of semantic units: text, information flow pattern and message.

4.3.2 Interpersonal meaning

The basic semantic unit of interpersonal meaning in SFL is a proposition or proposal. When a clause is used to exchange information, the semantic function of the clause is a proposition. On the other hand, the semantic function concerned is referred to as a proposal if a clause is used in the exchange of goods-&-services. Given that any language is used for the exchange of information and goods-&-services, this differentiation of semantic unit is valid in Chinese.

The proposal or proposition in Chinese has different speech functions in terms of the social-contextual options of role assignment and the commodity exchanged. In particular, the four speech functions concerned in Chinese language are offer, command, statement and question. The semantic unit of proposal or proposition is also concerned with the semantic system of modality, which is the intermediate meaning between positive and negative poles. If the expression is a proposition, the intermediate meaning is modalization which consists of probability and usuality. In the case of proposal, the intermediate meaning is referred to modulation which includes obligation and inclination. Section 3.4 has described the grammatical realizations of modality system in Chinese by reference to those in English.

A proposal or proposition in Chinese semantic system involves only one speaker. In Chinese texts, proposals and propositions are combined to form a larger unit of interpersonal system. The combination is named 'exchange pattern' in SFL (Halliday and Matthiessen, 2004). This larger unit of the semantic system in Chinese is illustrated by Example 4.2.

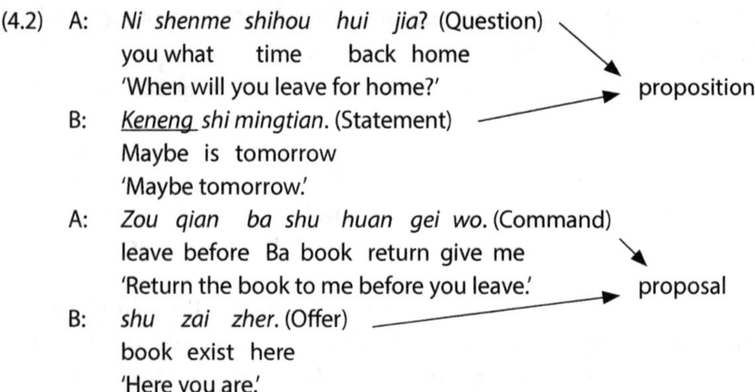

Example 4.2 shows that the exchange pattern is formed by four propositions or proposals which respectively have the speech functions of question, statement, command and offer. Furthermore, it is noticed that the underlined modal verb of *keneng* (maybe) is used to express the meaning of modality. The pattern of exchange in Chinese is, therefore, constructed by a sequence of proposition or proposal with various speech functions and modality meanings.

4.3.3 Ideational meaning

Figures are basic semantic units within the ideational metafunction of Chinese. Similar to that in English, a figure in Chinese is typically a 'configuration of a process, participants involved in it and any attendant circumstances' (Halliday and Matthiessen, 2004: 169). Human experience is construed by the ideational semantic systems in Chinese as four primary types of figure: doing (including happening), sensing, saying and being (including having). There are also intermediate types of figure lying at the borderline of the primary types in Chinese.

According to SFL theory, the experiential meanings in any language are expressed by semantic units of three orders of complexity: sequence, figure and element. These units are connected by a constituency structure: sequences consist of figures while figures consist of the elements of participant, process and circumstance. The ideational meaning in Chinese is construed by these semantic units.

The discussion of clause complex in Section 3.5.1 shows that there are two types of sequence: projection and expansion, and the figures in these types of sequence may be related equally or unequally. Chinese is very similar to English in terms of projection and expansion relations. The projection relation concerns the projecting of idea and locution, while the expansion relation can be further divided into three subtypes of elaboration, extension and enhancement. However, it seems that the scope of expansion relation in Chinese is not as broad as that in English. In particular, some expanding meanings in English are construed by Chinese at the rank of figure.

The discussion above shows that the general framework of semantic systems in Chinese is similar to that in English. Actually, we can apply the semantic categories initially developed for English to the analysis of semantic systems in Chinese. However, a framework of semantic categories is far from enough for the thorough understanding of semantic meanings in a language. There are always inherent properties in any semantic network that is determined by the historical and cultural background of the language involved. The semantic systems in Chinese are briefly displayed in Figure 4.1 (below).

4.4 Transgrammatical semantic domains in Chinese

I have clarified the nature of GM in Chinese and set up the semantic and lexicogrammatical system networks in the language. In order to identify GM in Chinese, it is necessary to describe how the remapping between semantic and lexicogrammatical systems occurs in the language. It is by no means difficult

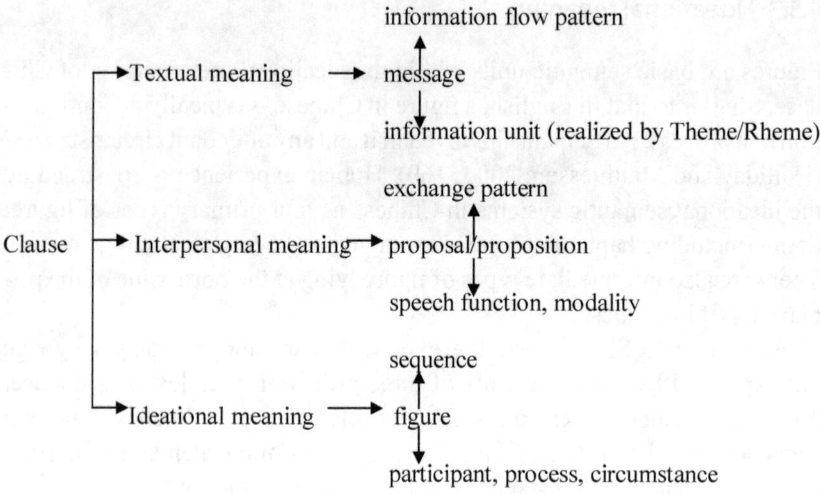

Figure 4.1: Semantic systems in Chinese

to find the remapping phenomenon between semantics and lexicogrammar in Chinese by making reference to previous research of GM. However, previous research of GM is carried out by examining the semantic and lexicogrammatical systems in English. Given the distinctions between English and Chinese in their semantics and lexicogrammar, any exploration of GM in Chinese reasoning along the same line of studying GM in English might deviate from the real situation of GM in the language. As such, the realizational relationship between semantics and lexicogrammar in English should not be used for the identification of GM in Chinese. Instead of making an assumption that the remapping between semantics and lexicogrammar exists in Chinese, I begin the identification of GM in Chinese with the exploration of transgrammatical semantic domains in the language.

Transgrammatical semantic domains refer to semantic domains realized by more than one grammatical category (Halliday and Matthiessen, 2004). It provides a foundation for the remapping between semantic and lexicogrammatical systems in a language. This is because the metaphorical realization of a semantic unit occurs only when the semantic domain is manifested by more than one grammatical category. In other words, the different grammatical categories realizing the same semantic unit create an environment for the remapping between semantics and lexicogrammar. The examination of transgrammatical semantic domains in Chinese, therefore, is a reliable approach to achieve the goal of identifying GM in the language.

Four transgrammatical semantic domains are observed in the semantic systems of Chinese: expansion, projection, speech function and modality.

This observation is largely based on the systemic functional framework developed for Chinese analysis in Chapter 3. For example, the realization of modality domain is examined on the basis of the discussion of modality system in Section 3.4.

4.4.1 Expansion

The discussion in Section 3.5 reveals that the semantic domain of expansion in Chinese is first realized by the grammatical category of clause complex. Similar to English, the expansion relation between figures in Chinese is frequently manifested by Conjunctions and conjunctive Adjuncts which connect clauses into clause complex. However, Conjunctions and conjunctive Adjuncts in Chinese are only involved in the manifestation of two subtypes of expansion: extension and enhancement (see Table 3.4). When Chinese figures with an elaborating relation are combined to form a sequence, there is no linking element in the clause complex concerned. Additionally, Conjunctions and conjunctive Adjuncts are not compulsory for the manifestation of expansion relation when the clauses involved are linked paratactically. As is often the case, the expansion relation in a Chinese sequence is understood by resorting to the meaning of the whole clause complex. Chinese and English thus have different preferences for deploying Conjunctions and conjunctive Adjuncts in expansion manifestations.

The expansion in Chinese is also realized in the grammatical regions of clause and nominal group. In a clause domain, both grammatical categories of Process and Circumstance are capable of manifesting the meaning of expansion. Circumstances in Chinese realize two subtypes of expansion relation: extension and enhancement. According to the classification of circumstances in Section 3.2.3, the meaning of extension is expressed by the circumstance of Accompaniment. The meaning of enhancement, on the other hand, is realized by the circumstances of Location, Cause and Source. The correspondence between expansion relations and Circumstances is revisited in Section 5.3.4 to categorize GM in Chinese.

The realization of expansion in the grammatical category of Process is divided into two forms. First, the expansion meaning is realized by the Processes in relational clauses of intensive, possessive and circumstantial in Chinese. More precisely, the intensive Process embodies elaboration meaning, possessive Process extension meaning and circumstantial Process enhancement meaning. It is worth noting that enhancement relation is not manifested in Chinese so extensively as in English because the circumstantial relational clause in Chinese covers a smaller semantic domain than that in English (see Section 3.2.2.1).

The second form of expansion manifestation in Process is concerned with the Serial Verb Construction (SVC) in Chinese. An SVC is 'a sequence of verbs which act together as a single predicate, without any overt marker of coordination, subordination, or syntactic dependency of any other sort' (Aikhenvald, 2006: 1). SVCs in Chinese can be used to manifest the expansion meaning within one clause. This situation is exemplified by the following comparison of clause complex and clause.

(4.3) Clause complex: *Ta de jiang le, suoyi women gongxi ta.*
he receive award Asp. so we congratulate him
'He received the award, so we congratulate him.'

SVC: *Women gongxi ta de jiang.*
We congratulate him receive reward
'We congratulate him on receiving the award.'

The comparison illustrates that the expansion relation between two figures can be realized by a series of verbs in the SVC. Strictly speaking, an SVC is a particular grammatical category lying between clause complex and clause. Section 8.2.3.2 discusses the features of Chinese SVCs in more detail.

In the grammatical domain of nominal group, the expansion relation in Chinese is manifested by modifiers which elaborate, extend or enhance the Thing in a group. The modifiers involved in this kind of expansion manifestation can be constituted by embedding clauses or groups. Significantly, all the modifiers in a Chinese nominal group occur before the Thing in the group. This special order of grammatical constituents greatly affects the structure of nominal groups in Chinese.

4.4.2 Projection

The semantic domain of projection in Chinese is realized by grammatical categories of clause complex, clause and nominal group. The meaning of projection is realized in a clause complex by dividing the whole nexus into projected clause and projecting clause. The projecting part of the clause complex is a verbal or mental clause which reports or quotes the content in the projected part. Unlike the manifestation of expansion in a clause complex, no linking element is used to indicate projecting relation between clauses. The projection meaning is thus realized by the interaction between two clauses, while the expansion is manifested by Conjunctions and conjunctive Adjuncts which connect two clauses.

The projection meaning is manifested in a Chinese clause by the element of Circumstance. According to the classification of Circumstances in

Section 3.2.3, the Circumstance of Source is involved in the expression of the projecting meaning in Chinese. This kind of Circumstance is generally used to point out the Sayer or the Senser of the main process. For example:

(4.4) *Anzhao Lord Kelvin de guandian, taiyang shi zhire qiti goucheng de qiuti.*
according to Sub. opinion the sun is hot gas constitute Sub. sphere
'According to Lord Kelvin, the sun is a sphere of hot gas.'

When the projection is realized by a nominal group, the projected clause is embedded in the nominal group with Heads like *xiangfa* (idea) and *shuofa* (saying). Compare the following clause complexes and nominal groups which realize similar meaning of projection.

(4.5) Quote: *Galileo shuo, 'suoyou wuti yi tongyang sudu xialuo.'*
Galileo say all object at same speed fall
'Galileo said, "all objects fall at the same speed".'

Galileo guanyu suoyou wuti yi tongyang sudu xialuo de shuofa
Galileo about all object at same speed fall Sub. saying
'Galileo's saying that all objects fall at the same speed'

Report: *Galileo renwei suoyou wuti yi tongyang sudu xialuo.*
Galileo believe all object at same speed fall
'Galileo believes that all objects fall at the same speed.'

Galileo guanyu suoyou wuti yi tongyang sudu xialuo de xiangfa
Galileo about all object at same speed fall Sub. idea
'Galileo's idea that all objects fall at the same speed'

As illustrated by the comparison, the original projection relation between two clauses is embodied by the Head in the nominal group which has the meaning of reporting or quoting. The Sayer or the Sensor in the projecting clause is transferred as the modifier in the nominal group. In the case that the Sayer or the Sensor can be recovered by reference to the preceding clause, they are often omitted in the nominal group.

4.4.3 Modality

The discussion of Chinese modality systems in Section 3.4.3 shows that modal verbs, adverbs, full verbs and even Mood particles are involved in the expression of modal meaning. In terms of grammatical category, the semantic domain of modality is realized by clauses, verbal groups and adverbial groups in Chinese.

When the meaning of modality is construed by a Chinese clause, three forms of expression are involved. The most frequently used grammatical form is a verbal or mental clause serving as the projecting part in a clause complex. In this case, the meaning of modality is manifested as the subjective expression from the Sayer or the Sensor in the clause. The structures of *shi ... de* and *you ...* which respectively constitute relational and existential types of clauses in Chinese are used to express modality meaning objectively. The Chinese clauses involved in the manifestation of modality share the common feature of stating the meaning of modality explicitly. I discuss structures of *shi ... de* and *you ...* at greater length in Section 4.6.3, considering that they are critical for the identification of interpersonal GM in Chinese.

The grammatical categories of verbal group and adverbial group are also used for the expression of modality. Given that modal verbs and adverbs for the purpose of modality expression have been described in Section 3.4.3, they are not revisited in this discussion. However, it is worth noting that these modal verbs and adverbs always state the meaning of modality implicitly.

4.4.4 Speech function

According to SFL theory, the speech function is realized by the grammatical system of Mood. The description in Section 3.4.2 shows that the Mood system in Chinese is constituted of special structures, Mood elements and particular types of clause. In this sense, the semantic domain of speech function in Chinese also ranges over more than one grammatical category.

The majority of speech functions in Chinese are realized by the Mood particles located at the end of clauses. As mentioned in Section 3.4.1, there are four main Mood particles in Chinese: *ma*, *ne*, *ba* and *a/ya*. The Chinese clauses ending with these particles involve three types of Mood: declarative, imperative and interrogative. Moreover, the Mood particles in Chinese are probably used to realize different speech functions according to the context of a dialogue. The systemic deployment of Mood particles in the expression of speech function is further explored in Section 4.6.2.

In contrast to Mood particles which are widely deployed in realizing various types of speech function, clauses involved in the manifestation of speech function are restricted to the meanings of command and question. To be more specific, the command and question are realized by a projecting clause with the Mood of declarative, rather than imperative and interrogative. The realization is represented by Example 4.6.

(4.6) Command: *Wo juede ni gai xiuxi yixia.* (declarative)
I feel you should rest a while
'I think you should take a short rest.'

Question: *Wo xiang ni hui anshi daoda.* (declarative)
I think you will on time arrive
'I think you will arrive on time.'

In these clause complexes, the speech functions of Command and Question are realized by the projecting clauses *wo juede* (I feel) and *wo xiang* (I think). The projecting clause functions to soften the forcefulness of a proposition or proposal with Command and Question meanings. Example 4.6 also shows that the speech functions realized by a projecting clause overlap with the meaning of modality. This reflects the fact that there is not a clear-cut boundary between the speech function and modality in Chinese propositions or proposals. This point is not discussed in detail in this book because it is not one of the primary concerns of the study. Finally, the speech function in Chinese is realized by special structures like 'A-not-A' in interrogative clause. Section 5.4.1 discusses the speech functional formulae deployed in Chinese in detail.

The description above shows that four semantic regions are realized by more than one grammatical category in Chinese. Various ranks of grammatical category in Chinese are interrelated by the common function of realizing transgrammatical semantic domains. As mentioned, the transgrammatical semantic domains create an environment for the realignment of realizational relationship between semantic units and grammatical categories. A sequence with expansion or projection meaning in Chinese can be realized by a clause or a nominal group. Similarly, a figure in Chinese can be realized by a nominal group which maintains the expansion or projection meaning of the original figure. With regards to speech function and modality, they are generally involved in the upgrading grammatical movement from clause to clause complex. For example, a proposition with the particular meaning of modality and speech function can be realized by a clause complex. In sum, the examination of transgrammatical semantic domains indicates that there are remapping relations between semantic and lexicogrammatical strata in Chinese. In other words, the phenomenon of GM exists in Chinese.

4.5 Congruent and metaphorical realizations

The existence of GM in Chinese is confirmed by examining the transgrammatical semantic domains in Section 4.4. In order to explore GM in Chinese in more detail, a comprehensive description of the congruent and metaphorical realizations of semantic meanings in Chinese is needed. This section discusses how various semantic choices in ideational and interpersonal dimensions are congruently and metaphorically realized by lexicogrammatical categories.

4.5.1 Congruent realizations

As illustrated in literature review, the term 'congruent' appears in different GM studies with different meanings. It is by no means easy to provide a concise definition for the congruent realizations of semantic system in a language. The congruent realizations in this study refer to the typical or unmarked lexicogrammatical form of a semantic meaning in Chinese. In practical analysis, the congruent expressions of ideational semantic units in Chinese are described by reference to the framework developed by Halliday and Matthiessen (1999). The congruent realizations of interpersonal systems of modality and speech function are determined by following the study of Halliday and Matthiessen (2004). To begin with, the congruent realizations of ideational semantic units in Chinese are presented.

The congruent realizations of ideational meaning in Chinese are represented along two lines: rank and element. In the case of rank, the semantic units of sequence, figure and element are congruently realized by clause complex, clause and group in Chinese grammatical systems, which are illustrated as shown in Figure 4.2.

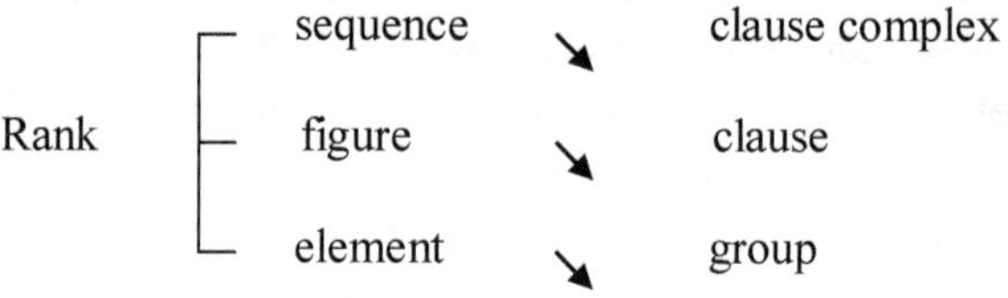

Figure 4.2: Congruent realizations of semantic units in Chinese

Corresponding to the congruent realizations of semantic units, the elements making up a figure or a sequence are respectively construed by different kinds of word, group and phrase in Chinese. There are four basic semantic elements in the ideational system of Chinese, namely process, participant, circumstance and relator. Since the element of participant is further divided into quality and thing, the congruent realizations of different elements can be presented as Figure 4.3.

Compared to those of the ideational system, the congruent realizations of interpersonal system are more difficult to define. Congruent realizations of a particular speech function are often not used in real dialogues due to the need of politeness or the difference in social status between speaker and listener. Thus, the most frequently used expressions may not be congruent realizations. However, Halliday (1984) notices that speakers of a language

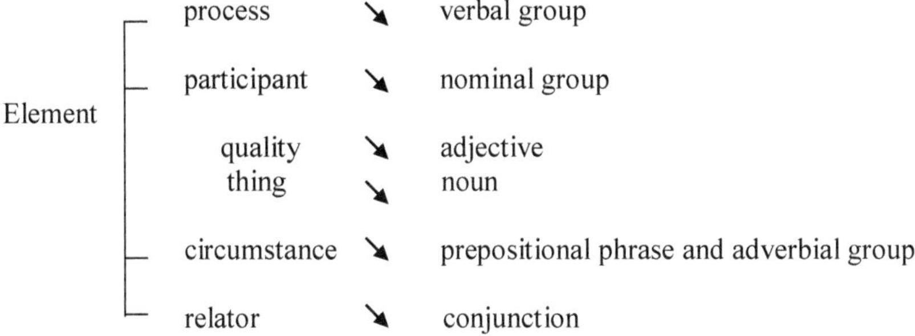

Figure 4.3: Congruent realizations of semantic elements in Chinese

should be aware of what is the congruent mode of any speech function. For instance, 'however rarely we may actually use an imperative in giving orders, we have a feeling that it is in some sense the unmarked way of doing so' (Halliday, 1984: 14).

According to this principle, it is easy to define that the speech functions of statement, command, and question are congruently realized by the Mood of declarative, imperative and interrogative in Chinese. However, the congruent realization of offer is less determinate because both declarative and interrogative clauses in Chinese are the unmarked expressions of the speech function. Halliday (1994: 95) claims that in English 'for offers there is no distinct mood category at all'. This conclusion is also valid for the speech function of offer in Chinese. The congruent realizations for the options in speech function network are displayed in Figure 4.4.

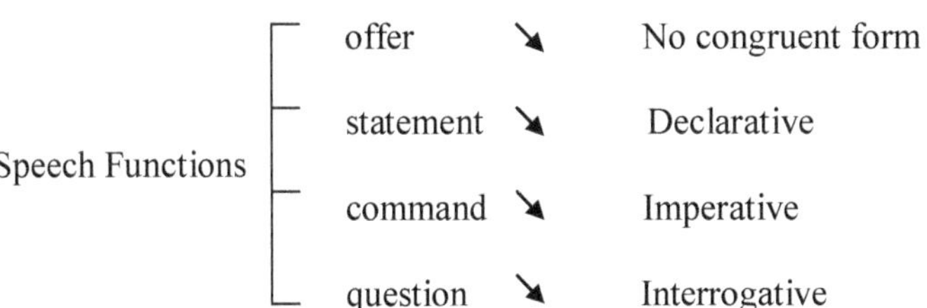

Figure 4.4:Congruent realizations of speech functions in Chinese

Halliday and Matthiessen (2004) propose that the modality of a proposal or proposition is congruently realized by the grammatical elements within a clause. Based on the discussion of modality in Section 3.4, the congruent realizations of modality system in Chinese are presented in Figure 4.5.

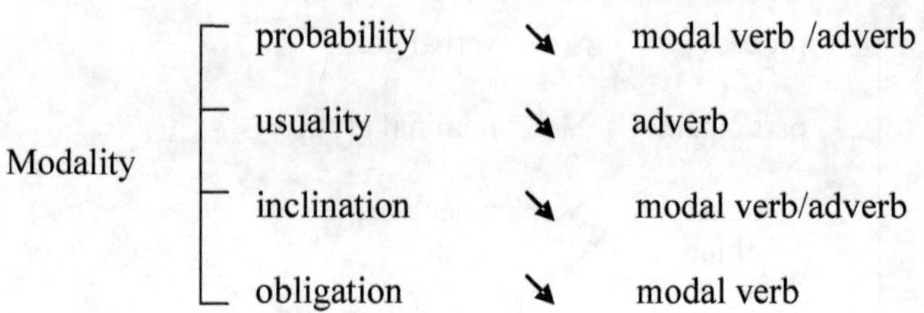

Figure 4.5: Congruent realizations of modality in Chinese

4.5.2 Metaphorical realizations

With the discussion of transgrammatical semantic domains and the description of congruent realizations, it is easy to define the metaphorical realizations of ideational and interpersonal meanings in Chinese. The transfer between congruent and metaphorical realizations is essentially a variation occurring at the lexicogrammatical stratum. In order to describe the metaphorical realization of semantic meanings in Chinese, I examine what kinds of grammatical variation occur in the creation of ideational and interpersonal GM.

A. Ideational strand

In the ideational strand of meaning, a sequence is metaphorically realized by a clause or a nominal group. A figure is metaphorically realized by a nominal group, while the elements forming a figure are metaphorically realized by the words in a nominal group. This realizational relationship is summarized in Figure 4.6.

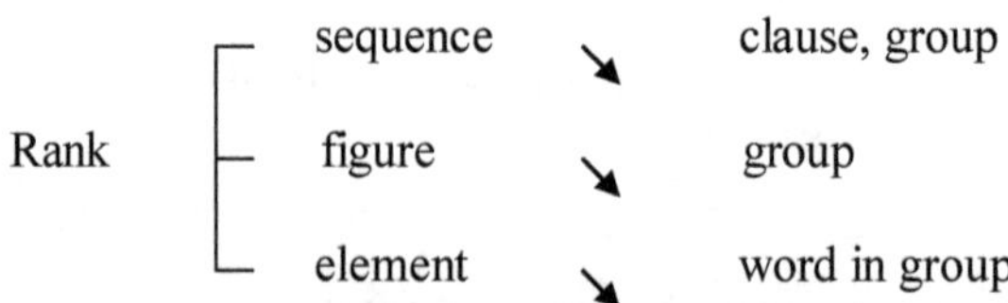

Figure 4.6: Metaphorical realizations of semantic units in Chinese

The comparison of congruent and metaphorical realizations of ideational meaning shows the downranking grammatical movements occurring in the process of realizing ideational metaphor in Chinese. In particular, ideational metaphor in Chinese involves four kinds of downranking movements: (1)

from clause complex to clause; (2) from clause complex to group; (3) from clause to group; and (4) from group to word. These movements are illustrated with their examples in Table 4.1.

Semantic units to be construed	*Downranking grammatical shift*	*Examples*
Sequence	(1) Clause complex ↓	*Wendu shenggao, suoyi tiji pengzhang.* Temperature increase so volume expand 'The temperature increases, so the volume expands.'
	Clause	*Wendu shenggao daozhi tiji pengzhang.* temperature increase cause volume expand 'The increase of temperature leads to the expansion of volume.'
	2) Clause complex ↓	*Wendu shenggao, tiji pengzhang.* temperature increase volume expand 'Because the temperature increases, the volume expands.'
	Group	*Wendu shenggao yinqi de tiji pengzhang.* temp. increase cause Sub. volume expand 'The volume expansion caused by temperature increase.'
Figure	(3) Clause ↓	*Wendu shenggao daozhi tiji pengzhang.* temperature increase cause volume expand 'The increase of temperature leads to the expansion of volume.'
	Group	*Wendu shenggao yinqi de tiji pengzhang.* temp. increase cause Sub. volume expand 'The volume expansion caused by the temperature increase.'
Element	(4) Group ↓	*Wendu shenggao (daozhi tiji pengzhang).* temperature increase cause volume expand 'The increase of temperature (leads to the expansion of volume).'
	Word in group	*Wendu shenggao (yinqi de tiji pengzhang)* temp. increase cause Sub. volume expand '(the volume expansion caused by) the temperature increase.'

Table 4.1: Downranking grammatical movements in Chinese

Corresponding to these downranking grammatical movements, the elements of sequence and figure are realized metaphorically in the following patterns of metaphorical realization:

(a) the meaning of a quality can be realized as a noun;
(b) the meaning of a process can be realized as a noun/verb functioning as the modifier in a nominal group or a nominal group;
(c) the meaning of a circumstance can be realized as a verbal group, a noun/verb functioning as the modifier in a nominal group, or a nominal group;
(d) the meaning of a relator can be realized as a prepositional group, a verbal group, a noun/verb functioning as the modifier in a nominal group, or a nominal group.

There are metaphorical realizations which occur as the accompaniment of the realizations described above. First, the meaning of a thing can be realized as a modifier in a nominal group when its corresponding process is nominalized. Second, a verb or a noun can be attached to a nominalization to indicate that the original meaning is metaphorically realized. In this case, the noun or the verb has no congruent form. In sum, 13 types of grammatical variations are involved in the metaphorical realizations of semantic elements in Chinese. The grammatical variations concerned are presented in Table 4.2.

The description of grammatical variations also illustrates the possible shifts between different semantic elements in Chinese. In particular, there are six groups of semantic shift: (1) a relator can be reconstrued in the form of any other semantic element; (2) a circumstance can be reconstrued as a process, a quality or a thing; (3) a process can be reconstrued as a quality or a thing; (4) a quality can be reconstrued as a thing; (5) a thing can be reconstrued as an expansion of thing; (6) a 'Ø' semantic domain can be reconstrued as a thing or a process. This identification of semantic shifts in Chinese provides a theoretical foundation for the categorization of ideational GM in the next chapter (see Section 5.2).

B. Interpersonal strand

The grammatical variations involved in the metaphorical realizations of interpersonal system are quite different from those in the dimension of ideational meaning. First, the downranking grammatical movement is not observed. When a projecting clause is involved in the expression of mood and modality meanings, the grammatical variations show a tendency of 'upgrading'. Second, the clear shift between individual grammatical categories does not exist. Generally speaking, the metaphorical expressions are realized by the variations between different grammatical domains, in which both individual categories and special structures are involved. To begin with, the grammatical variations concerned with speech function realization are shown in Table 4.3.

Semantic element to be realized metaphorically	*Grammatical variation (congruent – metaphorical)*	*Examples*
thing	noun – modifier in nominal group	*tiji (pengzhang) – tiji(pengzhang)* volume (expand)volume (expansion)
quality	adjective – noun	*chengshu – chengshu* mature maturity
process	verbal group – nominal group	*jiashi – jiashi* drive driving
	verbal group – modifier in nominal group	*huanxiang - huanxiang (de)* imagine imaginative (SUB)
circumstance	prep./adverbial group – nominal group	*huanman – disu* slowly low speed
	prep./adverbial group – modifier in nominal group	*zai shan xia – shan xia (de)* at hill below hill below (SUB)
	prep./adverbial group – verbal group	*yi ... wei canzhao – canzhao* with as reference refer to
relator	conjunction – noun	*yinwei – yuanyin* because reason
	conjunction – modifier in nominal group	*suoyi – daozhi (de)* so resultant (SUB)
	conjunction –– verb	*suoyi – daozhi* so caused
	conjunction – prep./adverbial group	*yinwei – yi .. wei yuanyin* because with as reason
'Ø' (no congruent form)	+ noun	*... de xianxiang* SUB phenomenon
	+ verb	*you ...* have

Table 4.2: Grammatical variations in metaphorical realizations of elements

Projecting clause and special structure are of particular importance to the metaphorical realizations of modality meaning in Chinese. The projecting clause is deployed to express the subjective and objective modality explicitly. However, it cannot be used for expressing every kind of modality in Chinese. It is observed that the meanings of usuality and inclination are not construed in the form of projecting clauses in Chinese. According to Palmer (2001) and Tsang (1981), usuality and inclination are typically concerned with the Subject of a clause instead of to the speaker. On the contrary, probability and obligation in most cases relate directly to the speaker of a clause. Thus, usuality and inclination are 'semantic domains where the

Speech functions to be construed	*Grammatical variation*	*Examples*
Offer	*No Shift*	
Command	(1) Imperative ↓	*He yi bei shui.* drink one Meas. water 'Drink a cup of water.'
	Interrogative	*Yao he bei shui ma?* want drink Meas. water Ma 'Would you like a cup of water?'
	(2) Imperative ↓	*He yi bei shui.* drink one Meas. water 'Drink a cup of water.'
	Declarative	*Zhe you yi bei shui.* here exist one Meas. water 'There is a cup of water.'
Statement	(3) Declarative ↓	*You daoli.* exist reason 'It is reasonable'
	Interrogative	*Nandao meiyou daoli?* do you think not exist reason 'Don't you think it's reasonable?'
Question	(4) Interrogative ↓	*Hangban shenme shijian daoda?* flight what time arrive 'When will the flight arrive?'
	Declarative	*Wo xiang zhidao hangban de daoda shijian.* I want know flight Sub. arrival time 'I want to know the arrival time of this flight.'

Table 4.3: Grammatical variations in the metaphorical realization of speech functions

speaker cannot readily pose as an authority' (Halliday, 1994: 358). In this case, a projecting process, which ordinarily involves the attitude of speaker, is not applicable to the expression of usuality and inclination.

One particular point in the realization of modality in Chinese is the use of structures of *shi* ... *de* and *you* .... Although the structures could be translated as 'it is ...' and 'there is ...' in English, they are not projecting processes because they cannot instate another clause as a locution or an idea. In addition, the structure of *shi* ... *de* can be used to construe metaphorically every modality in Chinese from an impersonal prospective. The detailed exploration of these structures is conducted in Section 4.6. The grammatical variations in metaphorical realization of modality are summarized in Table 4.4.

Modalities to be construed	*Grammatical variations*				
	Congruent realization ⟶			*Metaphorical realization*	
	Modal verb	*Adverb*	*Mood particle*	*Projecting process*	'shi...de' 'you...'
Probability	*keneng* (can) *hui* (can) *gai* (should)	*yiding* *kending* *biding* *zhun* (must)	*'ba'*	*wo* *xiangxin* (believe) (I) *guji* (estimate) *xiang* (think) *renwei* (reckon)	*shi kending de* (is must Sub.) *you keneng* (have possibility)
Usuality		*yizhi* (always) *jingchang* (usually) *youshi* (sometimes)			*shi changyou de* (is often Sub.)
Inclination	*yao* (will) *xiang* (wish) *yuanyi* (will) *ken* (will)	*yiding* *pian* *fei* (must)			*shi ziyuan de* (is willing Sub.)
Obligation	*bixu* (must) *gai* (should) *keyi* (may) *yinggai* (should)			*wo* *yaoqiu* (require) (I) *qiangpo* (comple) *rang* (let) *yunxu* (permit)	*shi bixu de* (is necessary Sub.) *you biyao* (have necessity)

Table 4.4: Grammatical variations in the metaphorical realization of modality

4.6 Critical lexicogrammatical phenomena for GM identification

The description of metaphorical realizations shows that certain lexicogrammatical phenomena are critical for the identification of GM in Chinese. To be more specific, there are three phenomena which are respectively concerned with the metaphorical realizations of ideational and interpersonal meanings in Chinese. First, the phenomenon of transcategorization is the basis of the grammatical variations occurred in the reconstrual of ideational semantic elements. Second, the use of Mood particles is the most distinctive characteristic in the realization of speech functions in Chinese. Finally, the structures of *shi* ... *de* and *you* ... are important in identifying the metaphorical expressions of modality. The use of Mood particle and *shi* ... *de* and *you* ... structures have been briefly discussed in Section 3.4. This section describes them in more detail to facilitate the identification of GM in Chinese.

4.6.1 Transcategorization in Chinese

According to Halliday and Matthiessen (1999: 242), the phenomenon of transcategorization 'implies two things: (i) that each etymon belongs inherently to a major class; and (ii) that at least some etymons can be transferred to another class'. The grammatical variation involved in the metaphorical realization of a semantic element is in fact the transfer between Chinese words in different classes. In addition, the transfer serves as the foundation of the downranking grammatical movement occurred in ideational GM. The transcategorization is thus crucial for the identification of ideational GM in Chinese.

Chinese is typologically distinguished from English with respect to its lack of morphological indicators for different classes of word. With this feature, the transfer of a word from one class to another in Chinese is generally realized by the syntactic means instead of by derivational morphemes as in English. Thus, it is frequently observed that Chinese words with different grammatical functions are similar in their forms. I first discuss the transfer from verb/adjective to noun because nominalization is predominant in metaphorical realizations. Following this, I explore how the noun and verb in Chinese function as modifiers in nominal groups.

A. From verb/adjective to noun

The discussion in Section 3.2.2.1 reveals that adjectives and verbs in Chinese share many common features. The formal similarity between adjectives and verbs determines that they are transferred to nouns through the same method. The transfer from verb/adjective to noun can be further divided into two subtypes depending on whether the verb/adjective changes its form. First, the verb/adjective can be transferred to noun without changing its form, as illustrated by the following examples:

(4.7) *weimiao* – *weimiao* (adjective to noun)
delicate delicacy
gongping – *gongping* (adjective to noun)
fair fairness
kaolü – *kaolü* (verb to noun)
consider consideration
panduan – *panduan* (verb to noun)
judge judgement

Second, verbs and adjectives in Chinese are nominalized by adding lexemes like 性 *xing* (property), 率 *lü* (rate) or 度 *du* (degree) to them. This kind of nominalization is exemplified by the transfers below:

(4.8) *keneng* – *kenengxing* (adjective to noun)
possible possibility
chenggong – *chenggonglü* (verb to noun)
succeed probability of success

The nouns ending in *xing*, *lü* or *du* are generally the result of westernization of modern Chinese (Kubler, 1985). This kind of nouns is used more extensively in scientific writings than in other registers of Chinese.

B. Noun and verb as modifiers in nominal groups

When nouns and verbs in Chinese are used as modifiers in a nominal group, they are not changed into adjectives. However, this kind of transfer is functionally concerned with the grammatical shift from Thing/Process to Quality. Similar to those in English, nouns and verbs functioning as modifiers are sometimes placed before the Head of a nominal group without any indicator such as *ketang guancha* (classroom observation). However, the majority of these modifiers are indicated by the subordinating particle *de*, which is represented in the following examples:

(4.9a) *shunxu* *de* *bianhua* (noun as modifier)
sequence Sub. change
'the change of sequence'

(4.9b) *zhendong* *de* *zhuangtai* (verb as modifier)
vibration Sub. state
'the state of vibration'

The use of particle *de* for various functions has always been a key issue in previous research of Chinese (for example, Chao, 1968; Li and Thompson, 1981). I focus my discussion on its function of indicating modifier because this function is critical for recognizing GM instances in Chinese. The subordinating particle *de* is indicated by the abbreviation of 'Sub.' throughout this book, as shown in the examples above.

It is worth noting that nouns and verbs functioning as modifiers without *de* are generally more closely knit with the headword (Li and Thompson, 1981). The nominal group in the structure of 'noun/verb + noun' is ordinarily used to categorize the Thing in the group. The noun and verb followed by *de* have the function of clarifying the noun they modify.

The lexicogrammatical phenomenon of transcategorization affects the semantic systems in Chinese. The semantic nature of transcategorization is clear in some of the shifts from one grammatical category to another. Take the transfer from *chenggong* (succeed) to *chenggonglü* (probability of success) for example, the semantic nature of the words is apparently changed. In other cases, however, the nature of the change is less clear. Halliday (1998) claims that the semantic meanings of English words like 'development', 'shakiness' and 'awakening' can be explained as a 'junction' of two semantic elements. This ambiguity of semantic meaning is also observed in the Chinese words like *sikao* (consideration), *yundong* (movement) and *fanyi* (translation). As discussed in Chapter 2, the remapping of semantics and lexicogrammar accounts for the appearance of such words with junctional meaning.

4.6.2 Mood particles

As far as the realization of speech function is concerned, the most distinctive feature of the Mood system in Chinese is the systematic deployment of Mood particles. As mentioned in Section 3.4.1, there are four Mood particles which are used most frequently in Chinese, i.e, 吗 *ma*, 呢 *ne*, 吧 *ba* and 啊/呀 *a/ya*. These particles function to indicate various kinds of Mood in Chinese clauses. I describe the use of these Mood particles on the basis of previous studies of *yuqi ci* (Mood word) in Chinese (Chao, 1968; Li and Thompson, 1981).

A. Ma

The particle *ma* is distinctive in two points: first, it functions exclusively as a question marker; second, *ma* cannot co-occur with other forms of Chinese questions. Unlike other Mood particles, *ma* never appears in declarative and imperative clauses. The particle *ma* also has the function to convert any declarative utterance into an interrogative clause. The discussion in Section 3.3.3 shows that declarative and interrogative clauses in Chinese share similar structures. In this case, the presence of *ma* in the final position of a clause signals the interrogative nature of the clause, as shown in Example 4.10.

(4.10a)	*Mingtian*	*women*	*qu*	*gugong.*
	tomorrow	we	go to	Forbidden City

'We will go to the Forbidden City tomorrow.'

(4.10b)	*Mingtian*	*women*	*qu*	*gugong*	*ma?*
	tomorrow	we	go to	Forbidden City	Mood particle

'Should we go to the Forbidden City tomorrow?'

Section 3.3.3 has divided interrogative clauses into three groups: question-word, A-not-A and particle interrogatives. *Ma* does not occur with A-not-A or question-word interrogatives in practical expressions. Li and Thompson

(1981) claim that A-not-A and question-word interrogatives already contain the information which indicates the interrogative nature of the clause. Thus, 'there is no need for the presence of *ma*, whose sole function is to mark an utterance as a question' (Li and Thomson, 1981: 307).

B. Ne

The Mood particle *ne* has the function of signalling both declarative and interrogative clauses. When it is used as the final particle of a declarative clause, it 'has the effect of calling on the hearer to pay particular attention to the information conveyed by the sentence' (Li and Thompson, 1981: 300). This can be illustrated by a contrast of declarative clauses with and without the Mood particle *ne*.

(4.11a)	*Zhe*	*tiao*	*jie*	*you*	*wu*	*gongli*	*chang*
	this	Meas.	street	exist	five	kilometre	long

'This street is five kilometres long.'

(4.11b)	*Zhe*	*tiao*	*jie*	*you*	*wu*	*gongli*	*chang*	*ne*
	this	Meas.	street	exist	five	kilometre	long	Mood particle

'This street is as much as five kilometres long.'

The use of *ne* in Example 4.11b strengthens the assertion of the expression and attracts the attention of the reader to the length of the street. The complete information conveyed by clause (4.11b) can be paraphrased as 'mind you/listen, the street is five kilometres long'.

Ne cannot by itself change a declarative clause into an interrogative clause. It only occurs in A-not-A, question-word or elliptical interrogatives, as shown by the following examples created by Li and Thompson (1981: 305–306).

(4.12a)	*Ni*	*xihuan*	*bu*	*xihuan*	*ta*	*ne?*
	you	like	not	like	him/her	Mood particle

'Do you like him/her?'

(4.12b)	*Ta*	*yao*	*chi*	*shenme*	*ne?*
	he/she	want	eat	what	Mood particle

'What does s/he want to eat?'

(4.12c)	*Ni*	*ne?*
	you	Mood particle

'How about you?'

C. 'Ba'

According to Li and Thompson (1981), the semantic meaning of *ba* is best described as 'don't you think so?' or 'do you agree' in English. Thus the interrogative clauses with *ba* have the effect of soliciting approval or agreement. More importantly, when the Subject of a clause is first person plural or a second person, the interrogative with *ba* often realizes the speech function of command. See Example 4.13.

(4.13a) *Women zou ba?*
we go Mood particle
'Shall we go?' – (Let's go.)

(4.13b) *Ni shui ba*
You sleep Mood particle
'Why don't you sleep?' – (You sleep.)

Example 4.13 shows that the real function of the expressions is to give a command although the force of utterance is reduced. This explains why *ba* is labelled an 'advisative' particle by Chao (1968: 807). Generally, *ba* cannot be added to question-word, A-not-A and Mood particle interrogatives in Chinese. The possible reason is that the function of various kinds of interrogative is to request information, while the clause with *ba* only asks listeners to agree to some statement (Li and Thompson, 1981).

D. A/Ya

The particle *a/ya* is used at the final position of Chinese clauses to indicate interrogative and imperative Moods. In interrogative clauses, *a/ya* 'performs the function of reducing the forcefulness of the message conveyed' (Li and Thompson, 1981: 313). It is thus frequently placed after an interrogative clause to soften the query and can be translated into 'excuse me' or 'by the way' in English. The following examples are A-not-A and question-word interrogative clauses with *a/ya*.

(4.14a) *Ni xiang bu xiang mama a/ya?*
you think not think mother Mood particle
'Do you miss your mother?'

(4.14b) *Ni zai na a/ya?*
You at where Mood particle
'Where are you?'

When *a/ya* occurs with imperatives, it functions to reduce the forcefulness of imperative expressions. This can be shown by the comparison of Examples 4.15a and 4.15b.

(4.15a) *Ni gaosu wo*
you tell me
'You tell me.'

(4.15b) *Ni gaosu wo a/ya.*
you tell me Mood particle
'You can tell me.'

When particle *a/ya* is used in Example 4.15b, the forcefulness of command is greatly reduced. More precisely, the clause construes the meaning of a suggestion or an encouragement.

To summarize the use of Mood particles, the relationship between different Moods and particles is shown in Table 4.5.

Particles / *Moods*	Ma	Ne	Ba	A/Ya
Declarative		+		
Interrogative	+	+	+	+
Imperative				+

Table 4.5: Deployment of Mood particles in Chinese

The overview of Mood particles indicates that these particles can express different Moods without changing the main structure of the clause. It is also observed that the Mood particles are often concerned with metaphorical realizations of speech functions in Chinese. For example, the interrogative clause ending in *ba* construes the semantic meaning of command. This characteristic of Mood particles determines that they are critical for identifying interpersonal GM instances in Chinese.

4.6.3 *Shi … de* and *you …* structures

As pointed out in Section 4.5.2, the modality meanings in Chinese are metaphorically realized by projecting process, *shi … de* structure, *you …* structure and Mood particle. This section examines *shi … de* and *you …* structures in detail to see how they construe metaphorical expressions in Chinese.

A. Shi … de *structure*

The structure of *shi … de* is generally deployed to emphasize the specific information or attitude of a speaker. When the structure is used to emphasize information, it functions as the Attribute of a relational process in Chinese:

(4.16) *Zhe shi wo song ni de.*
this is I give you Sub.
'This is what I am giving to you.'

Its function of expressing attitude involves the metaphorical expression of modality. In particular, *shi … de* is located in the final position of the whole expression and the Modal verb or adverb with modal meaning is inserted between *shi* and *de*. The structure can express each type of modality, as shown in the following examples.

(4.16a) Probability: *Anshi wancheng renwu// shi kengneng de.*
on time complete task is possible Sub.
'It is possible to complete the task on time.'

(4.16b) Usuality: *Ta chidao //shi jingchang de.*
he late is usual Sub.
'It is usual for him to be late.'

(4.16c) Inclination: *Ta shangke// shi ziyuan de.*
he go to school is willing Sub.
'He goes to school on his own will.'

(4.16d) Obligation: *Anshi wancheng renwu// shi yinggai de.*
on time complete task is necessary Sub.
'It is necessary to complete the task on time.'

In order to negate the modal meaning construed by *shi* ... *de*, the negative marker must be included in the structure and positioned before modal verbs. Take probability and obligation for examples:

(4.17a) Probability: *Anshi wancheng renwu// shi bu kengneng de.*
(negative) on time complete task is not possible Sub.
'It is not possible to complete the task on time.'

(4.17b) Obligation: *Anshi wancheng renwu// shi bu yinggai de.*
(negative) on time complete task is not necessary Sub.
'It is not necessary to complete the task on time.'

B. You ... *structure*

In addition to *shi* ... *de* structure, modality in Chinese is sometimes metaphorically realized by *you*... structure. However, the structure is only involved in the metaphorical realizations of probability and obligation in Chinese. For example:

(4.18a) Probability: *You keneng// ta yijing zou le.*
exist possibility he already leave Asp.
'There is the possibility that he has already left.'

(4.18b) Obligation: *You biyao// rang ta zhidao.*
exist necessity let him know
'There is the necessity to let him know.'

In Examples 4.18a and 4.18b, the verb *you* is glossed as exist and *you* ... structure is literally translated as 'there is' in English. However, it should be noted that *you* ... structure does not form an existential clause in Chinese. In contrast to the existential clause, *you* ... structure is used to establish a relation between two entities.

The examination of '*shi* ... *de*' and '*you* ...' structures shows that they state the modality meaning in the form of 'isolated expression'. According to Halliday and McDonald (2004), the relational process in Chinese regularly functions as the extension of other types of process. This study claims that *shi* ... *de* and *you* ... structures are special forms of relational clause which extend other clauses in Chinese. In other words, the modality meanings construed by *shi* ... *de* and *you* ... structures are expressed explicitly. In this point, they are very similar to the projecting clause in Chinese which also construes modality meaning explicitly.

4.7 Summary

The discussions in this chapter are centred on the theme of identifying GM in Chinese. First, the three motifs of identifying GM in Chinese are specified by revisiting the findings of previous GM studies falling into three phases. The semantic system network in Chinese is then established in terms of ideational, textual and interpersonal meanings. Together with the grammatical systems developed in Chapter 3, the semantic network established in this chapter provides a theoretical background for examining the realignment between semantics and lexicogrammar in Chinese. Following this, the chapter confirms the existence of GM in Chinese by examining the transgrammatical semantic domains in the language. This examination of transgrammatical semantic domains avoids the danger of imposing the features of GM in English on the GM identification in Chinese. Furthermore, the congruent and metaphorical realizations of semantic systems in Chinese are described by focusing on the grammatical variations involved. This comprehensive description of congruent and metaphorical realizations is fundamental for further analysis of GM in this study. Finally, this chapter discusses three lexicogrammatical phenomena which are critical for identifying GM instances in Chinese.

In addition to the main theme of identifying GM in Chinese, Chapter 4 illustrates the distinctive features of semantic and lexicogrammatical systems in Chinese. These features greatly affect the construction of metaphorical expressions in the language. For example, the three grammatical phenomena discussed in Section 4.6 distinguish the metaphorical realizations in Chinese from those in English. In this sense, the work in this chapter provides a starting point for the comparison of GM in English and Chinese.

5 Categorization of grammatical metaphor in Chinese

5.1 Introduction

This chapter discusses the categorization of ideational and interpersonal GM in Chinese by specifying the metaphorical realizations defined in Chapter 4. The GM categories and subcategories described in this chapter provide a guide to Chapters 6 and 7 which contain quantitative analyses of the properties of GM in Chinese. I first categorize ideational GM according to a framework developed on the basis of the shift between different semantic elements. Interpersonal GM is then differentiated by examining the grammatical methods involved in the metaphorical realizations of speech function and modality.

5.2 Framework for categorization of GM in Chinese

This section outlines the framework to be used for the categorization of ideational and interpersonal GM in Chinese. The framework is developed by referring to the previous classification of GM in English and the description of metaphorical realizations in Chapter 4.

5.2.1 Framework for Ideational GM categorization

Ideational GM in English has been classified from two perspectives: the downranking grammatical movement and the metaphorical shift between semantic elements. These two approaches are integrated in this study to classify ideational GM in Chinese. Ideational GM in Chinese is first categorized in terms of the shift between semantic elements. The discussion of metaphorical realizations in Section 4.5 shows that the 13 types of semantic shift proposed by Halliday (1998) exist in Chinese. I thus classify ideational GM into 13 categories in terms of elemental shift. The downranking grammatical movement is taken into account in the detailed discussion of each category

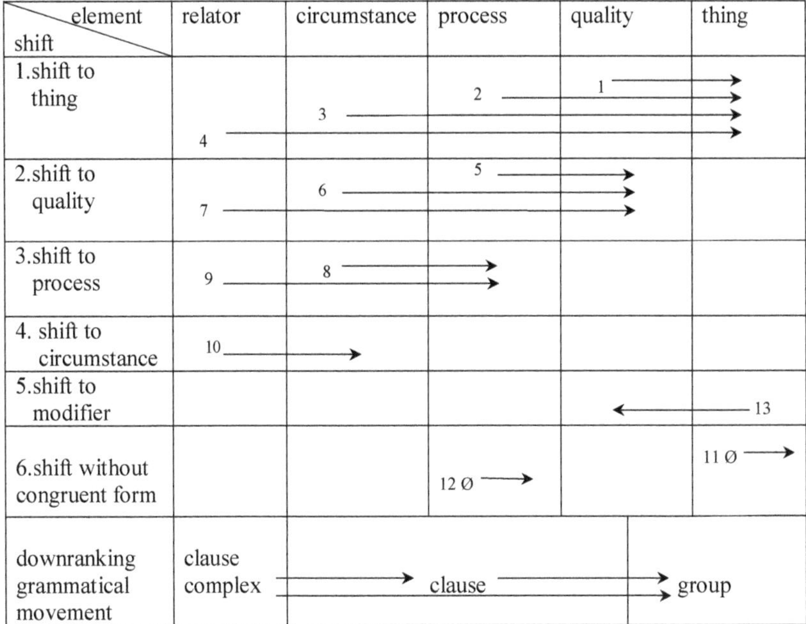

Figure 5.1: Framework for ideational GM categorization in Chinese

of ideational GM. The various categories of ideational GM in Chinese and their locations in the downranking grammatical movement are presented in Figure 5.1.

In Figure 5.1, there are 11 major GM categories which correspond with 11 possible shifts between five semantic elements and two minor GM categories which have no corresponding congruent domains. These categories of ideational GM in Chinese are sorted into six groups in terms of the destination of semantic shift: (1) shift to thing; (2) shift to quality; (3) shift to process; (4) shift to circumstance; (5) shift to modifier; and (6) shift without congruent form. The shifts with the same destination generally share a similar motivation of metaphorical expressions. The recognition of different groups of ideational GM, therefore, provides a foundation for the further exploration of the linguistic properties of Chinese. For instance, the extent of 'thinginess' in Chinese can be defined by quantifying ideational GM instances in different groups. This point is explored in Chapter 6 which discusses the use of GM instances in authentic texts.

In addition to the grouping of ideational GM categories, I subdivide each category of GM listed in Figure 5.1. Halliday and Matthiessen (1999) differentiate various categories of ideational GM in English into subcategories on the basis of the shift between grammatical functions (see Section

2.3.1 for a detailed description). I subdivide the categories of ideational GM in Chinese by following Halliday and Matthiessen's (1999) method. That is, the GM categories in Chinese are specified on the basis of two linguistic facts. On the one hand, a semantic element may be realized as different grammatical functions in different ranks of grammatical unit. For instance, the element of quality is realized as Epithet in a nominal group and Attribute in a clause. The GM categories concerned with quality are thus differentiated in terms of Epithet and Attribute. On the other hand, a semantic element may be realized by a combination of grammatical functions. For instance, the element of process can be realized by the combination of Auxiliary, Event and Extension. There are thus three subcategories of the semantic shift from process to thing: (1) the shift from Auxiliary to Thing; (2) the shift from Event to Thing; and (3) the shift from Event + Extension to Thing (see detailed discussion in Section 5.3).

The discussion above gives rise to the consideration of the distinctions between English and Chinese in the differentiation of GM categories. For example, the ideational GM category 2 in English has the subtype of Catenative to Thing which could be illustrated by expressing the meaning of 'try to' with 'attempt' or 'want to' with 'desire' (Halliday and Matthiessen, 1999). This subtype of ideational GM does not exist in Chinese because of the absence of catenative expressions in the language (see Section 7.3.2 for details). This sort of distinction is also observed in the subtypes of other categories of ideational GM in the two languages. The differences between English and Chinese in GM categorization are further discussed in Chapter 8.

5.2.2 Framework for Interpersonal GM categorization

The categorization of interpersonal GM is more complicated than that of ideational GM for two main reasons. First, interpersonal meanings in a language are more complex than ideational meanings in terms of the number of choices in semantic system networks. Second, the two types of interpersonal GM, i.e., metaphor of mood and metaphor of modality, do not have a consistent pattern of grammatical movement. The metaphor of modality is featured by the upgrading movement from clause to clause complex. The metaphor of mood, however, involves both grammatical movements from clause to clause complex and those from clause to clause.

The characteristics of interpersonal GM determine that it cannot be classified with a framework based on the shifts between semantic elements. I thus develop a framework for the categorization of interpersonal GM in Chinese by focusing on the grammatical realizations of interpersonal meaning. In particular, the metaphor of mood is categorized by specifying the

Mood choices involved in the metaphorical reconstrual of speech functions. The metaphor of modality, on the other hand, is categorized by differentiating the grammatical methods which realize four types of modality metaphorically. This framework is presented in Table 5.1.

Interpersonal GM	*Categories*
Metaphor of mood	1. Expressing command with interrogative Mood
	2. Expressing command with declarative Mood
	3. Expressing statement with interrogative Mood
	4. Expressing question with declarative Mood
Metaphor of modality	1. Metaphorical realizations of probability
	2. Metaphorical realization of usuality
	3. Metaphorical realizations of obligation
	4. Metaphorical realizations of inclination

Table 5.1: Framework for interpersonal GM categorization in Chinese

5.3 Categorization of Ideational GM

This section describes each category of ideational GM by locating them in a larger linguistic environment. For instance, the shift from process to thing is described in the grammatical movement from clause to nominal group in Chinese. This method integrates the two types of grammatical movements involved in ideational GM, namely, the movement of grammatical units and the movement of grammatical elements. As mentioned in Section 1.3, the examples of ideational GM are selected from scientific textbooks. The provenance of each example of ideational GM is indicated according to the labels of textbook in Table 1.1. The congruent and metaphorical expressions in the examples are distinguished from the perspective of logogenesis. The expressions coming earlier and later in a text are recognized respectively as congruent and metaphorical realizations.

5.3.1 Shift to thing

The shift to thing is more important than other groups of ideational GM because the GM instances in this group involve nominalization. Ravelli (1985: 59) claims that nominalization is 'the instance of metaphor of which there is the greatest cultural awareness'. Halliday (1998: 211) also asserts that 'the noun is the most metaphorically attractive category: everything else can end up as a noun'. As shown in Figure 5.1, the instances of ideational GM with thing as destination covers four categories respectively numbered from 1 to 4. These categories of ideational GM and their subtypes are examined here one by one.

(1) Quality to Thing

This category of ideational GM involves the reconstrual of quality as thing. The semantic element of quality is construed as Epithet in a nominal group and Attribute in a clause. This determines that ideational GM category 1 in Chinese is further differentiated into two subcategories: (i) from Epithet to Thing and (ii) from Attribute to Thing. An Epithet serves as the modifier in a nominal group, while an Attribute only appears in a relational process with ascriptive meaning. This distinction determines that the subcategory (i) occurs in the rank of group, as shown in the following example:

(5.1) *jingzhi* *wuti*
static object
'objects at rest'
Epithet Thing
↘
Epithet Thing
wuti *(de)* *jingzhi*
body (Sub.) rest
'the rest of objects'

In contrast, the subcategory (ii) is concerned with the downranking shift from clause to nominal group. This situation is illustrated by Example 5.2.

(5.2) *Wuti* *wanqu.*
object curved
'The object is curved.'
Carrier Attribute
↓
Epithet Thing
wuti *de* *wanqu*
object Sub. curvature
'curvature of object'

As a semantic element, a quality lies somewhere between a thing and a process and its status in different languages varies considerably (Halliday and Matthiessen, 1999). Qualities in English are more closely related to things and contribute primarily to the construction of participants. Halliday and Matthiessen (1999: 206) claim that 'English favours construing a quality as Epithet in a nominal group, and the class of adjective is clearly related to that of noun'. By contrast, the quality in Chinese is typically construed as Attribute in a clause rather than as Epithet in a nominal group. For example, Newton's third law of mechanics is expressed in an English textbook and a Chinese textbook respectively as follows:

(5.3) If one body (A) exerts a force on another body (B), then B must exert an equal and opposite force on A. (Gamow and Cleveland, 1976: 49)

Liang ge wuti zhijian de zuoyongli he fanzuoyongli zong shi
Two piece body between Sub. force and anti-force always is

daxiao xiangdeng, fangxiang xiangfan, zuoyong zai tong yi tiao
magnitude same direction opposite act on same one piece

zhixian shang.
line above

'The force and anti-force between two bodies are always same in magnitude, opposite in direction and act along the same line.'

The comparison of English and Chinese expressions shows that the qualities with the meaning of 'equal' and 'opposite' are respectively realized as Epithet and Attribute in the two languages.

The preference for construing a quality as Attribute in Chinese may engender a relatively higher quantity of GM instances in subcategory (ii) than in subcategory (i). This assumption is testified through a quantitative analysis of the GM deployment in authentic texts (see Section 6.4). Another point concerned with the subcategories is that Chinese adjectives functioning as Epithet and Attribute are distinctive in the way of assigning qualities to things. Generally speaking, the Epithet is generally deployed to sort things into classes, while the Attribute is used to describe the property of a thing.

(2) Process to Thing

This category of ideational GM occurs most frequently and acts as the moving force of other GM categories in Chinese. The element of process is realized by a verbal group whose structure has been discussed in Section 3.5.3.2. The discussion reveals that the verbal group in Chinese is constructed by the components of Auxiliary, Event and Extension. These grammatical functions can be transferred as Thing in three directions: (i) Event to Thing; (ii) Event + Extension to Thing; and (iii) Auxiliary to Thing.

The subcategory of Event to Thing is concerned with the nominalization of various types of process in Chinese. That is, GM instances in this subcategory can be analysed in terms of how each type of clause (material, mental, relational, behavioural, verbal or existential) is metaphorically realized as a nominal group. The metaphorical realizations of various clause types are displayed by the following examples.

(5.4) Material:
Daidian wuti xianghu paichi huo xiyin.
Charged body each other repel or attract
'Electrically charged bodies repel or attract each other.'
Actor Cir:Manner Process (Event)
↓
Classifier Epithet Thing
daidain wuti de xianghu paichi huo xiyin [SP1]
Charged body Sub. each other repulsion or attraction
'repulsion or attraction between electrically charged bodies'

(5.5) Mental:
Thomson *quexin fu lizi de cunzai.*
Thomson believe negative particle Sub. existence
'Thomson believes the existence of negative particles.'
Sensor Process (Event) Phenomenon
→
Deictic Epithet Thing
Thomson dui *fu lizi de quexin* [UP2]
Thomson to negative particle Sub. belief
'Thomson's belief of negative particles'

(5.6) Relational: (Identifying)
A *biaoshi meiri wendu.*
A represent everyday temperature
'A represents the daily temperature.'
Token Process Value
(Event) →
Classifier Epithet Thing
A dui meiri wendu de biaoshi [SC1]
A to everyday temperature Sub. representation [modified]
'The representation of A to daily temperature.'

(5.7) Behavioural:
Renlei zai kongqi zhong huxi.
human being in air inside breath
'Human beings breathe in the air.'
Behaver Cir:Location Process (Event)
↘
Classifier Epithet Thing
Renlei zai kongqi zhong de huxi [SC1]
human being in air inside Sub. breath
'the breath of human beings in the air'

(5.8) Verbal:

Baogao shuo cunzai xin lizi.
paper say exist new particle
'The report says that there is a new particle.'
Sayer Process (Event) Verbiage

Epithet Epithet → Thing
baogao zhong cunzai xin lizi de guandian [UP2]
report in exist new particle Sub. view
'the view on the existence of a new particle in the report'

(5.9) Existential:

Shui fenzi zhong you qing lizi.
water molecule inside have hydrogen ion
'There are hydrogen ions in a water molecule.'
Cir: Location Process (Event) Existent

Epithet Epithet → Thing
shui fenzi zhong qing lizi de cunzai [UC1]
water molecule inside hydrogen ion Sub. existence
'the existence of hydrogen ions in a water molecule'

The description of grammatical transfer from Event to Thing shows that this subcategory of ideational GM involves each type of process in Chinese. By contrast, the subcategory of Event + Extension to Thing is mainly observed in the metaphorical realization of material processes. See Example 5.10.

(5.10) Material:

Bingshan zai gao wen xia rong jie.
iceberg at high temperature under melt away
'The iceberg melts at a high temperature.'
Participant Cir: Location Process (Event + Extension)

Epithet Classifier Thing
gao wen xia de bingshan rong jie [SP2]
high temperature under Sub. iceberg melting away
'the melting away of the iceberg at a high temperature'

The shift from Auxiliary to Thing involves the nominalization of Modal verbs in Chinese. As discussed in Section 3.4, the Modal verbs in Chinese are concerned with the construal of modality and ability meanings. Thus, the shift from Auxiliary to Thing is considered from these two perspectives. First, the metaphorical reconstrual of ability is shown Example 5.11:

(5.11) Ability:
Gai shebei neng fenjie shui fenzi.
this device can break down water molecule
'This device can break down water molecules.'
Actor Process (Auxiliary + Event) Goal

Classifer Epithet → Thing
Gai shebei fenjie shui fenzi de nengli [UC2]
this device break down water molecule Sub. ability
'the ability of this device to break down water molecules'

The metaphorical realizations of modality are more complex than that of ability because modal verbs are deployed to express probability, inclination and obligation meanings in Chinese (for details, see Table 4.4). The shifts concerned in the three types of modalities are exemplified as follows:

(5.12) Probability:
Yali keneng zengda.
pressure can increase
'It is possible that the pressure increases.'
Actor Process (Auxiliary + Event)

Epithet Thing
yali zengda de kenengxing [SC2]
pressure increase Sub. possibility [modified]
'the possibility of pressure increase'

(5.13) Inclination:
Women yuanyi bangzhu bieren
we will help others
'We are willing to help others.'
Actor Process (Auxiliary + Event) Goal

Deictic Epithet → Thing
women bangzhu bieren de yiyuan
we help others Sub. desire
'our desire for helping others'

(5.14) Obligation:
Bixu jiangdi moca xishu.
must reduce friction coefficient
'The coefficient of friction must be reduced.'
Process (Auxiliary + Event) Goal

Epithet → Thing
jiangdi moca xishu de biyao [SP2]
reduce friction coefficient Sub. necessity
'the necessity of reducing the friction coefficient'

It is worth noting that the meaning of modal verbs in Chinese is frequently reconstrued as 'isolated clauses'. As discussed in Section 4.5, this kind of realization concerns the interpersonal meaning of the modal verbs. The modal verbs presented in the above examples are treated as a constituent of process and their functions are limited in the dimension of ideational meaning. The metaphorical realizations of their interpersonal meanings are explored further in Section 5.4.

(3) Circumstance to Thing

Section 3.2.3 reveals that Circumstances in Chinese are divided into three types in terms of their structures, i.e., (1a) those realized by prepositional phrases with the structure of 'minor Process + Participant + Facet'; (1b) those realized by propositional phrases with the structure of 'minor Process + Participant'; and (2) those realized by adverbial groups. When different types of Circumstance are reconstrued as other semantic elements, they have distinctive inclinations of destination. As far as the shift from circumstance to thing is concerned, it is observed that only the circumstances in type (1b) can be metaphorically realized. The circumstances in type (2) are not involved in the semantic shift from circumstance to thing because adverbs in Chinese cannot be nominalized. In addition, the circumstances in type (1a) are normally transferred into the semantic element of quality (see Section 5.3.2). These two kinds of reconstrual are obviously not the content of this discussion.

The metaphorical realizations of circumstances in type (1b) are reconstrued in two methods. On the one hand, only the minor Process in a prepositional phrase is involved. The major Process in congruent expressions is embedded as the Epithet of a nominal group in metaphorical realizations, as shown in Example 5.15.

(5.15) *Genju* *Maxwell fangcheng,* *cunzai* *dianci* *bo.*
depending on Maxwell equation exist electro-magnetic wave
'Depending on Maxwell equation, there exist electro-magnetic waves.'
Circ: Source (minor Proc. + Partic.) Process Existential

Identified Proc. Identifier
(Epithet Thing)
Dianci *bo* *cunzai* *de* *genju* *shi* *Maxwell* *fangcheng*
electro-magnetic wave existence Sub. basis is Maxwell equation
'The basis of the existence of electro-magnetic waves is Maxwell equation.'
[UP2]

On the other hand, the minor Process and the Participant in a prepositional phrase are transferred together. In this case, the major Process is maintained in the metaphorical realizations, while the Circumstance is reconstrued as a new Participant. This is shown by Example 5.16.

(5.16) *Yanjiu renyuan an gai yuanli jiangdi moca de yingxiang.*
research person follow this principle minimize friction Sub. effect
'Researchers minimize the effect of friction according to this principle.'
Actor Circ: Instrument Process Goal
(minor Proc. + Partic.)

Actor Process Goal
Gai yuanli de yingyong jiangdi le moca de yingxiang.
This principle Sub. application minimize Asp. friction Sub. effect
'The application of this principle minimizes the effect of friction.'

[UP1]

Examples 5.15 and 5.16 show that the reconstrual of a circumstance as a thing in Chinese may be accompanied by a change of process type of the original expression. Conversely, it is possible that the intention of expressing the original meaning in different type of process gives rise to the reconstrual of a circumstance as a thing.

(4) Relator to Thing

In Section 3.5, Conjunctions and conjunctive Adjuncts used for the realization of relator are described in terms of various types of expansion relations in Chinese. It has been pointed out that relator is not a compulsory constituent of a sequence in Chinese. In many cases, sequences can be realized as clause complexes without the presence of any Conjunction. It is thus possible that the thing in a metaphorical expression is realized by compensating the meaning of 'covert' relator. In this case, the shift from relator to thing can be examined from two perspectives: the nominalization of 'covert' Conjunction and the nominalization of 'overt' Conjunction.

In order to express metaphorically the meaning of a clause complex without a Conjunction, the meaning of 'covert' relator must be added to make the clause complete. This can be illustrated by the following example:

(5.17) *Wendu shenggao, Brown yundong de chengdu jiaqiang.*
temperature increase Brown motion Sub. intensity increase
'The temperature increases, so the intensity of Brownian motion increases.'
Actor Process (Conj.) Actor Process

Classified Proc. Classifier
Epithet Thing
Wendu shenggao de jieguo shi Brown yundong chengdu de jiaqiang.
Temperature increase Sub. result is Brown motion intensity Sub. increase
'The result of the temperature increase is the intensity increase of Brownian motion.'

[UC1]

It should be noted that the sequence may also be realized as a nominal group. Thus, the semantic shift from relator to thing does not necessarily engender the movement from clause complex to clause.

In the case that the meaning of a clause complex with Conjunctions is expressed in a metaphorical form, the 'overt' relator is realized in the same way as 'covert' relator. However, we have to take into account the existence of double Conjunctions in Chinese. The nominalizations of single and double Conjunctions are illustrated in Examples 5.18 and 5.19.

(5.18) Single Conjunction
Yinwei E1 he E2 de fangxiang xiangtong, zong dian chang wei E1 +E2.
since E1 and E2 Sub. direction same total electric field is E1 + E2
'Since E1 and E2 are in the same direction, the total electric field is E1+E2.'
Conj. Carrier Attribute Token Process Value

Token Process Value
(Epithet (rank shifted) Thing)
Zong dian chang wei E1+E2 de yuanyin shi E1 he E2 de fangxiang xiangtong.
total electric field is E1 + E2 Sub. reason is E1 and E2 Sub. direction same
'The reason that the total electric field is E1 + E2 is E1 and E2 are same in direction.'

[UP2]

(5.19) Double Conjunctions
Ruguo yong shouzhi peng qiu, jiuhui zhonghe qiu shang de dianhe.
if with finger touch ball so neutralize ball on Sub. electron
'If the ball is touched with a finger, its electron will be neutralized.'
Conj. Cir: Manner Process Goal Conj. Process Goal

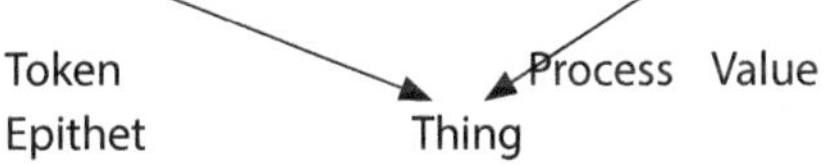

Token Process Value
Epithet Thing
Shouzhi peng qiu de jieguo shi qiu shang de dianhe bei zhonghe
finger touch ball Sub. result is ball on Sub. electron Bei neutralize
'The result of touching the ball with a finger is the neutralization of its electron.'

[SP2]

These examples demonstrate that either single or double Conjunctions can be transferred as nouns although the meaning of double Conjunctions must be reconstrued by one noun. Furthermore, all examples above are involved in the reconstrual of enhancement relation. This is not to say that only relators expressing this kind of logical relation shift to thing. As revealed in Table 3.4, Conjunctions in Chinese are deployed to express both extension and enhancement relations. The clause complex involved in extension relation is normally compacted into a nominal group. Correspondingly, the relator in question is generally realized as Thing in a nominal group, as shown in Example 5.20:

(5.20) *Zengda dianlu qiangdu huo jiangdi juli.*
increase current strength or reduce distance
'to increase the strength of the current or reduce the distance'
Process Goal Conj. Process Goal

Epithet Epithet → Thing
zengda dianlu qiangdu he jiangdi juli de dengxiaoxing [UP1]
increase current strength and reduce distance Sub. equivalence
'the equivalence of the increase of current strength and the reduction of distance'

So far, the four categories of ideational GM involved in the semantic shift to thing have been described. Each category of the semantic shift is further classified into subcategories in terms of the transfer between grammatical functions. In the following section, the semantic shift to quality is described in the same way.

5.3.2 Shift to Quality

As Figure 5.1 shows, there are three kinds of semantic elements which can be reconstrued as qualities: process, circumstance and relator. The shift to quality thus covers three categories of ideational GM: process to quality, circumstance to quality and realtor to quality. Those GM categories are numbered respectively as (5), (6) and (7) in this study. As mentioned above, the quality in Chinese functions as Epithet in a nominal group and Attribute in a relational clause. For this reason semantic elements of process, circumstance and relator can be metaphorically realized as Epithet or Attribute in different linguistic environments. As with the shifts starting from process and circumstance, I discuss only the reconstrual of them as Epithet in nominal groups. The reason is that only this kind of reconstrual involves downranking grammatical movement, which is a critical criterion in identifying ideational GM.

(5) Process to Quality

The GM instances in this category are further classified into three groups in terms of grammatical movement: (i) Event to Epithet, (ii) Event + Extension to Epithet and (iii) Auxiliary to Epithet. The subcategory Event to Epithet occurs in every type of process in Chinese, as shown in the following examples:

(5.21) Material:
Liang ge qiu xianghu paichi.
two piece ball each other repel
'The two balls repel each other.'
Actor Cir:Manner Process

Epithet Numerative Thing
paichi de liang ge qiu [SP1]
repulsive Sub. two piece ball
'the two repulsive balls'

(5.22) Mental:
Einstein jiading guangsu bubian.
Einstein hypothesize the speed of light same
'Einstein hypothesizes that the speed of light is constant.'
Sensor Process Phenomenon

Deictic Epithet Thing
Einstein jiading de bubian guangsu [UP1]
Einstein hypothesized Sub. same the speed of light
'the constant speed of light hypothesized by Einstein'

(5.23) Relational:
G daibiao zhongli.
G represent gravity.
'G represents gravity.'
Token Process Value

Classifier Epithet Thing
G daibiao de zhongli. [SP2]
G represent Sub. gravity
'the gravity represented by G'

(5.24) Behavioural:
Newton zai pingguo shu xia sikao.
Newton at apple tree under think
'Newton thinks under an apple tree.'
Behaver Cir: Location Process

Deictic Epithet Epithet Thing
Newton zai pingguo shu xia sikao (de wenti) [SP1]
Newton at apple tree under think (Sub. question)
'(the question) Newton thinks under a apple tree'

(5.25) Verbal:
Shouce jieshi shiyan buzhou.
guidebook describe experiment procedure
'The guildbook describes the procedure of the experiment.'
Sayer Process Verbiage

Epithet Epithet Thing
Shouce zhong jieshi de shiyan buzhou [UC1]
guidebook in described Sub. experiment procedure
'the experiment procedure described in the guidebook'

(5.26) Existential:
Jinshu zhong cunzai ziyou dianzi
Metal inside exist free electron
'There are free electrons in metals.'
Cir: Location Process Existent

Epithet Epithet Thing
cunzai yu jinshu zhong de ziyou dianzi [UC1]
exist in metal inside Sub. free electron
'free electrons existing in metals'

The subcategory of Event + Extension to Epithet is most frequently observed in the metaphorical realization of a material process, as shown in Example 5.27.

(5.27) Material:
Jinshu yin zishen zhongliang zhe duan.
metal because own weight break crack
'The metal breaks because of its own weight.'
Participant Cir: Cause Process (Event + Extension)

Epithet Epithet Thing
yin zishen zhongliang zhe duan de jinshu [SC2]
because own weight break crack Sub. metal
'the metal which breaks because of its own weight'

The subcategory of Auxiliary to Epithet is concerned with the transfer from a modal verb to a modifier of noun. In particular, the Auxiliary with the meaning of probability, inclination or obligation can be realized as Epithet.

(5.28) Probability:

Guang xian keneng jizhong zai mou quyu.
light ray can concentrate in certain area
'The light rays could be concentrated in a certain area.'
Actor Process Cir: Location

Epithet Epithet Thing
Guang xian jizhong de keneng quyu [UP1]
light ray concentrate Sub. possible area
'the possible area in which the light rays concentrate'

(5.29) Inclination:

Gai dianzi yao yan guidao yundong
the electron will along orbit move
'The electron will move along an orbit.'
Actor Process Cir: Location Process

Epithet Epithet Thing
Dianzi yundong de yuding guidao [UC1]
electron movement Sub. intended orbit
'the intended orbit of electron movement'

(5.30) Obligation:

Zheshe jiao bixu shi 30°.
deviation angle must is 30°
'The angle of deviation must be 30°.'
Token Process Value

Epithet Numerative Thing
Yaoqiu de 30° zheshi jiao [SP2]
required Sub. 30° deviation angle
'the required 30° angle of deviation'

(6) Circumstance to Quality

Circumstances in Chinese are divided into three types according to their typological structures discussed in Section 3.2.3. Types (1a) and (1b) are respectively expressed by prepositional phrases with the structures of 'minor Process + Participant + Facet' and 'minor Process + Participant', while type (2) is realized by an adverbial group. As mentioned above, the metaphorical realizations of various types of circumstance are different in terms of reconstrual method. When the circumstance in type (1a) is reconstrued as a quality, the minor Process is frequently omitted. Simultaneously, the Participant and the Facet within the circumstance are realized as an Epithet in metaphorical expressions. Look at the following example:

(5.31) *Guang bo zai zhenkong zhong chuanbo*
light wave in vacuum inside transmit
'The light wave transmits in vacuum'
Actor Circ: Location Process
(minor Proc. + Partic. + Facet)

Epithet Classifier Thing
zhenkong zhong guang bo de chuanbo [UP1]
vacuum inside light wave Sub. transmission
'the transmission of the light wave in vacuum'

In the reconstrual of this type of circumstance, the Facet is generally moved to the metaphorical realization without change of form.

The reconstrual of circumstances in type (1b) is distinguished from that in type (1a) in that the minor Process in question is transferred as Epithet and the Participant within the circumstance becomes a modifier in a nominal group.

(5.32) *Genju Einstein de guandian, shijian gainian he kongjian gainian keyi tidai.*
According to E Sub. view Time notion and space notion may interchange
'According to Einstein's view, the notions of time and space may be interchanged.'
Circ: Source Actor Process
(minor Proc. + Partic.)

Deictic Epithet Classifier Thing
Einstein tichu de shijian he kongjian de huhuanxing [UP2]
Einstein claim Sub. time and space Sub. reciprocity
'the reciprocity of space and time claimed by Einstein'

Finally, the metaphorical realization of a circumstance in type (2) only involves adverbs in Chinese. In the reconstrual of this type of circumstance, the adverb concerned is transferred into an adjective. In addition, the shift from a type (2) circumstance to a quality is featured by their tendency to co-occur with the shifts from semantic element of quality or process to thing. These shifts are exemplified as follows:

A. Accompanying the shift from quality to thing

(5.33) *Shijian he kongjian miqie lianxi.*
time and space intimately connected
'Time and space are intimately connected.'
Carrier Circ: Manner Attribute

Classifier Epithet Thing
Shijian kongjjan de miqie lianxi. [UP1]
time space Sub. intimate connection
'the intimate connection between time and space'

B. Accompanying the shift from process to thing

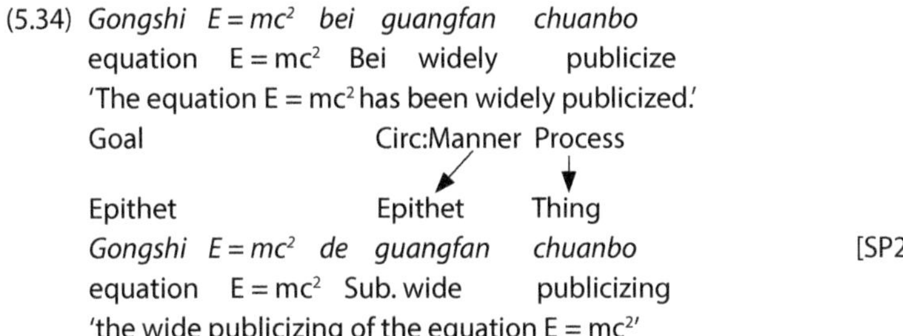

The discussion above indicates that ideational GM category 6 can be divided into three subcategories which respectively involve circumstances in types (1a), type (1b) and type (2).

(7) Relator to Quality

The shift from relator to quality has two destinations on account of the grammatical functions of quality. In particular, a relator could be metaphorically realized as an Epithet in a nominal group or an Attribute in a relational clause. These two subcategories of shift from realtor to quality are described respectively. Subcategory (i) refers to the grammatical transfer from Conjunction to Attribute. The Attribute involved is normally indicated by the attributive particle *de*. See Example 5.35.

(5.35) *Sheng yuan yidong jiakuai, tongshi shengyin pinlu bian gao.*
sound source move faster and sound frequency become high
'The source of sound moves faster, and the frequency of sound becomes greater.'
Actor Process Conj. Actor Process
Carrier Proc. Attribute
Sheng yuan yidong he pinlu biangao shi duiying de
sound source movement and frequency increase is corresponding Particle
'the movement of sound source and the increase of frequency are corresponding.' [UP2]

It is worth noting that a Conjunction in the congruent expressions of this subcategory of GM instances maybe single, double or 'covert'. The meaning of a 'covert' Conjunction must be represented in GM instances, as shown in Example 5.36.

(5.36) *Yali jiada, moca li jiada.*
pressure increase friction force increase
'If the pressure increases, the friction force will increase.'
(Conj.)Actor Process Actor Process
→
Carrier Process Attribute
moca li jiada he yali zengda shi guanlian de [SP2]
friction force increase and pressure increase is connected Sub.
'the increases of friction force and pressure are connected.'

Subcategory (ii) refers to the grammatical transfer from Conjunction to Epithet. Similar to subcategory (i), it is also concerned with the single, double and 'covert' Conjunctions. Only an example of single Conjunction is displayed here.

(5.37) *Dang liang ge yuanquan chongdie, tamen xianghu ganrao.*
when two piece circle overlap they each other interfere
'When two circles overlap, they interfere each other'
Conj. Actor Process Actor Cir:Manner Process
→
Epithet Epithet Thing
Liang ge yuanquan chongdie chansheng de ganrao [UP1]
two piece circle overlap produce Sub. interference
'the interference resulted by the overlap of two circles.'

Examples 5.36 and 5.37 reveal that both extension and enhancement relations are involved in the shift from relator to quality. The relator with an extension meaning is generally realized as an Attribute in a relational clause, while the relator with an enhancement meaning is reconstrued as an Epithet in a nominal group.

5.3.3 Shift to Process

Two categories of ideational GM in Chinese involve the semantic shift to process, namely, circumstance to process and relator to process. They are category (8) and category (9) in the framework of ideational GM categorization.

(8) Circumstance to Process

Circumstances and processes are largely construed by prepositions and verbs in Chinese. The prepositions in Chinese, as revealed in Section 3.2.3, are derived from verbs. Many prepositions have characteristics of verbs and can be used as verbs that have similar meanings. This feature of Chinese prepositions determines that the shift from the circumstance realized by a prepositional phrase to process is less recognizable than other types of semantic shifts. Generally speaking, only a circumstance with the meaning of source or causality is transferred to process. For example:

(5.38) *Yizhao shiyan shouce, wendu yao yange kongzhi.*
According to experiment guidebook temperature must strictly control
'According to experiment guidebook, the temperature must be controlled strictly'
Circ: Source (minor Proc. + Partic.) Goal Pro- Cir: Manner -cess.
→
Initiator Process (Actor) Cir:Manner Process Goal
Shiyan shouce yaoqiu (women) yange kongzhi wendu
experiment guidebook require (us) strictly control temperature
'The experiment guidebook requires us to control the temperature strictly.'
[SC2]

(5.39) *Youyu di wen qiti shousuo.*
because of low temperature gas shrink
'The gas shrinks because of the low temperature.'
Circ: Cause (minor Proc. + Partic.) Actor Process
→
Actor Process Goal
Di wen daozhi qiti shousuo [SC1]
low temperature engender gas shrink
'The lower temperature engenders the shrinkage of gas.'

Circumstances and processes are the semantic elements in the same rank of expression. The shift from circumstance to process engenders the transfer between figures, as shown in Examples 5.38 and 5.39. However, the shift from circumstance to process is accompanied by a compression of process. The original minor process is reconstrued as a major process, while the original major process is rankshifted as the participant of a metaphorical expression. In this sense, the shift from circumstance to process has the common feature of rankshift found in ideational GM. As a corollary to this point, if the shift from circumstance to process occurs without the simultaneous embedding of the original major clause, the congruent figure will be realized as a clause complex. This kind of transfer is apparently not concerned with the ideational GM because a figure is reconstrued as a sequence in this case.

Finally, it is worth noting that the shift from circumstance in the form of adverbial group to process never occurs. This is because there is no possibility of transferring adverbs into verbs in Chinese.

(9) Relator to Process

The shift from relator to process usually occurs in the reconstrual of semantic unit in higher rank, where two nominalized processes are joined by a verbalized relator. This type of shift is a grammatical resource for realizing a sequence as a clause and maintaining the semantic relations within a figure. The instances of this category of ideational GM are concerned with the metaphorical reconstrual of expansion sequences in which figures are connected by semantic relations of different types. In Chinese, only the logico-semantic relations of extension and enhancement are involved in the shift from relator to process. The following examples represent this situation.

(5.40) Single Conjunction

Yinwei zhongli xiyin, shizi zuo paowuxian yundong.
Because gravity pull stone make parabola movement
'Because the stone is pulled by gravity, it moves in a parabola'
Conj. Actor Process Actor Process

Actor Process Goal
Zhongli de xiying daozhi shizi de paowuxian yundong [SP1]
gravity of pull lead to stone Sub. parabola movement
'The pull of gravity leads to the parabola movement of a stone.'

(5.41) Double Conjunctions

Celiang danwei yue xiao, celiang jieguo yue zhunque.
measure scale more small measure result more accurate
'The smaller the measure scale, the more accurate the measure result.'
Carrier Conj. Attribute Carrier Conj. Attribute

Actor Process Goal
Celiang jingdu qujue yu celiang danwei. [UC1]
Measure accuracy depend upon measure scale
'The measure accuracy depends upon measure scale.'

This category of ideational GM is not observed frequently in Chinese (see Section 6.4.1). However, the significance of the shift from realtor to process is that it is the driving force of other categories of ideational GM. This point is further explored in terms of the interdependency between different categories of GM in Chapter 6.

5.3.4 Shift to Circumstance

This group of shift only involves one category of ideational GM in Chinese. As indicated in Figure 5.1, it is the shift from relator to circumstance which is numbered category (10).

(10) Relator to Circumstance

The reconstrual of a relator as a circumstance involves the downranking grammatical movement from clause complex to clause. The instances of the shift can be differentiated in terms of logico-semantic relations. The majority of the instances in this category express enhancement relation, while a few instances are concerned with the relation of extension.

In the case of extension relation, the Conjunction in a clause complex is transferred into a preposition which occurs in the circumstance of Accompaniment. With respect to enhancement relation, the shift between relator and circumstance is more complex. Halliday (1994) divides the enhancement relation into four types: (a) spatio-temporal; (b) manner; (c) causal-condition; and (d) matter. In the sense of semantic meaning, each of these types of enhancement relators corresponds to one or several types of circumstance. Given that the meaning of a relator cannot be realized by the Circumstances of Matter and Manner in Chinese, the shifts from relator to circumstance in the language are concerned with two subtypes of enhancement relation. The correspondence between various expansion relations and different types of circumstance in Chinese are summarized in Table 5.2.

Expansion relation	*Circumstance*	
Extension	Accompaniment	
Enhancement – spatio-temporal	 Location (Place, Time)	 – causal-condition Cause, Source

Table 5.2: Correspondence between expansion relation and circumstance in Chinese

The semantic shift from the relator with extension meanings to the circumstance of Accompaniment is illustrated by the following example:

(5.42) *Shoure wuti tiji bianda, tongshi tamen de midu bianxiao.*
heated body volume increase at the same time their Sub. density decrease
'The volume of heated bodies increase and their density decreases.'
Actor Process Conj. Actor Process

Circ: Accompaniment Actor Process
Sui tiji bianda, shoure wuti de midu bianxiao. [UP1]
with volume increase heated body Sub. density decrease
'With the increase of their volume, the density of heated bodies decreases.'

The shifts from relators in enhancement sequences to different types of circumstance are shown by the examples below:

(5.43) Spatio-temporal relation
Dang yeti duiliu shi, re chuanbo jiasu
when liquid convect time heat propagation accelerate
'When the liquid convects, the propagation of heat accelerates.'
Conj. Actor Process Actor Process
↓
Circ: Location Actor Process
Zai yeti duiliu zhong, re chuanbo jiasu. [UC2]
In liquid convection inside heat propagation accelerate
'In the process of liquid convection, the propagation of heat accelerates.'

(5.44) Causal-condition relation
Yinwei yali fasheng le bianhua, shengyin de sudu shou yingxiang.
because pressure occur Asp. change sound Sub. speed receive effect
'The speed of sound is affected because the pressure is changed.'
Conj. Actor Process Actor Process
↓
Cir: Cause Actor Process
Youyu yali de bianhua, shengyin de sudu shou yingxiang
Because of pressure Sub. change sound Sub. speed receive effect
'Because of the change of pressure, the speed of sound is affected.' [UP1]

5.3.5 Shift to Modifer

The GM categories discussed above reflect the primary motif of the drift towards thing in the ideational GM of Chinese. There also exists the semantic shift where the modifier of a thing is a destination. According to Halliday and Matthiessen (1999: 264), this category of GM refers to 'the move from "thing" into what might be interpreted as a manifestation of "quality"'. This category of GM is numbered (13) in Figure 5.1.

(13) Thing to Quality
The instances in this category of ideational GM are concerned with the reconstrual of participant role as various kinds of modifier. To be more specific, a thing can be metaphorically realized as Epithet, Classifier or Deictic. The shift from thing to quality is the secondary metaphor of other categories of ideational GM. It usually occurs as the accompaniment of category 1 or category 2, resulting in a GM cluster of category 1 + category 13 or category 2 + category 13. The examples below illustrate how category 13 is combined with other categories of ideational GM.

Combining with category 1

(5.45) *Fangxiang buke yuce.*
direction not predictable
'The direction is unpredictable.'
Carrier Attribute
↓ ↘
Epithet Thing
Fangxiang de bukeyucexing [UP1]
direction Sub. unpredictability
'the unpredictability of direction'

Combining with category 2

(5.46) *Reliang fushe.*
heat radiate
'Heat radiates.'
Actor Process
↓ ↘
Classifier Thing
reliang de fushe [SP1]
heat Sub. radiation
'heat radiation'

The examples illustrate that the GM instances in category 13 occur only as secondary metaphors that accompanies the types of metaphor which involve the shift to thing, especially category 1 and category 2.

As mentioned, the destination of the shift could be Epithet, Deictic or Classifier. The movements from Thing to Epithet and Classifier are illustrated in Examples 5.45 and 5.46. Here's one example of the grammatical shift from Thing to Deictic.

(5.47) *Kepler jisuan xingxing guidao.*
Kepler calculate planet orbit
'Kepler calculates the orbit of a planet.'
Actor Process Goal
↓
Deictic Epithet Thing
Kepler dui xingxing guidao de jisuan [UP1]
Kepler to planet orbit Sub. calculation
'Kepler's calculation of the planet orbit'

Based on the analysis above, the shift from thing to quality is divided into three subcategories in terms of grammatical shift: (i) Thing to Epithet; (ii) Thing to Classifier; and (iii) Thing to Deictic.

5.3.6 Ideational GM without congruent form

In addition to the major categories of ideational metaphor listed in Figure 5.1, there are two types of ideational GM in Chinese which have no corresponding congruent form. Similar to the instances of the shift from thing to quality, metaphorical expressions involved in these types occur in combination with other metaphorical shifts. These two categories of ideational GM are numbered (11) and (12) in Figure 5.1.

(11) Addition of Thing

The instances in this category of ideational GM are concerned with the attachment of noun to a metaphorical expression. The noun involved is a 'dummy noun introduced in the nominalising of another process' (Halliday, 1998: 233). In other words, the most important characteristic of the noun is that it never refers to any thing in the preceding nominalization. This type of ideational GM is exemplified by the following transfers from clause to nominal group.

(5.48) *Shengyin bei fanshe.*
sound Bei reflect
'Sound is reflected.'
Goal Process
↓
Classifier Thing Thing (additional)
Shengyin fanshe de xianxiang [SP1]
sound reflect Sub. phenomenon
'the phenomenon of sound reflection'

(5.49) *Sudu gaibian.*
velocity change
'The velocity changes.'
Actor Process
↓
Classifier Thing Thing (additional)
Sudu gaibian de daxiao [SP1]
velocity change Sub. size
'the rate of velocity change'

In these examples, the nouns of *xianxiang* (phenomenon) and *daxiao* (size) are added to metaphorical shifts from process to thing. Without them, the metaphorical transfer from clause to nominal group may exist in its own right.

(12) Addition of Process

In English, there is a very common form of expressions which is exemplified by 'have a bath', 'do some work', 'make a mistake' or 'take a rest' (Halliday, 1994). In these expressions, the verbs are empty in lexical meaning and simply indicate the occurrence of certain process. Meanwhile, the real meanings of the expressions are realized by the nouns functioning as Range. Halliday (1994: 348) claims that 'this entire set of expressions is really incongruent'. This category of ideational GM is also observed in Chinese though it is not used as widely as that in English. For example:

(5.50) *Wendu* *yingxiang* *shiyan* *jieguo.*
temperature affect experiment result
'The temperature affects the result of the experiment.'
Actor Process Goal
→
Actor Goal Process Range (Thing)
Wendu *dui shiyan* *jieguo* *you* *yingxiang* [SC1]
Temperature to experiment result have effect
'The temperature has an effect on the result of experiment.'

In this example, the Process in the congruent clause is realized in the form of Process + Range. The addition of verb *you* (have) is the dependent metaphor of the shift from process to thing.

5.3.7 A summary of ideational GM categories

Up to this point, 13 categories of ideational GM in Chinese and their subcategories have been analysed on the basis of the framework described in Section 5.2. To facilitate further studies in this field, these ideational GM categories and subcategories in Chinese are presented in Table 5.3.

In Table 5.3, all 13 categories of ideational GM and their subtypes are tabulated on the basis of the detailed discussion in Section 5.3. The examples are the expressions analyzed in this section, which are simplified to suit the space constraints of Table 5.3.

5.4 Categorization of interpersonal GM

In this section, interpersonal GM in Chinese is categorized by differentiating the metaphorical realizations of the semantic systems of speech function and modality. These two types of interpersonal GM are referred to metaphor of mood and metaphor of modality in Chinese. I distinguish the metaphorical and congruent realizations of an interpersonal meaning on the basis of the grammatical variations listed in Tables 4.3 and 4.4. For example, an expression is recognized as congruent if its modality meaning is realized by the grammatical elements within a clause. It is worth noting that the meaning of the examples in this section must be understood by referring to particular contexts.

Shift of semantic element			*Shift of grammatical function*	*Example*
#	*Cong.*	*Meta.*	*Cong. Meta.*	
1	quality	thing	i) Epithet – Thing ii) Attribute – Thing	*jingzhi* (static) – *jingzhi* (rest) *wanqu* (curved) – *wanqu* (curvature)
2	process	thing	i) Event – Thing ii) Event + Extension – Thing iii) Auxiliary – Thing	*biaoshi* (represent) – *biaoda* (representation) *Rong jie* (melt away) – *rong jie* (melting away) *keneng* (can) – *nengli* (ability)
3	circ.	thing	i) minor Proc. – Thing ii) minor Proc. + Partic. – Thing	*genju* (depending on) – *genju*(foundation) *an gai yuanli*(according to that principle) – *gai yuanli de yinyong* (that principle Sub. application)
4	relator	thing	Conj. – Thing	*yinwei* (since) – *yuanyin* (reason)
5	process	quality	i) Event –Epithet ii) Event + Extension – Epithet iii) Auxiliary – Epithet	*paichi* (repel) – *paichi* (repulsive) *zhe duan* (break crack) – *zhe duan de* (break crack Sub.) *yao* (will) – *yuding* (intending)
6	circ.	quality	i) Partic. + Facet – Epithet/Classifier ii) minor Proc. + Partic. – Epithet/Classifier iii) Manner – Epithet	*zai zhenkong zhong* (in vacuum inside) – *zhenkong zhong* (vacuum inside) *genju Einstein de guandian* (according to E. Sub. theory) – *Einstein tichu de* (E. claim of) *guangfan* (widely) – *guangfan* (wide)
7	realtor	quality	i) Conj. – Attribute ii) Conj. – Epithet	*tongshi* (and) – *duiying de* (corresponding Sub.) *dang* (when) – *shengcheng de* (produced Sub.)
8	circ.	process	minor Proc. – Process	*yizhao* (depending on) – *yaoqiu* (require)
9	relator	process	Conj. - Process	*yinwei* (because) - *daozhi* (lead to)
10	relator	circ.	i) Conj. – minor Proc. (Accompaniment) ii) Conj. – minor Proc. (directional Location) iii) Conj. – minor Proc. (Cause, Source)	*tongshi* (and) – *sui* (with) *dang* (when) – zai (in) *yinwei* (because) – *youyu* (because of)
11		+ thing	+ Thing	*fanshe* (reflect) – *fanshe de xianxiang* (reflection Sub. phenomenon)
12		+ process	+ Process	*yingxiang* (affect) – *you yingxiang* (have effect)
13	thing	quality	i) Thing – Epithet ii) Thing – Classifier iii) Thing – Deictic	*fangxiang* (direction) – *fangxiang de* (direction Sub.) *sudu* (velocity) – *sudu gaibian* (velocity change) Kepler – Kepler

Table 5.3: Categories and subcategories of ideational GM in Chinese

5.4.1 Metaphor of Mood

Section 4.5 reveals that there is no one-to-one match between the grammatical system of Mood and the semantic system of speech function in Chinese. When the relationship between them is considered in detail, two features are noted: (a) the same Mood selection can perform different speech functions; and (b) the same speech function can be performed by different Mood selections. I focus on the second feature to categorize the metaphor of mood. To be more specific, the metaphor of mood in Chinese is classified in terms of speech functions realized by various types of Mood. The categories of metaphor of mood are numbered from 1 to 4 in Table 5.1.

5.4.1.1 Metaphorical realization of command

As discussed in Section 4.5.2, an imperative is the most direct and typical way of expressing the speech function of command, hence, the congruent realization. However, it is well known that on many occasions the command is not expressed by imperative. According to Eggins (1994), the imperative is the typical choice for commanding family and friends, while declaratives and interrogatives are preferred to express commands in formal situations. In this sense, the metaphorical realizations of command involve the categories 1 and 2 of metaphor of mood.

(1) Expressing command with interrogative Mood

According to Liu and Pan (2004), the interrogative in Chinese is semantically equivalent to the request in many cases. The meaning of a command can be expressed in the form of interrogative in a particular context. This reconstrual of meaning in Chinese is illustrated by the following group of imperative and interrogative clauses with the same speech function of command.

(5.51) → *Zhunbei ni de baogao.* (Imperative)
prepare you Sub. report
'Prepare your report.'

→ *Ni de baogao zhunbei hao le ma?* (Interrogative: Mood particle)
you Sub. report prepare good Asp. Mood particle
'Are you ready with your report?'

→ *Ni de baogao zhunbei mei zhunbei hao?* (Interrogative: A-not-A)
you Sub. report prepare not prepare good
'Are you ready with your report or not?'

→ *Ni de baogao shenme shihou zhunbei hao?* (Interrogative: question-word)
you Sub. report what time prepare good
'When will you be ready with your report?'

These examples indicate that the speech function of command congruently realized by an imperative clause can be reconstrued in various types of interrogative clauses. Rather, the meaning of command can be metaphorically expressed by each type of interrogative in Chinese, i.e., question-word, A-not-A or Mood particle interrogatives.

Some specific patterns of expressions are deployed in Chinese to realize certain speech functions, which are referred to as speech-functional formulae by Halliday (1994). When the speech function of command is realized in the form of interrogative clauses, the most frequently used speech-functional formulae are as follows:

A. Hai bu ... *(yet not)*

The formula of *hai bu* ... (yet not) is the most salient one in the interrogative expressions with command meanings and could be translated into the English expression of 'why not …'.

(5.52) *Xiexie na ge jingcha.* (Imperative)
thank that Meas. policeman
'Say thank you to the policeman.'

Hai bu xiexie na ge jingcha ? (Interrogative)
yet not thank that Meas. policeman
(why not say thank you to the policeman?)

In some cases, the formula is preceded by the name of a person or a second personal pronoun. For example:

(5.53) *Ni kuai pao.* (Imperative)
you immediately run
'You run immediately.'

Ni hai bu kuai pao? (Interrogative)
you yet not immediately run
'why don't you run immediately?'

B. Nan dao ... *(difficult say)*

The formula *nan dao* is used in negative expressions indicated by *bu* (not) and frequently followed by the Mood particle *ma*. For example:

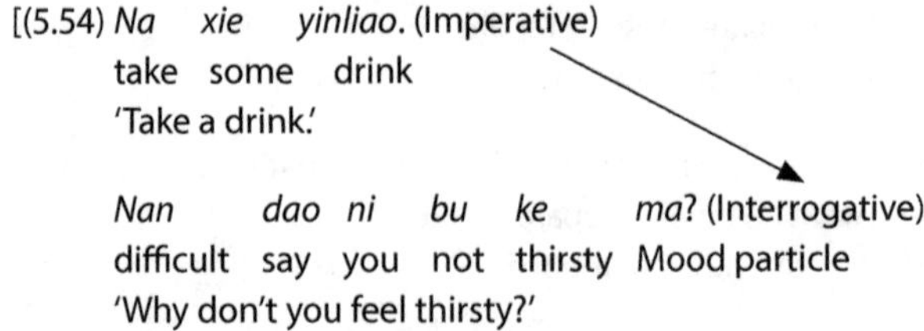
[(5.54) *Na xie yinliao.* (Imperative)
take some drink
'Take a drink.'

Nan dao ni bu ke ma? (Interrogative)
difficult say you not thirsty Mood particle
'Why don't you feel thirsty?'

*C. ...*Hao/xing/keyi ma *(good + Mood particle)*
With the Mood particle *ma*, the formula *...hao/xing/keyi ma* introduces interrogative clauses with the meaning of request. The Chinese clause with this formula could be expressed in English as 'Would you mind doing something.'

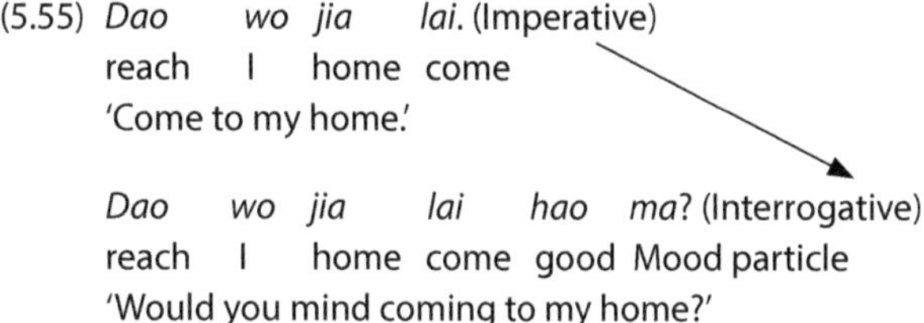

This analysis of speech-functional formulae reveals that the meanings of command are not reconstrued with just one method. The formulae *hai bu* and *hao ma* are attached to expressions which are originally imperative clauses. When the formula *nan dao* realizes the meaning of command by requesting a service from the listener, it is attached to an expression which does not have the meaning of command.

(2) Expressing command with declarative Mood
Compared with interrogative clauses, the utterances in a declarative form do not imply the meaning of command so obviously. In many cases, the speech function of command is realized by a declarative clause with reference to a particular context. The declarative clauses involved in the expression of command can be further divided into two types according to whether the emphasizing structure of *shi ... de* is deployed, as shown in Examples 5.56 and 5.57.

A. Normal structure

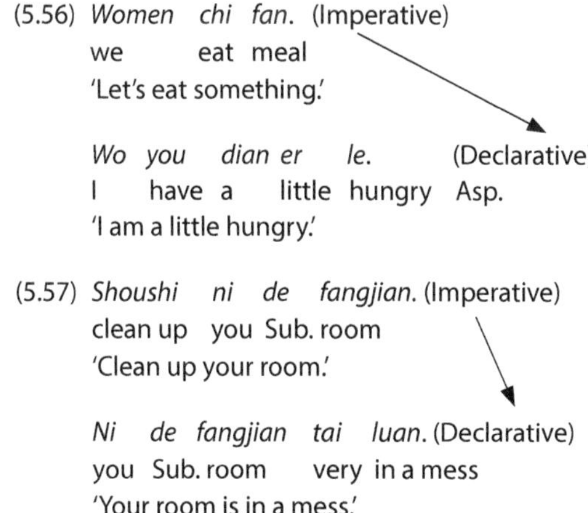

B. Emphasizing structure

(5.58) *Bu zhun zai zhe li xiyan.* (Imperative)
not permit in here inside smoke
'Do not smoke here.'

Zhe li shi yanjin xiyan de. (Declarative) [modified]
here inside is prohibit smoke Sub.
'Smoking is prohibited here.'

The inherent reason for expressing commands with interrogative and declarative Moods can be explored with reference to the politeness principle put forward by Brown and Levinson (1987). Generally speaking, the command metaphorically expressed by an interrogative or a declarative has a higher politeness class than the one congruently realized by an imperative.

5.4.1.2 Metaphorical realization of statement

The speech function of statement is congruently realized by a declarative clause. In addition, interrogative clauses in Chinese are frequently used to express the meaning of statement. In the sense of grammatical shift, the metaphorical realization of statement only involves the movement from declarative Mood to interrogative Mood. This type of grammatical movement is treated as category 3 of metaphor of mood in Table 5.1.

(3) Expressing statement with interrogative Mood

Rhetorical interrogatives are involved in the metaphorical realization of the speech function of statement in Chinese. This type of interrogative is distinguished from the normal interrogative in that the question is asked for a special purpose other than to obtain information. Normally, a speaker expresses a statement regarding his own opinion by using a rhetorical interrogative Mood choice. Many speech-functional formulae are deployed in Chinese to express statements with rhetorical interrogative clauses. The most frequently used formulae are as follows:

A. bu shi…ma? (not is … Mood particle)

(5.59) *Gen ni shuo guo le.* (Declarative)
to you talk already Asp.
'I've already talked to you.'

Bu shi gen ni shuo guo le ma? (Interrogative)
not is to you talk already Asp. Mood particle
'Haven't I talked to you?'

B. nan dao ... *(difficult say)*
The formula '*nan dao* ...' has been discussed in the analysis of commands realized in the form of interrogative Mood. In some contexts, it also functions to realize the speech function of statement.

(5.60) *Bu yiding qu tushuguan.* (Declarative)
not must go library
'We do not necessarily go to the library.'

Nan dao yiding qu tushuguan? (Interrogative)
difficult say must go library
'Is that necessary to go to the library?'

C. shenme *(what)*
This type of formula ordinarily appears in a relational process which is formed by a pair of Carrier and Attribute. It realizes the speech function of statement by negating the Attribute in an interrogative clause. In the following example, the meaning of *budui* (wrong) is negated.

(5.61) *Ta de kanfa shi dui de.* (Declarative)
he Sub. opinion is correct Sub.
'His opinion is correct.'

Ta de kanfa you shenme budui? (Interrogative)
he Sub. opinion have what wrong
'What's wrong with his opinion?'

D. Question-word

(5.62) *Zhe ge fangchengshi mei cuo.* (Declarative)
this Meas. equation not wrong
'This equation is not wrong.'

Zhe ge fangchengshi nali cuo le? (Interrogative)
this Meas. equation where wrong Asp.
'Where does the equation go wrong?'

5.4.1.3 Metaphorical realization of question
Compared to the other types of speech function, questions have relatively fewer forms of metaphorical realization. Only some declarative clauses with special structure can metaphorically realize the meaning of question. The expression of questions with these declarative clauses is referred to as category 4 in the classification of metaphor of mood.

(4) Expressing question with declarative Mood
The declarative clauses involved in the metaphorical expression of questions is characterized by the structure of '*Wo xiang zhidao/liaojie* ...'(I want to know/enquire ...). In other words, the declaratives concerned have the intension of obtaining information from the person addressed, which is shown in the following example.

(5.63) *Ni shenme shijian neng wancheng lunwen?* (Interrogative)
you what time can finish thesis
'When can you finish your thesis?'

Wo xiang zhidao ni wancheng lunwen de shijian. (Declarative)
I want know you finish thesis Sub. time
'I want to know the ending time of your thesis writing.'

To close the discussion of interpersonal GM in terms of mood, it is worth pointing out that any metaphorical realization of speech function is construed in a certain context. It is possible that the same clause expresses various types of speech function in different linguistic environments. For the convenience of discussion, this analysis exemplified the metaphorical forms of speech function without stating the context of these expressions. In the practical analysis of interpersonal GM in Chinese, the context in which metaphorical expressions occur must be taken into consideration. According to the discussion above, the categorization of metaphor of mood is summarized in Table 5.4.

5.4.2 Metaphor of modality

The metaphor of modality in Chinese is categorized in two steps. First, the metaphorical realizations of modality are classified in terms of the four types of modality in Chinese, namely, probability, usuality, obligation and inclination. Second, the metaphorical expressions concerned are subdivided by considering the grammatical methods involved in the metaphorical realization of particular modality meaning. As revealed in Section 4.5.2, the grammatical methods concerned are projecting process, *shi* ... *de* structure, *you* ... structure and Mood particle.

5.4.2.1 Metaphorical realizations of probability

Section 4.3.3 shows that all of the four grammatical methods are involved in the metaphorical realizations of probability in Chinese. To be more specific, probability can be metaphorically expressed by projecting process, *shi* ... *de* structure, *you* ... structure or the Mood particle of *ba*. This section examines the four types of metaphorical realization one by one.

Speech function	*Shift of Mood*	*Grammatical realizations*	
Command	(1) Imperative -Interrogative	(i) Normal interrogative	Question-word, A-not-A structure Mood particle
		(ii) Special formula	'*hai bu…*' (yet not); '*nan dao…*' (difficult say); '*…hao ma*'(good + Mood particle)
	(2) Imperative Declarative	(i) Normal declarative	
		(ii) Special formula	'*shi …de*' (is … Sub.)
Statement	(3) Declarative -Interrogative	(i) Normal interrogative	Question-word
		(ii) Special formula	'*bu shi…ma?*' (not is … Mood particle); '*nan dao …*' (difficult say); '*shenme*' (what);
Question	(4) Interrogative -Declarative	Special formula	'*Wo xiang zhidao/liaojie …*' (I want to know/enquire…)

Table 5.4: Categories of metaphor of mood in Chinese

(i) Expressing probability with projecting process

When probability is construed as a projecting process in Chinese, the metaphorical realization generally involves a mental process with a first person participant. The verbs *xiang* (think), *renwei* (reckon), *guji* (estimate) are used most frequently to construct the mental process involved. The probability meaning in Chinese is congruently realized by modal verbs and adverbs, which are functionally referred to as Finite and Adjunct in this study. The grammatical movements from Finite and Adjunct to mental clause are illustrated by Examples 5.64 and 5.65.

(5.64) *Ta keneng qu jisuanji zhongxin.*
he might go to computer center
'He might go to the computer center.'
Subject Finite Predicator Complement

Subject Predicator // Subject Predicator Complement
Wo xiang ta qu jisuanji zhongxin.
I think he go to computer center
'I think he goes to the computer center.'

(5.65) *Ta* *yiding* *zai* *8* *dian* *qian* *huilai*
He definitely in 8 o'clock before come back
'He definitely comes back before 8 o'clock.'
Subject Adjunct Adjunct Predicator

Subject Predicator// Subject Adjunct Predicator
Wo *xiangxing* *ta* *8* *dian* *qian* *huilai*
I believe he 8 o'clock before come back
'I believe he comes back before 8 o'clock.'

The projecting process in the above examples is the sole component used to metaphorically express the meaning of probability. In other cases, the projecting process presents together with a modal verb or adverb. The grammatical movement from congruent form to metaphorical expression which contains both projection and modal verb/adverb is exemplified as follows:

(5.66) *Ta* *hui* *chenggong.*
He will succeed
'He will succeed.'
Subject Finite Predicator

Subject Predicator// Subject Finite Predicator
Wo *renwei* *ta* *hui* *chenggong.*
I reckon he will succeed
'I reckon he will succeed.'

(ii) Expressing probability with Shi ... de structure

As discussed in Section 4.6.3, the structure of *shi...de* in Chinese is generally used to emphasize the information inserted between *shi* and *de*. When the information to be inserted involves comments addressed by a speaker, the structure expresses a modal meaning. Although the structure is generally translated as 'It is ...' in English, it is deployed with a broader semantic scope in Chinese. For example, any type of modality can be metaphorically realized in the form of '*shi ... de*', while the 'It is ...' structure in English is not involved in the expression of inclination. As far as the probability is concerned, almost every modal verb and adverb involved can be inserted into the *shi ... de* structure to form a metaphorical realization. The realizations with modal verb and adverb are shown respectively in the following two examples.

(5.67) *Xiangmu keneng zai san tian nei wancheng.*
Project can in three day inside complete
'The project can be completed in three days.'
Subject Finite Adjunct Predicator
→
Adjunct Predicator Complement // Pred. Complement
Zai san tian nei wancheng xiangmu shi keneng de.
In three day inside complete project is can Sub.
'It is possible to complete the project in three days.'

(5.68) *A dui yiding huosheng.*
A team certainly win
'Team A will certainly win.'
Subject Adjunct Predicator
→
Subject Predicator // Pred. Complement
A dui huosheng shi yiding de.
A team win is certainly Sub.
'It is certain that team A will win.'

(iii) Expressing probability with you ... structure

There is also the possibility to express probability through *you* ... structure in Chinese. To be more specific, the meaning of probability is construed as isolated processes, as shown in Example 5.69.

(5.69) *Ta keneng hui jia le.*
he probably go back home Asp.
'He probably went back home.'
Subject Finite Predicator Complement
↙
Pred. Complement//Subject Predicator Complement
You keneng ta hui jia le.
have possibility he go back home Asp.
'There is the possibility that a war breaks out between the two countries.'

Furthermore, the meaning of probability is sometimes construed more abstractly by treating the noun in question as a thing in the participant of an existential process. In this case, the noun involved is generally the one ended with the nominalizing morpheme *xing*. The metaphorical expression is an instance of ideational GM (see Section 5.3.1), for example:

(5.70) *Liang guo zhijian you baofa zhanzheng de kenengxing.*
two country between have break out war Sub. possibility
'Between the two countries, there is a possibility of breaking out a war.'

5.4.2.2 Metaphorical realizations of usuality

The structure of *shi* ... *de* is the only method for the metaphorical realization of usuality in Chinese. Adverbs, on the other hand, are the sole resource for the congruent construal of usuality in Chinese. Therefore, the metaphorical expression of usuality with *shi* ... *de* involves the grammatical movement from Adjunct to isolating process, which is represented as follows:

(5.71) *Tuixiaoyuan jingchang jiaban.*
salesman usually work overtime
'A salesman usually works overtime.'
Subject Adjunct Predicator

Subject Predicator //Pred. Complement
Tuixiaoyuan jiaban shi jingchang de.
salesman work overtime is usual Sub.
'It is usual for salesman to work overtime.'

It is necessary to point out that the metaphorical realization in the form of *shi* ... *de* is less preferred in Chinese. As is often the case, the modal meaning of usuality is realized through congruent expressions in the form of adverb.

5.4.2.3 Metaphorical realizations of obligation

The metaphorical realization of obligation involves three grammatical methods: projecting process, *shi* ... *de* structure and *you* ... structure. In addition, the obligation in Chinese is construed congruently through modal verbs. The metaphorical realization of obligation is therefore concerned with the grammatical movement from Finite to projecting process, *shi* ... *de* structure or *you* ... structure.

(i) Expressing obligation with projecting process

The projecting process involved in the expression of obligation is a mental process with first person as participant. For example:

(5.72) *Xueshengmen bixu zai 23 hao qian jiao zuoye.*
students must in 23 day before submit assignment
'Students must submit their assignments before 23.'
Subject Finite Adjunct Pred. Complement

Subject Pred.// Subject Adjunct Pred. Complement
Wo yaoqiu xueshegmen zai 23 hao qiang jiao zuoye.
I require students in 23 day before submit assignment
'I require my students to submit their assignments before 23.'

In many cases, the projecting process is expressed in a passive form because the relevant Subject is frequently not indicated in Chinese. The following expression is the modified version of GM instance in Example 5.72.

(5.73) *Xushengmen bei yaoqiu zai 23 hao qian jiao zuoyie.*
Students Bei require in 23 day before submit assignment
'Students are required to submit their assignments before 23.'

(ii) Expressing obligation with shi … de *structure*
The *shi ... de* structure associated with the expression of obligation is similar to the one used to construe probability meanings. The information inserted in the structure is also encoded in the form of modal verbs, as shown in Example 5.74.

(5.74) *Banche yinggai anshi daoda.*
shuttle bus should on time arrive
'The shuttle bus should arrive on time.'
Subject Finite Adjunct Predicator

Subject Adjunct Pred.// Pred. Complement
Banche anshi daoda shi yinggai de.
shuttle bus on time arrive is should Sub.
'It is sure that the shuttle bus arrives on time.'

(iii) Expressing obligation with you… *structure*
Like those expressing probability, the *you*... structure in the metaphorical realization of obligation is an isolated process. This is illustrated by the example below.

(5.75) *Women bixu zhichi zhengfu*
We must support government
'We must support our government.'
Subject Finite Predicator Complement

Pred. Complement// Pred. Complement
You biyao zhichi zhengfu
have necessity support government.
'There is a necessity to support our government.'

5.4.2.4 Metaphorical realizations of inclination

The only approach to realize inclination metaphorically in Chinese is *shi ... de* structure. As the meaning of inclination is congruently realized by modal verbs and adverbs, this category of modality metaphor involves the grammatical movement from Finite or Adjunct to *shi ... de* structure.

A. From Finite to Complement:

(5.76) *Ta* *ken* *bangzhu* *bieren*
he will help others
'He is willing to help others.'
Subject Finite Predicator Complement

Subject Predicator Comp.// Pred. Complement
Ta *bangzhu* *biren* *shi* *ziyuan* *de.*
He help others is willing Sub.
'He is willing to help others.'

B. From Adjunct to Complement:

(5.77) *Wo* *yiding* *anshi* *wancheng.*
I definitely on time complete
'I will definitely complete on time.'
Subject Adjunct Adjunct Predicator

(Sub.) Adjunct Predicator// Pred. Complement
(*Wo*) *anshi* *wancheng* *shi* *queding* *de.*
(I) on time complete is certain Sub.
'It is certain that I will complete on time.'

On the basis of the detailed description of metaphorical realizations of various types of modality in Chinese, I identify four categories of metaphor of modality. All these categories are differentiated further into subcategories in terms of the grammatical methods involved. All the GM categories and their subcategories are displayed in Table 5.5.

This section describes the categories and subcategories of interpersonal GM in Chinese in terms of metaphor of mood and metaphor of modality. The description shows that interpersonal GM is more difficult to specify than ideational GM in Chinese. This is because the semantic meanings and grammatical categories are connected in a more complicated pattern in the dimension of interpersonal meaning.

5.5 Summary

In the light of the description of semantic and lexicogrammatical systems and the discussion of metaphorical realizations, Chapter 5 provides a systematic account of the categories and subcategories of ideational and interpersonal GM in Chinese. Ideational GM in Chinese is classified into 13 categories in terms of the shift between semantic elements. Each category of ideational GM

Metaphor of modality category	*Subcategory*
1. Metaphorical realizations of probability	(i) projecting process; (ii) *shi* ... *de* structure; (iii) *you* ... structure;
2. Metaphorical realizations of usuality	*Shi*... *de* structure
3. Metaphorical realizations of obligation	(i) projecting process; (ii) *shi* ... *de* structure; (iii) you ... structure
4. Metaphorical realizations of inclination	*Shi* ... *de* structure

Table 5.5: Categories and subcategories of metaphor of modality in Chinese

is further differentiated according to the movement of grammatical functions. The interpersonal GM in Chinese is classified into metaphor of modality and metaphor of mood, each of which is further specified through an analysis of the grammatical methods involved. This study recognizes four categories of metaphor of mood which express various types of speech function in Chinese. There are also four categories of metaphor of modality respectively concerned with the realizations of the four types of modality in Chinese. Both the metaphor of mood and the metaphor of modality are subdivided to show how they are realized by different grammatical methods.

This chapter reveals that the categorization of GM in Chinese is greatly affected by the linguistic features of the language. More specifically, the typological features of various grammatical categories contribute most to the detailed categorization of GM in Chinese. For example, the ideational GM categories involving the element of process is specified by considering the particular structure of verbal groups.

The GM categories and subcategories recognized in Chapter 5 enrich the findings in Chapters 3 and 4 by describing GM in Chinese in more detail. More importantly, the categories and subcategories identified provide a theoretical foundation for the further analysis of metaphorical expressions in Chinese. Based on the findings in Chapter 5, the GM instances in real texts are recognized and quantified in Chapters 6 and 7 to explore the properties of GM deployment in Chinese.

6 The use of grammatical metaphor in written Chinese

6.1 Introduction

As shown in Chapter 2, ideational GM and interpersonal GM are respectively preferred in written and spoken languages. In order to conduct a thorough investigation on the use of GM in Chinese, it is necessary to collect and analyze a large quantity of language materials in both spoken and written modes. This is obviously not a task which can be accomplished in one chapter. This chapter focuses on the deployment of ideational GM, while the use of interpersonal GM in Chinese is explored in next chapter. Given the focus on ideational GM in this chapter, the 'GM' hereafter in this chapter refers to the metaphorical realizations in the ideational dimension if not specially noted.

The last two chapters have identified and categorized GM in Chinese with the purpose of establishing a theoretical framework for further analysis of the phenomenon. On the basis of the framework established, I explore the use of GM in written Chinese by analyzing the deployment of ideational GM in a data set formed by 37 texts from scientific textbooks. The analysis reveals the distribution of various types of ideational GM in Chinese and the interdependence between them. I also investigate the impacts of contextual and developmental factors on the use of ideational GM in Chinese through a comparison of GM degree in texts drawn from different genres and representing different stages of language development.

6.2 Language material and data collection

I employed a two-step method of data collection in this chapter. First, I selected the latest edition of scientific textbooks in Chinese as language material in order to enable an exploration of GM with respect to its register variables of mode and field. Second, the data set for detailed analysis was collected from the textbooks in terms of genre distribution.

6.2.1 Language material: Scientific writing in Chinese textbooks

In order to explore the use of GM in Chinese, the analysis in this chapter needs a special language material in which GM instances are widely deployed. On the other hand, the language material should be as typical as possible of Chinese to increase the reliability of findings in this chapter. In other words, the language material chosen for the analysis must satisfy the requirements of relevance and typicality. I chose scientific writings in Chinese textbooks as the large corpus from which the texts to be analyzed are drawn to balance these requirements. The reason for such a choice is explained by describing the features of Chinese writing in scientific textbooks.

6.2.1.1 Features of Chinese writing in scientific textbooks

The features of Chinese writing in scientific textbooks can be described from two perspectives in accordance with the requirements of relevance and typicality. Scientific writing in Chinese are closely tied up with the use of GM in terms of its register variables of mode and field. The review of contextual research of GM in Chapter 2 shows that the GM is a mode-oriented resource for organizing a text. Halliday (1985b) points out that written discourse has more instances of ideational GM than spoken language. With respect to the close relationship between ideational GM and written language, this chapter analyzes written texts in Chinese to investigate the deployment of ideational GM in Chinese.

The field of scientific writing is another significant consideration in choosing the language materials. This chapter needs a language material in which the instances of ideational GM are critical resources for text building. The literature review in Section 2.5.1 shows that the use of ideational GM is one of the most important linguistic features of scientific writings. The writings in the field of science generally involve a large amount of GM instances because taxonomizing and reasoning are the two main functions of ideational GM (Halliday, 1998). This correlation between ideational GM and the field of science explains why scientific writing is chosen as the language material in this chapter.

In addition, the scientific writing in textbooks is characterized by its typicality. This is because textbooks bear a unique social function of representing a sanctioned version of human knowledge and culture to each generation of students. This social function requires that textbooks must be designed and written carefully to transmit objective and factual information. Furthermore, any edition of modern Chinese textbooks is designed under the control of the Central Government in China. Therefore, the discourses in textbooks are possibly the most standard form of writing in Chinese.

The kind of language encountered in textbooks makes possible some way of expression and, simultaneously, prevents other ways of writing. In this sense, texts in schools are not just a vehicle for transmitting knowledge, but are also instruments for forming ways of writing. As far as the writing in scientific textbooks are concerned, they are typical writing model for students because 'most extended writing in science is in fact copied more or less directly from such books' (Martin, 1993b: 167). The reliance on the textbooks appears more pervasive and widespread in China since they are used by millions of students across the country. These characteristics of the scientific writing in textbooks determine that it is representative of written Chinese.

Taking all these factors into consideration, I chose scientific textbooks as the language material for GM analysis. It should be noted that there is the possibility of collecting Chinese writings across a range of registers to represent overall properties of Chinese. However, the corpus collected in such a way would be unmanageable for this study. More importantly, the exhaustive coverage of all text types causes difficulties in making generalizations because the linguistic properties of different registers of Chinese could greatly affect the deployment of GM instances.

6.2.1.2 Description of language material

In order to clarify the range of language material, the scientific textbooks must be further specified in terms of edition, subject and level. The language material is the latest edition of Chinese scientific textbooks which are used for the teaching of physics and chemistry in secondary schools and universities.

The writing for teaching is constantly being revised both from content and linguistic perspectives to reflect the developments in human knowledge, pedagogical methods, and in language itself. I adopted the latest edition of textbooks as the target of analysis to show the linguistic features of Chinese presently in use. Written Chinese from physics and chemistry textbooks was selected to balance possible differences in the distribution of GM in textbooks concerning various scientific subjects. It is worth noting that the main subjects of the science teaching in China are physics, chemistry and mathematics. The mathematics textbooks are not chosen for this study because mathematical language shows particular features in ideational, interpersonal and textual dimensions (O'Halloran, 2005).

The level of scientific textbooks is taken into consideration in choosing the language material because the GM deployment could be affected by language development. In mainland China, the systemic learning of scientific knowledge starts from secondary school and continues in university. There are two levels of scientific textbooks which are separately used by the students in secondary schools and universities. The two levels of textbooks compiled for the students of different ages are deliberately controlled in terms of complexity and abstraction. In other words, the same meaning could be expressed in a more complicated way in university textbooks than in secondary school textbooks.

Textbooks from each of the two educational levels were selected in this chapter. The secondary school textbooks are used by the fourth year students in secondary school (which spans six years) who are 15 years of age. The university textbooks are the learning material for the first year undergraduate students, who are generally 18 years old. This strategy of selecting language material at the two stages of education allows me to explore possible changes in the use of GM according to the level of sophistication of the intended audience. The detailed discussion of this point is presented in Section 6.4.3 from the perspective of ontogenesis.

6.2.2 Data collection

The extracts collected for the analysis in this chapter had to form a manageable data set to conduct the quantitative investigation of GM deployment. At the same time, this quantitatively small data set had to be representative of the language material in terms of the distribution of GM. This purpose was achieved by selecting extracts from different genres of writing in the scientific textbooks.

From the perspective of genre, texts in scientific textbooks fall into several types of writing which are distinctive in social purpose and generic structure. I selected various numbers of extracts from each type of genre in the scientific textbooks to make up a representative data set. The actual numbers of extracts in different genres were determined in accordance with the actual distribution of genres in the scientific textbooks. In order to do this, it was necessary to identify the genres in Chinese scientific textbooks and find out how these genres are proportionally distributed in the language material.

6.2.2.1 Genres in Chinese scientific textbooks

A framework for the genre identification in Chinese scientific textbooks is needed to examine the distribution of genres in the language material. Because of the absence of such research, I set up the framework by using the genre research on English textbooks in Martin (1993) and Veel (1997) as a guide. Martin (1993) claims that report, explanation and experiment are the most common types of genre particular to the science teaching field. Biography and exposition are the two other significant genres which are less common in the scientific textbooks. Additionally, each of all above genres is subject to further division into subgenres. Veel (1997) gives an account of the genres in secondary school science by describing the statement of social purpose and generic structure of each genre.

The framework for identifying genres in Chinese scientific textbooks is established by following the methods of Martin (1993) and Veel (1997). I described the primary function of each genre and differentiated the generic stages of genres involved according to the real situation of genres in Chinese. The major genres of report, explanation and experiment are divided into subgenres, while the minor genres of exposition and biography are not further categorized. The genres in Chinese textbooks and their generic structure are briefly described in Table 6.1.

No.	*Genre*	*Generic structure*
1	Report/Defining To define the scientific concept	General statement ^ Definition
2	Report/Classifying To classify different scientific concept	General statement ^ Statement of difference (1-n)
3	Report/Describing To describe the properties of an object	General statement ^ Description of properties (1-n)
4	Report/Decomposing To describe the composition of an object	General statement ^ Description of each part (1-n)
5	Explanation/Sequential To explain the sequence of activity	Phenomenon identification ^ Explanation of sequence (1-n)
6	Explanation/Causal To explain the reason of an occurrence	Phenomenon identification ^ Explanation of reason
7	Explanation/Theoretical To explain a theoretical principle	Phenomenon identification ^ Explanation of theory
8	Explanation/Consequential To explain the effects of certain event	Phenomenon identification ^ Explanation of effects
9	Experiment/Procedural To enable a scientific experiment	Aim ^ Materials needed ^ Steps
10	Experiment/Recount To recount the aim, steps and conclusion of a scientific activity	Aim ^ Record of Event ^ Conclusion
11	Exposition To present argument in favor of a position	Thesis ^ Arguments (1-n)
12	Biography To review the history of science	General statement^ Narrative

Table 6.1: Genres of scientific writings in Chinese textbooks

Table 6.1 shows that five types of genres are recognized in the scientific textbooks, in which three major types of report, explanation and experiment are subdivided. For the sake of convenience, the subtypes of major genres and minor genres are numbered together to indicate the 12 genres in Table 6.1. This table also illustrates the difference between the scientific writings in English and Chinese from the perspective of generic structure. Generally speaking, the genres in Chinese are relatively simpler in structure and contain fewer stages. For instance, there is a unique genre of report/defining in Chinese textbooks which defines scientific concepts in only two stages.

6.2.2.2 Genre distribution in language material

On the basis of the framework in Table 6.1, I selected a sample of writings from the textbooks to explore the distribution of genres in the language material. The genre distribution ascertained by examining the sample can be applied to the rest of the language material as long as the sample texts are sufficiently large to be representative. Five chapters of writing were selected randomly from each of the textbooks of physics and chemistry used in secondary school and university. In total, 20 chapters of writing which contain as many as 438 texts are involved in the exploration of genre distribution.

The genre of each text in the sample is identified by referring to the generic framework in Table 6.1. The frequency of occurrence of different genres in the sample is shown in Table 6.2.

Text / *Genre*	*Secondary school*			*University*		
	Phys.	*Chem.*	*Total*	*Phys.*	*Chem.*	*Total*
1. Report/Defining	20	6	**26**	19	6	**25**
2. Report/Classifying	10	11	**21**	8	15	**23**
3. Report/Describing	16	30	**46**	19	38	**57**
4. Report/Decomposing	7	4	**11**	6	4	**10**
5. Explanation/Sequential	12	8	**20**	13	21	**34**
6. Explanation/Causal	7	5	**12**	7	10	**17**
7. Explanation/Theoretical	7	4	**11**	25	9	**34**
8. Explanation/Consequential	8	11	**19**	5	7	**12**
9. Experiment/Procedural	8	12	**20**	2	1	3
10. Experiment/Reconunt	4	8	**12**	7	3	**10**
11. Exposition	2	3	5	2	1	3
12. Narrative	3	1	4	2	1	3
Total	104	103	207	115	116	231

Table 6.2: Genre distribution in sample texts

There are three points to be clarified in regards to the results of the genre count in Table 6.2. First, the numbers of genres are quantified respectively in the extracts from secondary school and university textbooks. The numbers of the same genre in the two levels of extracts reveals that secondary school and university textbooks give different priorities on genre deployment. The most salient difference is that the explanation/theoretical genre is highly preferred in university textbooks, while the experiment/procedural is more desired in the secondary school textbooks. These preferences, in a certain degree, reflect the different purposes of textbooks in transmitting knowledge. For instance, the preference on the explanation/theoretical genre in university textbooks is partly determined by the need of introducing more scientific theories.

Similar to the first point, the textbooks for different subjects are distinctive in genre distribution. The report/defining genre is deployed more frequently in physics textbooks. On the contrary, there is an inclination on the use of report/describing genre in the textbooks of chemistry. The variation of genre distribution in the textbooks of different subjects probably reflects the relationship between content and generic structure in written discourses.

Finally, Table 6.2 shows that the quantity of the texts belonging to exposition and biography is strikingly small compared with that in the genres of report, explanation and experiment. This observation supports Martin's (1993) claim that the genres of exposition and biography are used less commonly in scientific textbooks. Because the texts in these two genres appear in a very low frequency, they are not taken into account in the exploration of genre distribution.

The three points discussed above demonstrate the features of genre distribution in Chinese scientific writings. Although these features are not the focus in this study, genre research is an issue worth investigating in the further study of Chinese.

I calculated the distribution of genre to estimate the proportion of each type of genre in the language material. For example, each text of report/classifying genre is accompanied by about two texts of report/describing genre in secondary school textbooks. As such, the approximate proportion between these two genres in the textbooks is 1:2. The proportions between the other types of genre were measured in the same method. Given the low frequency of some types of genre, I only take in account the genres with more than ten texts (printed in bold) in the sample. The proportional distribution of various types of genre in the language material is presented in Table 6.3.

It is worth noting that the genre distribution in the language material is the result of approximate calculation. It is possible that the real genre distribution is slightly different from the numbers in Table 6.3. However, the

Types of Genre		*Secondary school*	*University*
Report	Defining	2	2
	Classifying	2	2
	Describing	4	5
	Decomposing	1	1
Explanation	Sequential	2	3
	Causal	1	1
	Theoretical	1	3
	Consequential	2	1
Experiment	Procedural	2	
	Recount	1	1

Table 6.3: Proportional genre distribution in language materials

distortion of calculation is greatly reduced because the genre distribution is estimated with a large sample of texts.

6.2.3 Resulting data

I selected extracts from each type of genre in Table 6.3 because the deployment of metaphorical expressions may differ across genres. Extracts from the ten types of genre were collected proportionally according to the genre distribution indicated in Table 6.3. Thus, the numbers of extracts in each type of genre vary from one to five, reflecting the proportion of the various genres in the language material.

In total, 37 extracts were collected with this method of data collection which comprised the data to be analyzed in terms of GM deployment. More precisely, 18 extracts in the data come from secondary school textbooks, while the other 19 extracts represent university textbooks. The extracts from the secondary school textbooks cover all the ten types of genre in Table 6.3. The texts from the university textbooks, on the other hand, involve nine types of genre in Table 6.3, reflecting the fact that the experiment/procedural genre occurs with a very low frequency in university textbooks.

The 19 extracts in the report genre and the 14 extracts in the explanation genre constitute the principal part of the data. The four extracts from the experiment genre are less important in terms of quantity. In light of the dominant role of report and explanation genres, the relationship between genre and GM deployment in Chinese is explored by comparing the extent of GM in extracts from these two genres. The data for analysis consists of 862 clauses with a total of 988 instances of ideational GM. The extent of

GM was calculated by relating the total number of GM instances to the total number of clauses in an extracts. Table 6.4 summarizes the occurrence of GM instances, the number of clause and the extent of GM in each extract of the data.

As shown in Table 6.4, each extract of data was assigned with a label which indicates the genre and source of the text. According to their source, the texts drawn from university and secondary school textbooks are presented as two groups, each of which consists of two smaller groups belonging to the subjects of physics and chemistry. The data set was thus divided into four parts in terms of level and subject.

6.3 Data treatment

The data consisting of 37 extracts is treated in two steps: (1) the identification of GM instances; and (2) the quantification of GM instances. The identification of GM instances is concerned with both individual GM instances and the syndromes of GM instances in the data. They were identified by referring to the definition and categorization of GM in Chapters 4 and 5. The definition and categorization are in turn testified in the process of recognizing GM instances. The quantification of GM instances in this study is conducted in a more exhaustive manner, compared to previous research on GM (Ravelli, 1985; Jones, 1991) in English. Some types of GM excluded in previous research are taken into account in this study.

6.3.1 Identification of GM instances

The identification of GM instances began with the division of Chinese extracts into clauses which serve as the basic unit of functional analysis. Following this, the clauses in an extract were further divided into grammatical elements on the basis of the framework for functional analysis of Chinese developed in Chapter 3. Then the individual GM instances in a clause were recognized according to the criteria of defining GM discussed in Chapter 4. The GM instances recognized were labeled with its category and subcategory by referring to the categorization framework established in Chapter 5. In sum, the identification of individual GM instances in the data heavily depends on the theoretical frameworks presented in Chapters 3, 4 and 5.

Except the first step of dividing a text into clauses, the recognition and labeling of GM instances are undertaken using *Systemics 1.0*, the software developed by Kay O'Halloran and Kevin Judd in 2002. The software is

Label	*Genre*	*Number of GM*	*Number of clause*	*Extent of GM*
Part A: Texts from University Textbooks of Physics				
I.U5a	Explanation/Sequential	31	17	1.82
II.U1a	Report/Defining	33	25	1.32
III.U7a	Explanation/Theoretical	32	15	2.13
IV.U1b	Report/Defining	37	22	1.69
V.U7b	Explanation/Theoretical	47	33	1.43
VI.U4a	Report/Decomposing	28	23	1.15
VII.U7c	Explanation/Theoretical	22	16	1.38
VIII.U2a	Report/Classifying	20	30	0.67
IX.U10a	Experiment: Recount	14	17	0.82
Part B: Texts from Secondary School Textbooks of Physics				
I. S3a	Report/Description	35	31	1.13
II. S3b	Report/Describing	22	23	0.96
III. S9a	Experiment/Procedural	14	15	0.93
IV. S1a	Report/Defining	29	33	0.88
V. S6a	Explanation/Causal	44	25	1.76
VI. S9b	Experiment/Procedural	20	25	0.80
VII. S2a	Report/Classifying	17	22	0.77
VIII. S1b	Report/Defining	27	22	1.23
IX. S5a	Explanation/Sequential	27	23	1.17
X.S8a	Explanation/Consequential	19	11	1.76
XI.S10a	Experiment/Recount	17	20	0.85
XII. S4a	Report/Decomposing	9	21	0.43
Part C: Texts from University Textbooks of Chemistry				
I. U2b	Report/Classifying	26	34	0.76
II. U3a	Report/Describing	21	21	1.00
III. U8a	Explanation/Consequential	34	23	1.48
IV. U6a	Explanation/Causal	25	19	1.93
V. U5b	Explanation/Sequential	39	30	1.30
VI. U3b	Report/Describing	41	20	2.05
VII. U3c	Report/Describing	39	28	1.39
VIII. U5c	Explanation/Sequential	21	16	1.31
IX. U3d	Report/Describing	17	25	0.52
X.U3e	Report/Describing	34	25	1.32
Part D: Texts from Secondary School Textbooks of Chemistry				
I. S5b	Explanation/Sequential	33	27	1.22
II. S3c	Report/Describing	31	29	1.07
III. S2b	Report/Classifying	17	23	0.74
IV. S8b	Explanation/Consequential	35	17	2.06
V. S7a	Explanation/Theoretical	18	17	1.06
VI. S3d	Report/Describing	17	26	0.65
Total	37 texts	988	862	

Table 6.4: Summary of occurrence of GM and the number of clause in data

a non-automated corpus annotation software designed to 'allow efficient and comprehensive discourse analysis of text from the perspective of SFL' (O'Halloran and Judd: 2002). However, the pre-programmed grammar is compiled for the analysis of English discourse. As the pre-programmed grammar can be modified, the grammar tree in *Systemics* was changed to include the GM categories for Chinese.

The GM instances belonging to different categories frequently present in the form of syndrome. The discussion in Section 5.3.7 shows that some categories of GM act as the driving force in the formation of GM syndromes in Chinese. However, the theoretical discussion only provides the conceptual framework for the description of GM syndromes in Chinese. In order to investigate the actual use of GM syndromes in Chinese, I identified the GM syndromes by observing the clusters of the individual GM instances in the data. The clusters of elemental GM appeared in the data were categorized in terms of the ranks where the metaphoric reconstrual takes place. To be more specific, the GM clusters were recognized as higher and lower rank syndromes, each of which is further divided into several syndrome types centered on certain categories of GM. The identification and categorization of GM syndromes in the data provide us an empirical basis for understanding the interdependence between different categories of GM in Chinese. In this sense, the analysis of GM syndromes applies and, more importantly, extends the findings in Chapter 5.

6.3.2 Quantification of GM instances

The quantification of GM instances in the data was divided into three steps. The first step aims to describe the incidences of GM instances in terms of group, category and subcategory. The GM instances were first counted according to their categories in individual extracts. The GM instances in different texts are then added up in terms of category to measure the numbers of each category of GM in the data. This provides a picture of the distribution of each elemental GM category in the general formation of metaphorical expressions in Chinese. For instance, the study reveals that the semantic shift from process to thing is the most extensively used GM category in Chinese.

Following this, GM instances were qualified according to groups and subcategories. First, the GM instances sharing the same destination of semantic shift were totalized to show how the GM groups with different degrees of 'thinginess' are deployed in Chinese. Second, I measured GM instances which take 'relator' as the starting point of a semantic shift. This measurement reveals how GM instances are involved in the logical progression of Chinese texts. Third, certain subcategories of GM instances were quantified to show how grammatical resources in Chinese are deployed to expand the meaning potential in the language.

The second step of GM quantification is conducted with the purpose of exploring the distribution of GM syndromes in Chinese. The clusters of GM instances in data were quantified according to the seven types of GM syndrome that were identified. The clusters of individual GM instances centered on the same GM category are counted as the same type of syndromes although they may differ in pattern. For example, the GM syndromes with the patterns of '13 + 6 + 2' and '6 + 2' (here '+' means 'occur together') are treated as the subtypes of the syndrome centered on GM category 2. It is also noted that higher rank syndromes are constructed by lower rank syndromes. In this case, the lower rank syndromes presented as the components of a syndrome higher in rank were not counted as independent GM syndromes. The reason for such a treatment is discussed at greater length in Section 6.4.2.2.

The last step in GM quantification is the measurement of the extent of GM use in the data. This study follows the method developed by Ravelli (1985) to measure the extent to which GM instances are deployed in an extract. This method demonstrates the extent of GM use by calculating the ratio of the number of GM instances in relation to the number of clauses in a given extract. As described in Section 6.2, the data in this study is deliberately chosen to form various groups of extracts different in genre and ontogenetic level. The frequencies of GM use were then compared in different genres and at different ontogenetic levels.

There are two issues which must be clarified in the quantification of GM instances: (1) the exclusion of certain types of GM; and (2) the treatment of GM recursion. Ravelli (1985) excludes certain types of GM instances in her analysis of GM in English texts, namely, *frozen*, *general*, *taxonomized* and *technical* GM. The present study also excludes the latter two types of GM from the quantification of GM instances in the data. However, the *frozen* and *general* types of GM in Chinese have been recognized as special categories of GM with reference to the framework developed by Halliday and Matthiessen (1999). For example, the *frozen* metaphorical expression of 'have a impact' and the *general* GM instance of 'phenomenon of' are recognized as GM categories 12 and 11 by Halliday and Matthiessen (1999). For that reason, the two types of GM are taken into account in the detailed counting of GM instances in this study. The recursion of GM means a metaphorical realization is realized metaphorically again (Ravelli, 1985). As one of the important aspects in the construction of metaphorical expressions, the phenomenon of recursion is observed in the present data. Following Ravelli (1985), this study treats the metaphorical expression engendered by GM recursion as a single instance of GM. In other words, a metaphorical expression is counted once only in the quantification of GM.

6.3.3 Presentation of data analysis

The GM analysis of all the extracts in the data is presented in Appendix A of this book. An individual extract was first segmented into clauses by inserting double vertical lines at the position of a clause boundary. GM instances identified were then underlined and marked with their categories and subcategories. The numbers of GM instances were tabulated in terms of their categories at the end of an extract. Following this, the ratio of the total number of GM instances to the total number of clauses in the extract was presented in a figure accurate to the second decimal place. For example, the GM instances identified and the ratio calculated in the extract 'S1a' are displayed as follows:

Category	1i	2i	5i	5ii	6iii	11	13i	13ii	Total	Clause
Number	4	9	4	2	3	1	2	4	29	33

Ratio of the number of GM instances to the number of clauses = 0.878

Given that the texts under discussion are selected from textbooks of physics and chemistry, formulas are sometimes present in the data. In these cases, the formulas are represented by the symbol (FORMULA) because they are not concerned with the analysis of GM.

The identification and quantification of GM instances is fundamental to the further discussion of GM in Chinese. The results of quantification are analyzed in terms of ranks and categories to describe the distribution of metaphorical expressions in Chinese. Furthermore, the GM deployments in the extracts with different contexts of culture and development levels are compared to show the impact of linguistic environment on the use of GM in Chinese.

6.4 Results and interpretation

In the following sections, the presentation and interpretation of the results obtained from data treatment concentrates on these three areas: (1) the distribution of GM in Chinese; (2) the syntagmatic interdependence of GM instances; and (3) the relationship between GM and linguistic environments.

6.4.1 GM distribution in Chinese

I first examine the numbers of GM instances in the 13 categories listed in Figure 5.1. The examination demonstrates the distribution of various GM categories in Chinese. The deployment of each GM category is discussed in detail to detect the underlying reasons for the distribution. The GM instances are then classified in different groups which share same starting point or destination of semantic shift. Following this, I describe the distribution of different groups of GM instances in the data. The description provides us the information on how the GM instances with specific functions are used, especially those involved in nominalization and logical progression. I also discuss the distribution of GM instances in certain GM subcategories tabulated in Table 5.3. The discussion reveals the involvement of grammatical resources in the expansion of meaning potential. For instance, it is possible to define which type of circumstance in Chinese is deployed most frequently in expressing things metaphorically.

6.4.1.1 Distribution of GM categories

A total of 989 instances of GM were found in the data. It is observed that some categories of GM instance occur with considerably higher frequency than other categories. More specifically, there are four GM categories which are quantitatively predominant in the general deployment of GM in Chinese. By contrast, the other nine categories are strikingly low in frequency. This distinction in incidence is attributable to the inherent properties of particular GM categories in Chinese.

The distribution of 13 GM categories is graphed in Figure 6.1 with the number of each choice added. The percentage of each GM category is displayed in Table 6.5 to two decimal places.

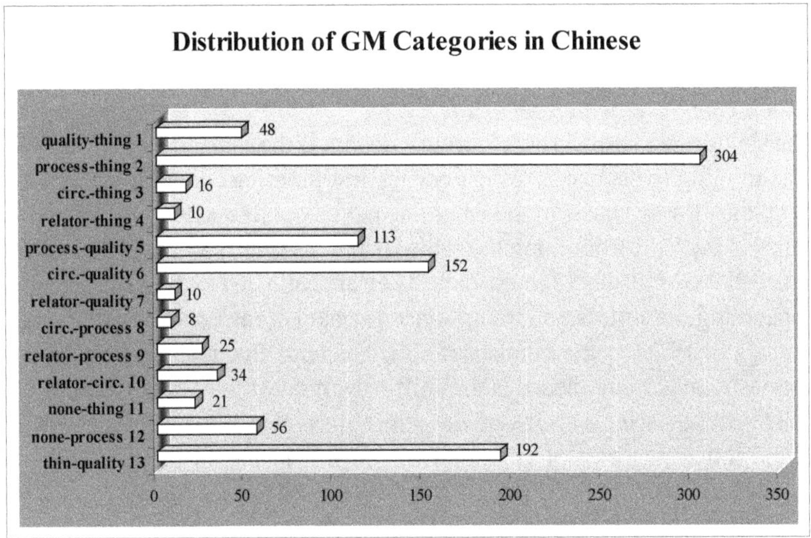

Figure 6.1: Distribution of GM categories in Chinese

Incidence	*Elemental GM categories*	*Percentage (%)*
High incidence	2. process-thing	30.74
	13. thing-quality	19.41
	6. circ.- quality	15.37
	5. process-quality	11.43
Low incidence	12. none-process	5.66
	1. quality-thing	4.85
	10. relator-circ.	3.44
	9. relator-process	2.53
	11. none-thing	2.12
	3. circ.- thing	1.62
	7. relator-quality	1.01
	4. relator-thing	1.01
	8. circ.-process	0.81

Table 6.5: Percentages of GM categories in Chinese

Figure 6.1 and Table 6.5 show that the numbers of GM instances in various categories vary from 304 to 8. The percentages of these categories, correspondingly, range from 30.74% to 0.81%. Table 6.5 also shows that the 13 categories of elemental GM could be divided into two sorts in terms of high and low incidence. To be more specific, there are nine GM categories which occur less than 56 times in the data while all the numbers of the other four types of GM instance are higher than 113. The GM categories with high and low incidence are respectively discussed to explore the reasons for such an observation.

A. GM categories with high incidence

The single most frequently occurring category is the semantic shift from process to thing (category 2) which occurs 304 times, accounting for 30.74% of all the GM instances in the data. The next most frequently occurring category is the shift from thing to quality (category 13): 19.41% or 192 of the entire 989 GM instances in the data. They are followed by the GM category concerning the shift from circumstance to quality (category 6) with the percentage of 15.37 or the number of 152. The least frequently used GM categories with high incidence is the shift from process to quality (category 5) which accounts for 11.43% of the entire instances with 113 occurrences. These four categories of GM instances together amount to about 77% of the overall total.

The semantic shift from process to thing is the most pervasive GM category in Chinese. The other three GM categories which are quantitatively important in Chinese involve the semantic shifts with the destination of quality. In other words, all the GM categories with high incidence involve the semantic shifts with the destinations of thing and quality. It is significant that thing and quality are two main elements of a nominal group. This indicates that the high incidence of these GM categories is concerned with the grammatical movement towards nominal groups. More precisely, these GM categories are engendered by the movement from clause to nominal group because the semantic shifts starting from relator are excluded from them. A close examination of the typical patterns of grammatical movement from clause to nominal group in Chinese explains this point more clearly.

In Chinese, there are two typical metaphorical movements from clause to group, each of which gives rise to different types of semantic shift. These patterns of movement and the GM categories involved are illustrated by Figures 6.2.

Pattern A

Yingpan	*gaosu*	*cunchu*	*shuju*
hard disk	at high speed	store	data
'Hard disks store data at high speed.'			
Participant	Circumstance	Process	Participant
Category13 ↓	Category 6 ↓	Category 13 ↓	Category 2 ↓
Quality 1	Quality 2	Quality 3	Thing
yingpan	*gaosu (de)*	*shuju*	*cunchu*
hard disk	high speed (SUB)	data	S storage
the high speed data storage by hard disk			

Pattern B

Yingpan	*gaosu*	*cunchu*	*shuju*
hard disk	at high speed	store	data
'Hard disks store data at high speed.'			
Participant	Circumstance	Process	Participant
Category 13 ↓	Category 6 ↓	Category 5 ↓	
Quality 1	Quality 2	Quality 3	Thing
yingpan	*gaosu*	*cunchu (de)*	*shuju*
hard disk	at high speed	store (SUB)	Sdata
the data stored at high speed by hard disk			

Figure 6.2: Two typical patterns from clause to group in Chinese

Figure 6.2 indicates that all the semantic shifts arising from the two typical patterns fall into GM categories of 2, 5, 6 and 13. The high incidence of these four GM categories shows that most GM instances in Chinese occur in the grammatical movement from clause to nominal group. The two patterns in Figure 6.2 also illustrate that the shift from process to thing and the shift from process to quality are more critical in the reconstrual of Chinese clauses since only these two shifts are compulsory in the process of metaphorical realization. In other words, the GM instances in categories 2 and 5 play leading roles in the relevant metaphorical expressions. This point is further explored in the discussion of interdependence between these GM categories (see Section 6.4.2.).

B. GM categories with low incidence

Table 6.5 shows that the proportions of GM categories with low incidence range from 5.66% to 0.81%. This observation is interpreted in relation to the properties of these categories of GM.

Categories without congruent form. First, the categories of 11 and 12 which include the GM instances without congruent form are investigated. The discussion in Section 5.3.6 reveals that these two types of GM are used as the attachments of a nominalization belonging to other GM categories. As a kind of reinforcing expression, the GM instances of the two categories are not compulsory for the relevant metaphorical rewordings. In this sense, the low frequency of the metaphorical expressions without corresponding congruent form is determined by their optional nature of deployment.

Categories starting from circumstance. Two GM categories occurred in a low frequency take circumstance as the starting point of semantic shift. In regards to the shift from circumstance to thing, its very low frequency is largely determined by the typological features of circumstance in Chinese. As discussed in Section 5.3.1, circumstances in Chinese fall into three groups in terms of their structures, namely (1a) 'minor Process + Participant + Facet', (1b) 'minor Process + Participant, and (2) adverbial groups. Only circumstances in group 1b can be metaphorically realized as a thing. Circumstances in group 1a are normally transferred into the semantic element of quality. Circumstances in group 2 are not involved in the semantic shift from circumstance to thing because adverbs in Chinese cannot be nominalized.

The low frequency of the shift from circumstance to process is tied up with the etymological relation between prepositions and verbs in Chinese. According to Li and Thompson (1981), many prepositions in Chinese have characteristics of verbs and can be used as verbs that have similar meanings. A circumstance realized by a prepositional phrase is frequently transferred as a process realized by a verb with the same morphological form as the preposition involved. In this case, the original clause is simultaneously extended into a clause complex. This kind of transfer does not appear to involve ideational GM because a figure is upgraded as a sequence. This means that the probability of realizing a circumstance metaphorically as a process is greatly reduced in Chinese.

Category of quality to thing. The GM category involving a shift from quality to thing needs special attention in the assessment of GM in Chinese because its incidence is unexpectedly low. The low frequency of this category of GM instances is related to the unique 'Carrier + Attribute' structure of ascriptive figures in Chinese, which is discussed in Section 3.2. In regards to this structure, the consideration of the shift from quality to thing is focused on how ascriptive figures are reconstrued as nominal groups. There are two patterns in transferring an ascriptive figure into a nominal group in Chinese, which are illustrated in Figure 6.3.

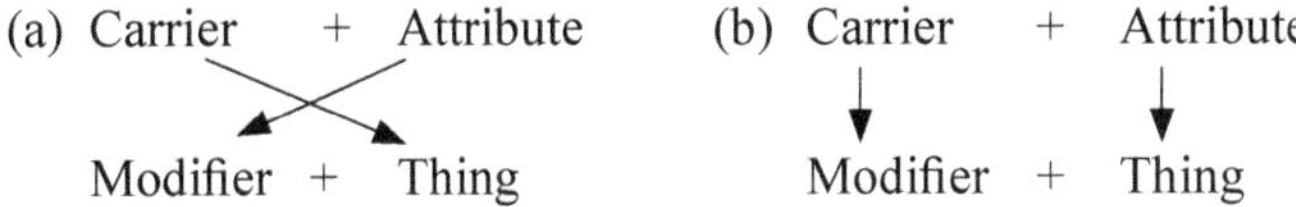

Figure 6.3: Two transferring patterns of ascriptive figures

According to the categorization of ideational GM in Chapter 5, only the transfer in pattern (b) is regarded as metaphorical realization of ascriptive figure. The transfer from clause to nominal group in pattern (a) is not identified as metaphorical reconstrual because it does not give rise to a metaphorical shift between grammatical functions. Halliday and Matthiessen (1999) point out that Chinese has the tendency to reconstrue quality in an ascriptive clause by following pattern (a). In other words, the low frequency of the shift from quality to thing is possibly related to the high incidence of pattern (a) construal. To verify this hypothesis, the number of transfers in pattern (a) was quantified in the present research. This pattern of transfers appears 89 times in the data, which is about twice as much as the GM instances involving the shift from quality to thing. Thus, the low incidence of GM category of quality to thing can be attributed to the preference in Chinese for pattern (a).

Categories starting from relator. The last four GM categories with a low incidence involve semantic shifts sharing the same starting point of relator. While all these categories appear infrequently, it is noticeable that the categories ending as circumstance and process occur twice as often as those in the categories with the destinations of thing and quality. In terms of 'distance' of metaphoric movements, the shifts with a shorter 'distance' are used more frequently than those with a longer distance, which are illustrated by Figure 6.4.

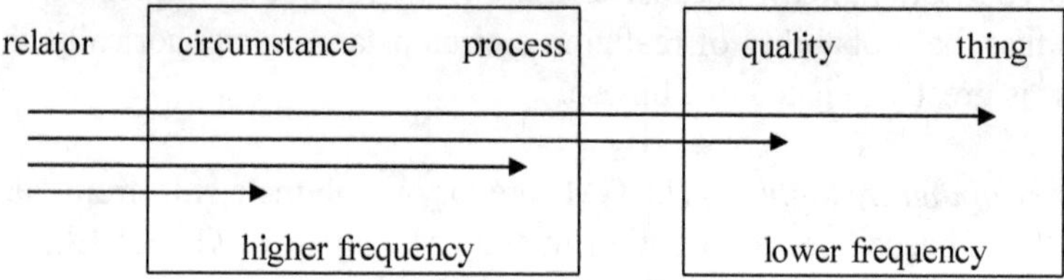

Figure 6.4: Frequency of GM categories starting from relator

Figure 6.4 shows that the categories with higher frequency are involved in the grammatical movement from clause complex to clause, while those with lower frequency are concerned with the movement from clause complex to group. It appears that a clause complex in Chinese tends to be reconstrued metaphorically as clause instead of group. Section 6.4.1.2 treats the GM instances in these categories as a whole group and discusses them from the perspective of logical progression.

The distribution of GM instances shows that there is a polarization of incidence in different GM categories. The discussion above reveals that this polarization is not a random phenomenon in Chinese. On the contrary, the low incidence of certain GM categories can be ascribed to the special properties of GM construction in the language. Additionally, it is worth noting that the significance of a certain GM category is not quantitatively determined. GM categories occurring in a low frequency could be more crucial in the metaphorical reconstrual of meanings. When a semantic shift from process to thing occurs in the movement from clause complex to clause, it is in effect motivated by the semantic shift starting from relator. That is, GM categories with a low incidence may be the driving force of those with a high incidence. The discussion of GM syndromes explores this problem in more detail.

6.4.1.2 GM instances in Groups

The GM instances are further classified into various groups in which the semantic shifts involved share a similar starting point or destination. The discussion of GM instances in groups reveals how the metaphorical expressions in Chinese are deployed in the two functions of ideational GM. Halliday (1998) identifies two functions of ideational GM: taxonomizing and reasoning, which are respectively concerned with the organization of the taxonomies and the logical progressions in a language. Since the function of taxonomizing depends on the resource of nominal groups in a language, the examination of the 'thinginess' degree of GM instances demonstrates the categorizing power of Chinese metaphorical expressions. The reasoning function, on the other hand, is explored by investigating GM instances involved in the expression of logical relations. In this case, I discuss various groups of GM instances from two perspectives: (1) the 'thinginess' degree of GM instances; and (2) the involvement in logical progression of GM instances.

A. The degree of 'thinginess'

According to Halliday and Matthiessen (1999), the primary motif of ideational GM is the drift towards 'thing'. Furthermore, 'the drift towards "thinginess" is the culminating and most clearly articulated form of a shift which can be characterized in more general terms as a shift towards the experiential' (Halliday and Matthiessen, 1999: 264). The semantic shifts to various semantic elements, therefore, represent different degrees of 'thinginess' in the general drift with things as terminal points. The examination of semantic shifts with different destinations provides us some information as to the way 'thinginess' is deployed in Chinese.

In Chapter 5, I classified GM instances into six groups: (1) shift to thing; (2) shift to quality; (3) shift to process; (4) shift to circumstance; (5) shift to modifier; and (6) shift without congruent form. Only GM instances in groups 1 to 4 are analyzed here to show the relationship between GM and 'thinginess' in Chinese. The GM instances belonging to groups 5 and 6 are not taken into account in the exploration of 'thinginess'. This is because the shift from thing to quality (group 5) is opposite in direction to the primary motif of the drift to thing. The shifts in group 6 which have no congruent form are generally used as the attachments of a nominalization to strengthen expressions. In other words, the GM instances in groups 5 and 6 are not directly concerned with the analysis of 'thinginess' in a language. The frequency of occurrence of each group of GM instances in the data is presented in Table 6.6.

Table 6.6 indicates that the GM instances with higher degree of 'thinginess' in groups 1 and 2 occur more frequently in the data. The GM instances

	Group 1 (shift to thing)	*Group 2 (shift to quality)*	*Group 3 (shift to process)*	*Group 4 (shift to circ.)*	*Group 5 (shift to modifier)*	*Group 6 (no cong. form)*
Number	378	275	33	34	192	77
Percentage	38.22%	27.80%	3.34%	3.44%	19.41%	7.79%

Table 6.6: GM groups with different degrees of 'thinginess'

involved in the semantic shifts to thing compose the most frequently used group of GM. The reconstruals of semantic elements as quality make up the GM group with a slightly lower frequency. Totally, the semantic shifts to thing and quality account for about 66% of the GM instances in the data. The shifts to process and circumstance engender less than 8% of the GM instances.

The percentage of GM instances in group 1 illustrates that the proportion of nominalization in Chinese is about 38%. In other words, about one-third of the GM instances in Chinese are realized in the form of nominalization. Coincidentally, Ravelli (1985) finds that the nominalization in English also accounts for about one third of all GM instances. However, it is worth noting that the proportion of nominalization in English and Chinese are calculated with different methods of GM quantification. Thus, the similarity in the percentage of nominalization does not necessarily imply that Chinese and English deploy nominaliztion to the same extent. In Section 8.3, this point is explored more extensively.

The percentage of GM instances in group 2 is relatively high if compared to that of other groups. This high proportion is closely related to the fact that the Head of a Chinese nominal group is typically preceded by its modifiers which can be realized by nominal elements, verbal elements and embedded clauses (Halliday and McDonald 2004). Although the Head of a Chinese nominal group can be modified by embedded clauses, the pressure of limiting the length of modifying elements greatly reduces the number of modifiers in the form of a clause. This means that the quality realized by a defining relative clause in an English nominal group is frequently construed by a verbal or nominal premodifier in its Chinese equivalent. The comparison of GM in English and Chinese in Chapter 8 reveals that GM instances in group 2 occur more frequently in Chinese than in English (see Section 8.3 for more detail).

Halliday and Matthiessen (1999: 264) claim that 'things are more easily taxonomized than qualities, qualities than processes, and processes more easily than circumstances or relations'. The GM instances in groups 1 and 2 have much more grammatical potential than those in other groups for being characterized and taxonomized. Put in another way, the taxonomizing function of GM is mainly concerned with the GM instances in groups 1 and 2. Given that more than 66% of the GM instances in the data fall into groups 1 and 2, it can be concluded that most individual GM instances in Chinese are used for the purpose of categorizing concepts or phenomena.

B. Logical progression

Processes are logically connected by relators to construct a flow of argument in a discourse. When the meanings of these relators are metaphorically construed by other semantic elements, the logical-semantic relation is maintained in the GM instances involved. As such, the GM instances involved in logical progression refer to all semantic shifts starting from a relator.

The metaphorical rewordings of relator occur 79 times or in about 8% of all the GM instances in the data. This means the GM instances involved in organizing logical progression are quantitatively less important in the general deployment of GM. This finding demonstrates that only a small portion of GM instances in Chinese are directly deployed to realize the reasoning function of GM.

It is worth noting that there are GM instances realizing both the two functions of GM. They are the nominalizations of relator, which appear with only ten occurrences in the entire data. This rare overlap of nominalization and logical progression indicates that the two functions of GM are generally isolated in Chinese.

The quantitative analysis of GM instances in various groups reveals that the number of GM instances involved in the function of taxonomizing is greater than those involved in the function of reasoning. This means the function of taxonomizing is quantitatively more preferred than the function of reasoning by the metaphorical expressions in Chinese. However, the quantitative evidence in the present study is not sufficient enough to demonstrate that the taxonomizing function of GM is more important than the reasoning function of GM in constructing a Chinese text. The reason is that the GM instances are treated as individual expressions in this section. In real texts, the GM instances occur in clusters controlled by certain categories of GM. The quantification of GM instances in isolation can not show the importance of certain metaphorical expressions in the forming of texts. I thus explore further the contributions of GM instances involved in taxonomizing and reasoning functions to the creation of Chinese texts in the discussion of GM syndromes.

6.4.1.3 GM Instances in subcategories

In Chapter 5, I divided GM categories into subcategories for the reason that the semantic elements involved in these categories are concerned with more than one grammatical function. For example, the element quality may alternatively be realized by the grammatical function of Epithet or Attribute. This section investigates the deployment of certain grammatical functions in the construction of GM in Chinese by quantifying GM instances in subcategories.

To begin with, I measure the numbers of two subcategories of the shift from quality to thing, namely, Epithet to Thing and Attribute to Thing. It is observed that in the 48 occurrences of the shift, 30 instances are concerned with the movement from Attribute to Thing, while the other 18 instances belong to the movement from Epithet to Thing. This observation supports the previous hypothesis that the movement from Attribute to Thing is deployed more frequently in Chinese (see Section 5.3.1).

The discussion in Section 5.3 shows that the metaphorical realization of a process in Chinese may involve Auxiliary, Event or Event + Extension. It is predicted that most metaphorical realizations of a process should be concerned with the grammatical movement from Event or Event + Extension because Event and Extension are the main components of a verbal group. This predication is tested by calculating the numbers of the movements occurring in relevant GM categories. In category 2 (process-thing), 273 GM instances are grammatical movements from Event + Extension to Thing and Event to Thing. The movement from Auxiliary to Thing, in contrast, occurs 31 times in the category. Of all the 113 GM instances in category 5 (process-quality), 110 occurrences are concerned with the movement starting from Event + Extension or Event. These results of calculation justify the hypothesis that the grammatical movement starting from Event or Event + Extension is predominant in the shifts starting from process.

The metaphorical realizations of a circumstance are more complex since they involve as many as eight grammatical functions, which fall into three groups in terms of structure (see Section 3.2.3). Significantly, the circumstances with different structures are concerned with different categories of GM. For instance, the circumstance of Manner only involves the shift from circumstance to thing. To show this feature of circumstance in Chinese more clearly, the match of relevant grammatical functions and GM categories is tabulated as follows:

Table 6.7 shows that only the circumstance in the grammatical form of 'Minor Process + Participant' is used in all three GM categories. On the other hand, category 6 deploys all kinds of circumstances, while the categories 3 and 8 are not concerned with the circumstances realized by

GM Category / *Cir. types*	*Category 3 (cir. - thing)*	*Category 6 (cir. - quality)*	*Category 8 (cir. - process)*
1a. + Participant with Facet (Location)		+	
1b. + Participant without Facet (Cause, Source, Matter Instrument, Comparison Accompaniment)	+	+	+
2. – Participant (Manner)		+	

Table 6.7: Match of circumstance and GM category

prepositional phrases in form of 'Minor Process + Participant + Facet' and adverbial groups. Quantitatively speaking, the three groups of circumstance specific in structure are involved in metaphorical shifts with similar frequency. In particular, the GM instances in groups 1a, 1b and 2 occur 55, 54 and 67 times respectively in the data. With respect to the detailed types of circumstance, Location (directional) and Manner are the grammatical functions relatively higher in frequency.

The present research quantifies GM instances in categories, groups and subcategories respectively. The quantification provides us a profile of the distribution of GM instances in Chinese. In addition, the quantifying work reveals how semantic and grammatical resources are employed in the interaction between semantics and lexicogrammar in the language. For example, it is found that the quantity of semantic shifts ending with quality and thing is greater than that of the shifts ending with other elements. The circumstances with different structures are metaphorically realized with almost equal quantity.

6.4.2 Syndromes of GM

The GM instances in Chinese have been discussed in Section 6.4.1 as individual linguistic phenomena. However, 'instances of grammatical metaphor typically occur not in isolation but in organic clusters or "syndromes"' (Halliday and Matthiessen, 1999: 249). In this section, the syndromes of GM in Chinese are identified and quantified to explore the syntagmatic relations of GM instances. First, the types of GM syndromes in Chinese are identified depending on the clusters of GM instances observed in the data. Second, the numbers of GM syndromes in the data are quantitatively analyzed to reveal the features of GM syndromes in Chinese.

6.4.2.1 Identification of GM syndromes

This study identifies 13 categories of ideational GM in Chinese. Some of these elemental GM categories occur independently, while others always appear in clusters. These clusters of GM categories are observed in two ranks of metaphoric movement: (I) from sequence to figure or element (higher rank); and (II) from figure to element (lower rank). As the syndromes in higher rank are more complex in structure, I start the exploration of GM syndromes with those at a lower rank.

A. Lower rank syndromes: from figure to element

When a figure is metaphorically construed as an element, a cluster of interrelated GM instances in different categories concurrently occur to reconfigure the original grammatical structure. Some categories of GM instance in the cluster are more critical and motivate the deployment of other categories of GM. For example, the analysis in Section 6.4.1 shows that the GM instances in categories 2 and 5 are the controlling categories in the two typical movements from clause to nominal group in Chinese. Because of the significance of controlling GM categories, the GM syndromes are differentiated in terms of these categories. Categories 1, 2 and 5 are the three controlling GM categories observed in the transfer from figure to element.

(1) Syndromes with category 2. The syndromes containing GM instances in category 2 generally occur in the cluster of (13) + (6) + (2), in which the category 6 is not compulsory. This cluster is further complicated by the GM subcategories involved and should be represented more precisely as the pattern of (13i)/(13ii)/13iii) + (6i)/(6iii) + (2i). Although the pattern could generate a set of subtypes of syndrome, the underlying principle of constructing syndromes are similar. Thus, all the subtypes of syndromes are illustrated by the Example 6.1.

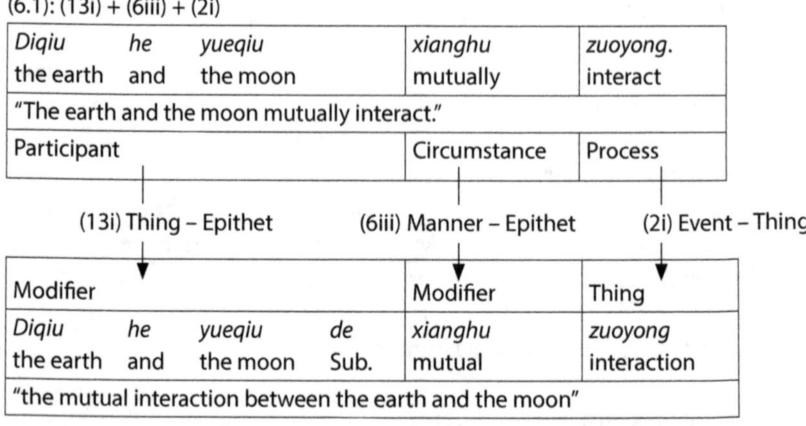
(6.1): (13i) + (6iii) + (2i)

Diqiu	*he*	*yueqiu*		*xianghu*	*zuoyong.*
the earth	and	the moon		mutually	interact
"The earth and the moon mutually interact."					
Participant				Circumstance	Process

Modifier				Modifier	Thing
Diqiu	*he*	*yueqiu*	*de*	*xianghu*	*zuoyong*
the earth	and	the moon	Sub.	mutual	interaction
"the mutual interaction between the earth and the moon"					

In this example, only one GM instance in category 13 or 6 is deployed to construct the metaphorical expression. It is possible that more than one GM instance of the two categories present in a syndrome with category 2. In addition, the sequence of the GM categories in this syndrome is not restricted to the form shown in Example 6.1. For instance, the GM instances of category 6 frequently present before the instance of category 13.

(2) Syndromes with category 5. In this type of GM syndromes, category 5 is used together with category 6 to form the syndrome pattern of (6) + (5). Frequently, the metaphors in category 13 could be added to extend the pattern as (13) + (6) + (5). Taking into account the subtypes of GM categories, the

syndromes generally occur in the structure of (13i) + (6i) + (5i/5ii), which is represented by Example 6.2.

(6.2): (13i) + (6i) + (5ii)

Lusu Halogen	*zai* *shui* *zhong* in water inside	*shengcheng* produce	*huahewu* compound
"Halogen produces compounds in water."			
Actor	Circumstance	Process	Goal

(13i) Thing – Epithet (6i) Location – Epithet (5ii) Event + Extension – Epithet

Modifier	Modifier	Modifier	Thing
lusu Halogen	*zai* *shui* *zhong* in water inside	*shengcheng* *de* produce Sub.	*huahewu* compound
"compounds produced by Halogen in water"			

[modified]

As shown in the example, this kind of syndrome is always accompanied by a movement from Participant in a clause to Thing in a nominal group. In the case that two Participants are involved in the GM syndromes of (6) + (5), one of them is construed as a Quality in the nominal group. In addition, the positions of GM instances in different categories are interchangeable. More importantly, category 6 is not compulsory for the occurrence of the GM syndrome with category 5. The GM instances in category 5 often occur alone and function as the Modifier in a nominal group. This determines that the frequency of syndromes in the pattern of (5) + (6) is fairly low. This point is revisited in the quantitative analysis of GM syndromes.

(3) Syndromes with category 1. The syndromes controlled by the GM category 1 are concerned with the downranking movement from relational process to nominal group. In terms of syndrome structure, this type of syndromes occurs in the pattern of (13) + (1). The most typical mode of the syndromes is illustrated by Example 6.3.

Similar to the GM instances in category 2 (process to thing), the metaphorical expressions belonging to category 1 are never used in isolation. Quite often, a GM instance in category 1 is accompanied by more than one GM instance in the other categories.

So far, three types of GM syndrome in lower rank have been described in terms of their controlling GM categories. The structure patterns of these GM syndromes are illustrated by examples of metaphorical reconstrual. It is

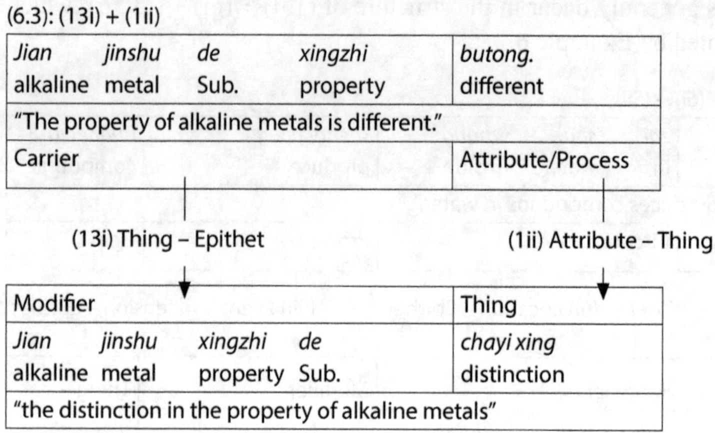

(6.3): (13i) + (1ii)

Jian *jinshu* *de* *xingzhi*	*butong.*
alkaline metal Sub. property	different
"The property of alkaline metals is different."	
Carrier	Attribute/Process

(13i) Thing – Epithet (1ii) Attribute – Thing

Modifier	Thing
Jian *jinshu* *xingzhi* *de*	*chayi xing*
alkaline metal property Sub.	distinction
"the distinction in the property of alkaline metals"	

[modified]

observed that GM categories 1 and 2 only occur in syndromes. The category 5 involving the shift from process to quality, on the contrary, could be used in isolation or in syndrome. This difference determines that GM syndromes with categories 1 and 2 are the dominant syndromes in the movement from figure to element.

B. Higher rank syndromes: from sequence to figure or element

In higher rank syndromes, a sequence is realized as a clause or a nominal group instead of a clause complex. The major motif of the realization is encapsulating the logical relation in clause complexes with the semantic shifts starting from relator. Thus, the GM categories of 4, 7, 9 and 10 serve as the controlling metaphors of higher rank GM syndromes.

Higher rank syndromes are characterized by the embedding of lower rank syndromes. This is because at least one of the clauses in a congruent clause complex is packed into the nominal group in metaphorical expression. Higher rank syndromes are thus the combination of GM categories starting from relator and the lower rank syndromes in terms of structure.

(1) Syndromes with category 4. Section 5.3.1 reveals that the GM instances in category 4 (relator to thing) are generally concerned with the encapsulation of enhancement relation in metaphorical expressions. This category of GM instances is deployed to indicate the causality between two elements or one element and one figure. The pattern of syndromes with category 4 can be represented as the following pattern:

(13) + (6) + (2) ╲
(13) + (6) + (5) — + (embedding clause) + (4)
(13) + (1) ╱

As the pattern shows, different lower rank GM syndromes can be linked to category 4 to form a higher rank syndrome. Category 4 is generally preceded by one lower rank GM syndrome and one embedding clause functioning as Modifier in a nominal group. The detailed structure of this type of syndromes is shown in Example 6.4.

(6.4)

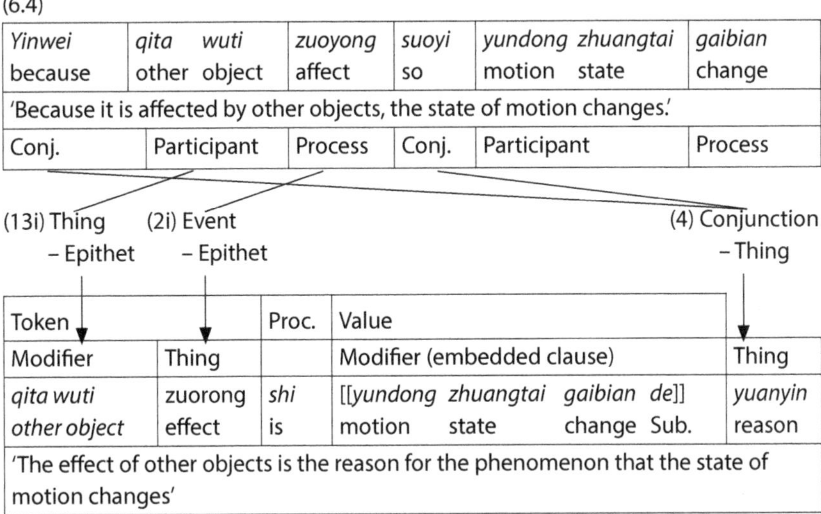

Yinwei because	*qita wuti* other object	*zuoyong* affect	*suoyi* so	*yundong zhuangtai* motion state	*gaibian* change
'Because it is affected by other objects, the state of motion changes.'					
Conj.	Participant	Process	Conj.	Participant	Process

Token		Proc.	Value	
Modifier	Thing		Modifier (embedded clause)	Thing
qita wuti *other object*	zuorong effect	*shi* is	[[*yundong zhuangtai gaibian de*]] motion state change Sub.	*yuanyin* reason
'The effect of other objects is the reason for the phenomenon that the state of motion changes'				

(2) Syndromes with category 9. The analysis in Section 6.4.1 shows that GM instances in category 9 (relator to process) occur with the greatest frequency of all the shifts starting from relator. The GM syndrome containing category 9 is the cluster of GM instances which occurs most frequently in the data. The pattern of this type of syndromes is as follows:

(13) + (6) + (2) ╲ ╱ (13) + (6) + (2)
(13) + (6) + (5) — (+ 9) — (13) + (6) + (5)
(13) + (1) ╱ ╲ (13) + (1)

The structure shows that all types of lower rank GM syndromes are involved in constructing the higher rank syndromes with category 9. A GM instance in category 9 ordinarily connects two lower rank GM syndromes, as shown in Example 6.5.

(6.5)

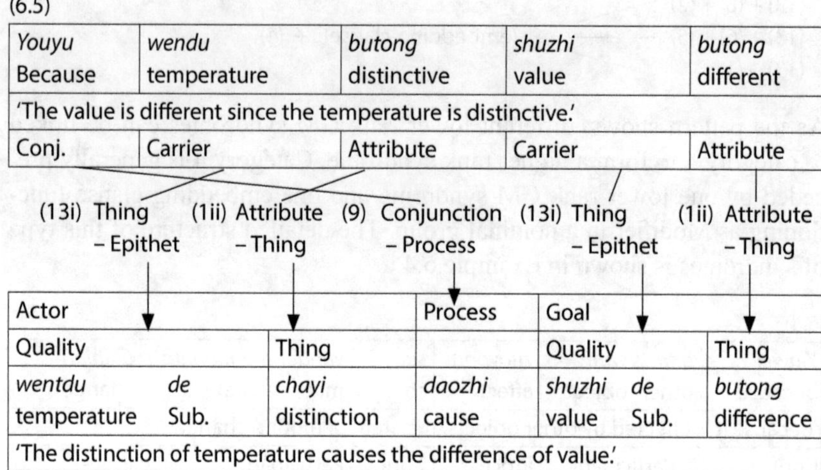

Youyu Because	*wendu* temperature	*butong* distinctive	*shuzhi* value	*butong* different
'The value is different since the temperature is distinctive.'				
Conj.	Carrier	Attribute	Carrier	Attribute

Actor		Process	Goal	
Quality	Thing		Quality	Thing
wentdu de temperature Sub.	*chayi* distinction	*daozhi* cause	*shuzhi de* value Sub.	*butong* difference
'The distinction of temperature causes the difference of value.'				

(3) Syndromes with category 7. The GM syndromes with category 7 generally occur in the movement from sequence to element, in which the relator is grammatically realized as the Epithet in a nominal group. Because Modifiers must be located before the Thing in a Chinese nominal group, the GM instances in category 7 precedes the syndromes in lower rank. This structure is shown by the following pattern:

(7) + (13) + (6) + (2)
(7) + (13) + (6) + (5)
(7) + (13) + (1)

The pattern shows that the GM instances in category 7 connect one embedded clause functioning as Epithet and certain type of lower rank syndrome. Here is an example:

(6.6)

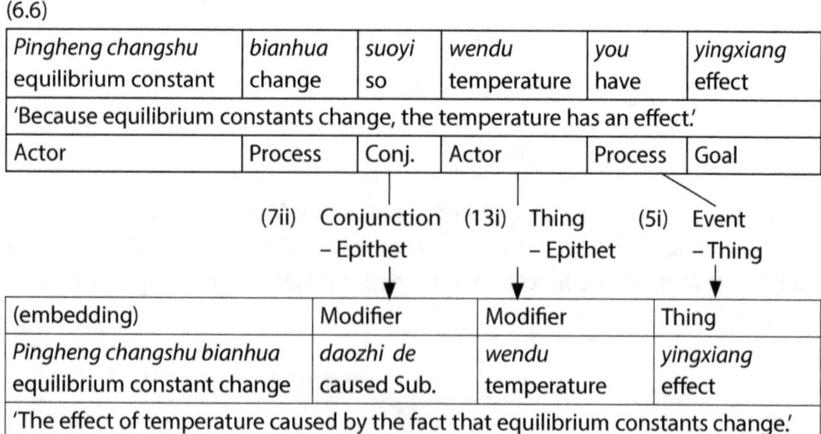

Pingheng changshu equilibrium constant	*bianhua* change	*suoyi* so	*wendu* temperature	*you* have	*yingxiang* effect
'Because equilibrium constants change, the temperature has an effect.'					
Actor	Process	Conj.	Actor	Process	Goal

(embedding)	Modifier	Modifier	Thing
Pingheng changshu bianhua equilibrium constant change	*daozhi de* caused Sub.	*wendu* temperature	*yingxiang* effect
'The effect of temperature caused by the fact that equilibrium constants change.'			

(4) Syndromes with category 10. The syndromes based on GM category 10 are concerned with the reconstrual of sequence as figure. The discussion in Section 5.3.4 indicates that the shift from relator to circumstance gives rise to the transfer from a major process to a minor process. The elements of a congruent clause are correspondingly realized as the components in a nominal group. Because GM category 10 appears before the lower rank syndrome involved, this type of syndromes has the following pattern:

(10) + (13) + (6) + (2)
(10) + (13) + (6) + (5)
(10) + (13) + (1)

I exemplify the syndromes with a GM instance of subcategory (10i) which refers to the grammatical movement from Conjunction to the circumstance of Accompaniment. In the example, the Actor and the Process in the clause is reconfigured as the Modifier and the Thing in a nominal group.

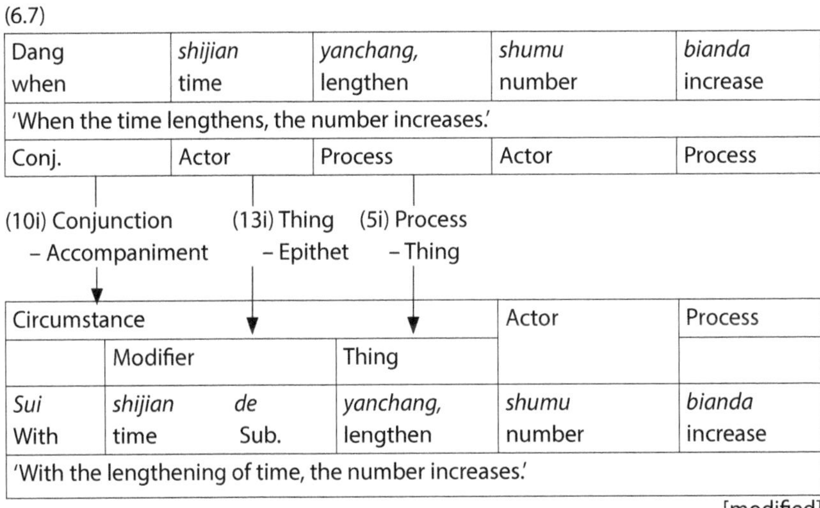

(6.7)

Dang when	*shijian* time	*yanchang,* lengthen	*shumu* number	*bianda* increase
'When the time lengthens, the number increases.'				
Conj.	Actor	Process	Actor	Process

(10i) Conjunction – Accompaniment ↓ (13i) Thing – Epithet ↓ (5i) Process – Thing ↓

Circumstance				Actor	Process
	Modifier		Thing		
Sui With	*shijian* time	*de* Sub.	*yanchang,* lengthen	*shumu* number	*bianda* increase
'With the lengthening of time, the number increases.'					

[modified]

The description above shows that higher rank GM syndromes are more complicated than lower rank GM syndromes in structure. The complexity of higher rank syndromes is largely engendered by the embedding lower rank syndromes. Thus, the analysis of higher rank syndromes is, to a certain degree, based on the discussion of lower rank syndromes. However, it must be pointed out that the lower rank syndromes involved in higher rank clusters do not exist in their own right because they arise from the encapsulation of logical-semantic relation in sequence. The lower rank syndromes occurring alone and those functioning as the components of higher rank syndromes are treated differently in the quantification of GM syndromes.

C. 'Favorite clause type' in Chinese

Halliday (1998) puts forward the concept of 'favorite clause type' in his exploration of GM in English scientific writing. This type of clause has the structure of 'one nominal group plus one verbal group plus a second nominal group or else a preposition phrase' (Halliday, 1998: 207). Although the 'favorite clause type' is very common in the scientific writings of English, it is absolutely not the most frequent form of expression in English. The significance of the 'favorite clause type' comes from the fact that it carries the most critical semantic load in developing scientific argument.

The examination of GM syndromes in this study demonstrates that the 'favorite clause type' also exists in the scientific writings of Chinese. In particular, it refers to the higher rank syndromes which are controlled by the GM category 9. The quantification of GM syndrome indicates that the syndromes with category 9 are very common in the rewording of sequence as figure. The instances of category 9 generally connect two nominal groups, forming the structure of 'Participant + Process + Participant'. This type of GM syndromes is not the most frequently used clause structure in the data. However, the 'favorite clause type' in Chinese is always used to summarize the preceding discussion and push forward the logical progression. Similar to the same structure in English, it is the most effective clause type in encapsulating logical-semantic relations.

In summary, this study recognizes seven types of GM syndromes in terms of the GM categories acting as the nucleus of the metaphor clusters. All the GM syndromes and their structures are shown in Table 6.8.

<table>
<tr><th colspan="2">GM syndromes</th><th>Structure</th></tr>
<tr><td rowspan="3">Lower rank</td><td>Syndromes with category 1</td><td>(13) + (1)</td></tr>
<tr><td>Syndromes with category 2</td><td>(13) + (6) + (2)</td></tr>
<tr><td>Syndromes with category 5</td><td>(13) + (6) + (5)</td></tr>
<tr><td rowspan="4">Higher rank</td><td>Syndromes with category 4</td><td>(13) + (6) + (2)
(13) + (6) + (5) + (4)
(13) + (1)</td></tr>
<tr><td>Syndromes with category 7</td><td>(13) + (6) + (2)
(7) + (13) + (6) + (5)
(13) + (1)</td></tr>
<tr><td>Syndromes with category 9</td><td>(13) + (6) + (2) (13) + (6) + (2)
(13) + (6) + (5) + (9) + (13) + (6) + (5)
(13) + (1) (13) + (1)</td></tr>
<tr><td>Syndromes with category 10</td><td>(13) + (6) + (2)
(10) + (13) + (6) + (5)
(13) + 91)</td></tr>
</table>

Table 6.8: Syndromes of GM in Chinese

6.4.2.2 *Quantification of GM Syndromes*

This section investigates how the seven types of GM syndromes are distributed in Chinese by quantifying the GM syndromes in the data. The distribution is then analyzed to evaluate the contribution of the GM categories in constructing Chinese texts.

A. Distribution of GM syndromes

It is revealed in the last section that part of the lower rank GM syndromes occurs as the components of higher rank GM syndromes. These lower rank syndromes are distinctive from those occurred independently by the fact that they are motivated by certain categories of GM. The lower rank syndromes occurring alone are named as 'independent' syndromes, while those functioning as the components of higher rank syndromes are referred to 'dependent' syndromes. Only the 'independent' lower rank syndromes are taken into account in the quantification of GM syndromes. The coalition/unity of different types of syndromes is another point to be noted in the quantification of GM syndromes. This study observes that two, or more than two, lower rank GM syndromes could be used together to form a larger combination of metaphorical expression. The different types of GM syndromes involved are respectively quantified in this study. The numbers of each type of GM syndromes across the whole data set are shown in the Table 6.9 together with their frequencies of occurrence.

GM syndromes types		*Number*	*Percentage (%)*
Lower rank	Syndromes with category 1	36	13.79
	Syndromes with category 2	123	47.13
	Syndromes with category 5	19	7.28
Higher rank	Syndromes with category 4	10	3.83
	Syndromes with category 7	10	3.83
	Syndromes with category 9	25	9.58
	Syndromes with category 10	34	13.03
Total		261	100

Table 6.9: Distribution of GM syndromes in Chinese

Table 6.9 demonstrates that the GM syndromes controlled by category 2 occur with the highest incidence in the data. The syndromes with categories 9 and 10 are used less frequently, which account for about 24% of the metaphorical clusters in the data. This observation shows that the most pervasive lower rank syndromes in Chinese are the clusters of GM instance which take the shift from process to thing as key metaphor. The most pervasive higher rank syndromes, on the other hand, are metaphorical clusters controlled by the shifts from relator to circumstance and process.

Given the fact that normally one GM syndrome consists of two or three GM instances, there is no question that most metaphorical expressions in the data are deployed in the form of syndromes. However, it is also possible that some GM categories do not occur in association with other GM categories. For instance, Table 6.9 shows that GM syndromes with category 5 occur in a very low frequency. This is because most of the GM instances in category 5 do not occur in the form of GM syndrome. The quantitative evidence in Table 6.9 thus pinpoints the most pervasive types of GM syndromes in Chinese, demonstrating that most GM instances in Chinese are present in the form of syndromes.

B. Analyzing the distribution of GM syndromes

This section analyzes the distribution of various types of GM syndromes to further reveal the properties of GM in Chinese. First, the analysis of GM syndrome distribution demonstrates the significance of different categories of GM instances in the construction of Chinese texts. According to Martin (1992: 490), GM is one of the texturing resources in the forming of English texts and 'it coordinates the synoptic systems and dynamic processes that give rise to text'. GM also contributes to the construction of Chinese texts through its power of creating taxonomies and establishing reasoning. However, the significance of GM instances in the forming of Chinese texts varies from category to category. The distribution of GM syndromes shows that three most frequently observed GM syndromes are controlled by GM instances in the categories of 2, 9 and 10. In these categories, only type 2 occurs with a high frequency in the data. The GM instances in categories 9 and 10, which act as the key metaphors in higher rank syndromes occur with a relatively smaller frequency. This finding shows that the contribution of a GM category to the construction of Chinese texts is not simply determined by its quantity.

Second, the description of GM syndromes shows that lower rank GM syndromes can occur in the form of 'dependent' syndromes and function as the constitutional components of the GM syndromes at higher rank. It is observed that as many as 165 'dependent' syndromes are deployed to construct the higher rank GM syndromes. In other words, the quantity of 'dependent' syndromes is even larger than the quantity of the 'independent' ones. Taking into account the quantity of GM categories 4, 7, 9 and 10, GM instances involved in the metaphorical reconstrual of sequence occur with a higher frequency than those involved in the reconstrual of figures. In other words, a larger part of GM instances in the data are involved in the manifestation of logical relations in the forms of clause or nominal group. This observation suggests that the need to encapsulate logical relations in texts acts as an important driving force for the use of GM in Chinese.

Third, the importance of two functions of GM could be assessed by analyzing GM syndromes. According to Halliday (1998), the lower rank syndromes are related with the taxonomizing function of GM, while the higher rank syndromes are tied up with the reasoning function of GM. Because the quantity of the 'dependent' syndrome is greater than that of the 'independent' syndrome in the data, the higher rank syndromes overrun the lower rank in terms of importance. Therefore, the reasoning function is a more important driving force in constructing scientific Chinese texts compared with the taxonomizing function.

6.4.3 Contextual and developmental considerations of GM in Chinese

In Sections 6.4.1 and 6.4.2, I discuss GM in Chinese as a stratal phenomenon without any consideration of its linguistic environment of deployment. Chapter 2 shows that the use of GM is closely related to context and language development. To investigate the effects of contextual and developmental factors on the use of GM in Chinese, I examine the deployment of GM instances in different data sets which are distinctive in context of culture and ontogenetic stage. First, I compare the extent of GM deployment in data sets belonging to report and explanation genres to show the effect of the context of culture. Second, I measure the GM deployment in data sets coming from secondary and university textbooks to illustrate the effect of language development. As mentioned, the degree of GM in a given text is illustrated by the ratio of the number of GM instances in relation to the number of the clauses.

6.4.3.1 GM and context of culture

The review in Chapter 2 indicates that the deployment of GM must be investigated by considering its immediate context of situation (register) and the more general context of culture (genre). In this study, all the extracts were selected from the register of science in Chinese to include as many GM instances as possible in a relatively small data set. The contextual variable of genre, on the other hand, is used as the criterion for sampling extracts from the scientific textbooks. The discussion in this section focuses on the assessment of contextual impact of genre difference on the deployment of GM in Chinese. The definition of genre as given by Martin (1992) refers to the staged, goal oriented social process that gives meaning and purpose to our linguistic behavior. Therefore, the analysis of GM in genre-specific extracts is designed to explore in what ways GM deployment is appropriate for the demands of general social purposes in Chinese language.

As shown in Section 6.2.2, the 37 extracts for analysis were selected from the genres of report, explanation and experiment. The 19 extracts in the report genre and 14 extracts in the explanation genre form the major part of the data. Only four or about 10% of the 37 extracts fall into the experiment genre. This section examines the GM deployment in the 33 extracts belonging to report and explanation genres due to statistical constraints. The extent of GM in each of the 33 extracts involved is calculated by dividing the total number of GM instances over the total number of clauses. Table 6.10 lists the GM occurrences in each extract.

In the second cell of Table 6.10, N1 stands for the total number of GM instances in a particular text, N2 for the number of clauses in that text and EM is the extent of metaphor. Table 6.10 shows that the extent of GM in the

Group 1 (Report genre)				*Group 2 (Explanation genre)*			
No.	*N1*	*N2*	*E.M.*	*No.*	*N1*	*N2*	*E.M.*
1	32	25	1.32	1	31	17	1.82
2	37	22	1.68	2	39	30	1.30
3	20	30	0.67	3	21	16	1.31
4	26	34	0.76	4	29	15	1.93
5	21	21	1.00	5	32	15	2.13
6	41	20	2.05	6	47	33	1.42
7	39	28	1.39	7	22	16	1.38
8	13	25	0.52	8	34	23	1.48
9	33	25	1.32	9	27	23	1.17
10	27	23	1.15	10	33	27	1.22
11	29	33	0.88	11	44	25	1.76
12	27	22	1.23	12	18	17	1.06
13	17	22	0.77	13	19	11	1.76
14	17	23	0.74	14	35	17	2.06
15	35	31	1.13				
16	22	23	0.96				
17	31	29	1.07				
18	17	26	0.65				
19	15	38	0.43				

Table 6.10: Extent of GM in extracts in report and explanation genres

33 extracts varies from 0.43 to 2.06. This means some extracts contain on average less than one GM instance in each clause while others contain more than two GM instances in each clause.

In order to investigate the differences between the two sets of data in terms of extent of GM, I carried out a statistical analysis. The EM measures in Table 6.10 form two groups of subjects, which represent the deployment of GM under the conditions of explanation genre and report genre. The groups, respectively consisting of 19 and 14 subjects, are constituted by small samples. In addition, the distributions of the population from which the samples are drawn are approximately normal and have almost equal variance. Therefore, I use a *t*-test to determine whether the means of the two groups of subjects differ significantly. The null hypothesis to be tested is that the mean number of DM is the same in two groups at the $p \leq 0.05$ level. The result of the calculation with Microsoft Excel is shown in Table 6.11.

t-Test: Two-Sample Assuming Equal Variances		
	Variable 1	*Variable 2*
Mean	1.037765789	1.557935714
Variance	0.165129667	0.120615427
Observations	19	14
Pooled Variance	0.146462405	
Hypothesized Mean Difference	0	
df	31	
t Stat	–3.85892205	
P(T<=t) one-tail	0.000269916	
t Critical one-tail	1.695518742	
P(T<=t) two-tail	0.000539832	
t Critical two-tail	2.039513438	

Table 6.11: *t*-test of GM degree in different genres

Table 6.11 shows that a value of 1.696 is needed in a one-tail test for significance at the $p \leq 0.05$ level. Since the *t*-test value of 3.859 is greater than the critical value, the null hypothesis can be rejected. Additionally, the value of the *t*-test is negative in the one directional calculation. This means that the extent of GM in the extracts from explanation genre is greater than that in the texts from report genre. Thus, the deployment of GM is related to the social purposes in different genres of Chinese writing. In other words, the GM deployment in Chinese is affected by the context of culture.

A possible reason for the greater use of GM in explanation genre is that the two genres of report and explanation have distinctive purposes of expression in scientific writings. Previous research on the two genres in scientific writing reveals that reports are generally involved in the description of how the world is organized while the explanations are used to explain why the world is organized in that way (Martin, 1993b). Because of this difference in purpose, the GM function of taxonomizing which achieves technicality with the resources of nominalization is more important in the genre of report. On the other hand, the GM function of reasoning for the purpose of logical relation encapsulation is highly preferred in the genre of explanation. Since the encapsulation of logical relations generally deploys more GM instances than the process of nominalization, the average number of GM instances in explanations is very likely to be greater than in reports. As a corollary to this, the occurrence frequency of GM instances in explanation extracts, as supported by the result of the *t*-test, is much higher than that in report extracts.

6.4.3.2 GM and language development

In addition to the context of culture, the present study also set out to investigate the variable of language development as another significant factor responsible for the variation in GM deployment. As mentioned in Chapter 2, the use of GM is closely associated with the development of language. The investigation of GM and language development focuses on the semogenic function of GM in terms of a time frame. The semiotic change in social context is modeled as an interaction among three kinds of semogenesis: phylogenesis, ontogenesis and logogenesis. This study examines the deployment of GM in different groups of texts from the perspective of ontogenesis because the data was selected from secondary school and university textbooks.

Previous research indicates that the quantity of GM increases with the ontogenetic development of language in children (Halliday, 1975; Derewianka, 1995). This study hypothesizes that the Chinese scientific writings in university textbooks have a higher degree of GM than those in secondary textbooks. To test the hypothesis, I compares the extent of GM in two groups of extracts selected from the textbooks for students of different ages. To be more specific, the 19 extracts representing the scientific writing in university textbooks constitute the first group. The 18 extracts selected from the secondary school textbooks make up the second group. The extent of GM in each extract of the two groups is illustrated in Table 6.12.

Group 1 (University)				*Group 2 (Secondary school)*			
No.	*N1*	*N2*	*E.M.*	*No.*	*N1*	*N2*	*E.M.*
1	33	25	1.32	1	29	33	0.88
2	37	22	1.68	2	27	22	1.23
3	20	30	0.67	3	17	22	0.77
4	26	34	0.76	4	17	23	0.74
5	21	21	1.00	5	35	31	1.13
6	41	20	2.05	6	22	23	0.96
7	39	28	1.39	7	31	29	1.07
8	13	25	0.52	8	17	26	0.65
9	33	25	1.32	9	15	38	0.43
10	27	23	1.15	10	27	23	1.17
11	31	17	1.82	11	33	27	1.22
12	39	30	1.30	12	44	25	1.76
13	21	16	1.31	13	18	17	1.06
14	29	15	1.93	14	19	11	1.76
15	32	15	2.13	15	35	17	2.06
16	47	33	1.43	16	14	15	0.93
17	22	16	1.38	17	20	25	0.80
18	34	23	1.48	18	17	20	0.85
19	14	17	0.82				

Table 6.12: Extent of GM in extracts from university and secondary textbooks

Table 6.12 shows that the extent of GM varies considerably across the extracts from secondary school textbooks (from 0.43 to 2.06), while the variance of GM use in the extracts from university textbooks is marginally smaller (from 0.67 to 2.13). This difference of variation appears to suggest that the scientific writing in university extracts is slightly more constant in the extent of GM deployment.

In detailed statistical analysis, the values of EM in the extracts from the university textbooks are treated as Group 1 with 19 subjects. Group 2 of subjects refer to the 18 EM values in extracts from secondary textbooks. The null hypothesis to be tested is that the samples come from scientific writings with the same mean of GM degree. The hypothesis is tested by a directional *t*-test operating with a significant level of 5%. The calculation result of *t* - test is shown in Table 6.13.

t-Test: Two-Sample Assuming Equal Variances		
	Variable 1	*Variable 2*
Mean	1.340168421	1.081775
Variance	0.207754128	0.174420398
Observations	19	18
Pooled Variance	0.191563459	
Hypothesized Mean Difference	0	
df	35	
t Stat	1.794887809	
P(T<=t) one-tail	0.040655975	
t Critical one-tail	1.68957244	
P(T<=t) two-tail	0.08131195	
t Critical two-tail	2.030107915	

Table 6.13: *t*-test of GM degrees in texts with different development stages

According to the result of *t*-test, the critical value of *t* is 1.690 for directional test, while the calculated value of *t* is 1.795. Since the calculated value exceeds the critical value, the null hypothesis is rejected. That is, the two groups of extracts come from scientific writings with different mean extents of GM. Considering that the test is directional and the calculated value of *t* is positive, it can be claimed that the extracts from university textbooks are more metaphorical than those from secondary textbooks. This conclusion justifies the hypothesis that the Chinese scientific writings in university textbooks have a higher degree of GM than those in secondary school textbooks. The deployment of GM in Chinese is, therefore, affected by the factor of language development.

The higher frequency of GM in the extracts from university textbooks is very likely related to the increase of 'technical knowledge' in the textbooks. From the point of view of ontogenesis, Halliday (1999) associates the reconstrual of experience in the form of GM with the emergence of technical knowledge. It is claimed that children begin to organize their knowledge around abstract entities by construing happening and quality as nouns in primary school and our experience is further construed with GM to develop logical progression in secondary school (Halliday 1999). In the process of language development, therefore, individuals have to use more abstract and metaphorical discourse to cope with increasing amount of technical knowledge. In the university textbooks which introduce more advanced science, there is a greater amount of technical knowledge than in the secondary school textbooks. Thus, the increase of technical knowledge in the university textbooks may give rise to the more frequent use of GM.

It is also noted that the calculated value of t is not considerably bigger than the critical value of t. This means the difference between the university and secondary school textbooks in the extent of GM is small. The relatively small difference is probably related to the close temporal distance between secondary school and university textbooks. As mentioned in the discussion of data collection, the university textbooks are used only about three years later than the secondary school textbooks. This suggests that it would be worthwhile carrying out a similar comparison with science textbooks that are used earlier in the secondary school system.

6.5 Summary

In this chapter, a data set consisting of 37 extracts from Chinese science textbooks has been analyzed to investigate the use of ideational GM in written Chinese. This analysis of GM in real text confirms the findings of the previous chapters and, more importantly, shows the properties of GM in Chinese and the relationship between the GM deployment in Chinese and its external environments.

By investigating how frequently different categories and syndromes of GM instances are used, this chapter has provided a quantitative profile of GM in Chinese. The profile first reveals that the semantic shift from process to thing is the most pervasive GM category in Chinese. Second, it has been found that about 38% of the instances take the form of nominalization. Third, the profile shows that most GM instances in Chinese occur in the metaphorical construal of figure as nominal group. All these findings are compatible with what has been found in previous research on GM in English (Ravelli 1985).

The quantitative profile also illustrates the special features of GM distribution in Chinese. The most salient points are the unexpectedly low frequency of semantic shift from quality to thing and the high occurrence of semantic shift ending as quality. These two points can be explained by the preference for one pattern of ascriptive figure reconstrual and the lack of postmodifiers in Chinese. More generally, the analysis has shown that the characteristics of GM distribution in Chinese are engendered by the typological properties of the language.

The investigation of GM syndromes extends and complements the findings in the quantification of categories. The observation of GM instances in data demonstrates that most of them occur in the form of clusters. These clusters are identified as seven syndromes, which center on certain categories. These findings support Halliday's (1998) claim that GM tends to occur in syndromes which are driven by controlling types of GM. More importantly, this study reveals that the significance of certain categories in constructing GM syndromes does not always correspond with their quantity. In particular, the quantification of syndromes shows that more than half of the instances in data are driven by categories occurring independently with a low frequency.

Apart from these major findings, the chapter has quantified different subcategories of GM in data. This provides information about how different types of Process, Quality and Circumstance are employed in the construction of different subcategories of GM. For instance, some types of Circumstance in Chinese are found to correlate with particular GM subcategories. This correlation is attributable to the distinction between different types of Circumstance in typological structure. To summarize, this chapter shows that GM distribution in Chinese is not random but determined jointly by the general tendencies of GM construction and the particular typological properties of the language.

In order to investigate the relationship between GM deployment and its external environment, I examined the extent of GM in extract groups different in genre and level of language development. The examination shows that the explanation genre uses more GM than the report genre. It further shows that GM deployment in the university textbooks is greater than that in the secondary school textbooks (albeit only slightly). These findings indicate that GM deployment is affected by generic structure and language development. More generally, the study suggests that investigation of GM in Chinese as a lexicogrammatical resource must take into consideration the particular linguistic environment in which the GM instances occur.

7 The use of grammatical metaphor in spoken Chinese

7.1 Introduction

Ideational GM is mainly deployed in prototypical written texts – like scientific, administrative and legal texts, while interpersonal GM is frequently observed in spoken discourses – like casual conversations and service encounters. This chapter focuses its analysis on the use of interpersonal GM in spoken Chinese to show the feature of meaning creation in the language. The exploration of interpersonal GM is more complicated than that of ideational GM for two reasons. First, there has been very little research on interpersonal GM both theoretically and empirically. This gives rise to the difficulty of discussing the phenomenon on the basis of a less rigid theoretical framework. Second, a research on interpersonal GM must be carried out by analyzing a corpus of spoken language, which is difficult to collect, transcribe and code.

The examination of interpersonal GM in this chapter is largely based on the discussion of GM identification and categorization in Chapters 4 and 5. It is the findings in these chapters that provide a theoretical framework for the discussion in this chapter. In order to reveal the features of interpersonal GM, a reliable and manageable corpus of spoken Chinese is needed to enable the detailed analysis. The written Chinese data set used in Chapter 6 is collected from scientific textbooks according to the distribution of genres. This approach for data collection is not used in this chapter due to the differences between spoken and written languages. I investigate the profile of GM deployment with a large corpus of spoken Chinese developed in mainland China. The corpus is used with the purpose of quantitatively analyzing interpersonal GM distribution in spoken Chinese. A small corpus formed by discourses extracted from the large one are manually analyzed to show the GM features not exposed through the automatic search of large corpus.

7.2 Spoken language and grammatical metaphor

Halliday and Matthiessen (2004: 626) claim that 'it is the pressure to expand the meaning potential that in fact lies behind the development of metaphorical modes of meaning'. Compared with written language, spoken language has a greater pressure in the expansion of meaning potential since it is faster in pace and shorter in the time of preparation. GM, as a critical way to construe additional layers of meaning and wording, surely contributes to the meaning expansion in spoken language. However, GM observed in spoken language is distinguished from that in written language in view of the fact that spoken and written languages are different in many aspects. In this section, the characteristics of metaphorical expressions in spoke Chinese are investigated to facilitate the following analysis.

7.2.1 Spoken and written languages

There have been many studies exploring the differences between spoken and written languages in the past few decades. These studies show that written language and spoken language differ from each other in more ways than just the medium in which they are presented. At lexical level, written texts have longer words, more attributive adjectives and more varied vocabulary and use fewer words referring to the speaker and fewer quantifiers and hedges (Drieman, 1962; Devito, 1966). Syntactically speaking, written language has more subordinate clauses than spoken language (O'Donnell, 1974; Kroll, 1977). Chafe (1982) argues that spoken and written language differ with regard to two sets of features through a comparative analysis of written and spoken text samples. One set of features is the opposition of fragmentation and integration, while the other set reflects an involvement vs. detachment dichotomy. According to Chafe (1982), the two sets of features are attributable to the two distinctions between spoken and written language: (1) speaking is faster than writing; and (2) speakers interface with their audience directly.

Halliday (1985) conducts the most thorough research on spoken and written language in the field of SFL. He examines the features of spoken language from the perspectives of language development, phonetic system and grammatical intricacy. Written language is discussed in relation to language evolution, functional variety, lexical density, etc. It is claimed that talking and writing are different modes for expressing linguistic meanings. They are used in different contexts and for different purposes. Unlike previous researchers, Halliday (1985) argues that it is wrong to think of the written language as highly organized, structured and complex while the spoken language is disorganized, fragmentary and simple. Instead, spoken and written languages have two kinds of complexity: 'the complexity of the written language is static and dense. That of the spoken language is dynamic and intricate. Grammatical intricacy takes the place of lexical density' (Halliday, 1985: 87).

The distinction between spoken and written mode in complexity is manifested differently in the form of GM. Ideational GM used in written language is one of the ways to achieve high lexical density, while interpersonal GM associated with spoken language increases grammatical intricacy. This is because ideational GM and interpersonal GM show different tendencies with respect to forming grammatical realizations to expand meaning potential. Ideational GM intends to downgrade the grammatical realization of certain semantic units, such as the realization of sequence in the form of clause. Interpersonal GM, on the other hand, has the tendency of upgrading the grammatical domain of a metaphorical realization. For example, the meaning of modality is realized by a clause instead of a modal Adjunct. The relationship between GM and language complexity is illustrated in Figure 7.1

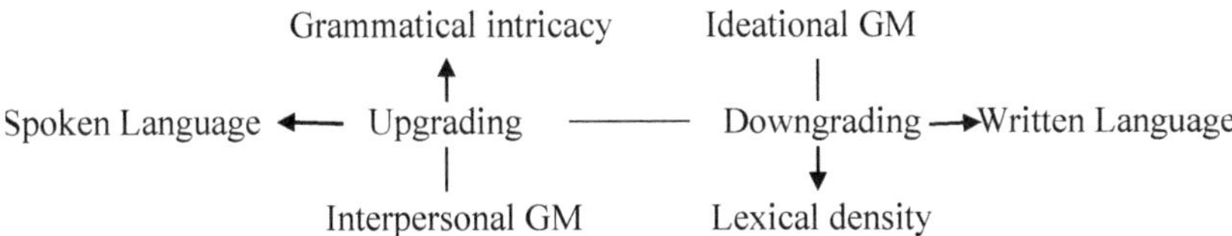

Figure 7.1: GM and complexity in spoken and written languages

In addition to the formal research on spoken language, there are many studies of spoken language carried out from a sociological or sociolinguistic perspective (see, e.g. Sacks *et al.*, 1974; Eggins and Slade, 1997). These studies show that the context of spoken language contributes centrally to the word choice in a discourse and the mode of interaction between speaker and addressee.

The findings of previous research on the differences between spoken and written languages are of importance for the present research in three aspects. First, an in-depth examination of the use of interpersonal GM will enhance our understanding of spoken language. As shown in Figure 7.1, interpersonal GM makes great contribution to the increase of grammatical intricacy in a spoken language. However, spoken discourses have not received as much attention from previous GM studies as written texts. The analysis in this chapter fills this gap by providing comprehensive description of how the meaning potential of a spoken language expands in a wide variety of ways. Second, any discussion on the features of interpersonal GM must rely on an analysis of authentic spoken discourses. The brief review of exiting studies shows that the understandings of linguistic characteristics in written language do not apply the same to spoken. Given that interpersonal GM is typically used in spoken language, a naturalistic corpus of spoken language is fundamental for a comprehensive research of the phenomenon. Finally, the features of interpersonal GM are closely related to typological properties and cultural context of a spoken language. For instance, the discussion in Section 4.6 has demonstrated that certain lexical and grammatical phenomena are critical for the identification of interpersonal GM in Chinese. The contextual and pragmatic studies of spoken language also highlight the need to consider language-external motives in the analysis of spoken discourses. The features of interpersonal GM are therefore attributable to the typological properties of a spoken language, the types of talks people engage in and the social context of spoken discourses.

7.2.2 Grammatical metaphor and spoken Chinese

As pointed out by DeFrancis (1984), the term 'spoken Chinese' suffers from a lack of precision in view of the wide varieties of speech that are usually subsumed under this name. The Chinese spoken in various parts of China is quite different in pronunciation, although they write in the same way as in standard Chinese (Mandarin). For example, the Chinese character with the meaning of nine is pronounced as 'jiu' in standard Chinese, but it sounds like 'gau' when pronounced in Cantonese. For this reason, communication among the Chinese sometimes does not go very smoothly if they are from different areas in China. In addition to pronunciation, Chinese dialects are different in vocabulary and grammar to a certain extent. For example, there are some pairs of words with the same meaning in Chinese, such as *da*o (to) and *zhi* (to). Usually *zhi* (to) is used in written texts, while *da*o (to) is used in speech. This study focuses its analysis on the use of interpersonal GM in Mandarin Chinese which is the most widely used Chinese variety in China. With this in mind, the Chinese corpus needed in this research should be a corpus of spoken Mandarin. Therefore, the spoken Chinese hereinafter refers to spoken Mandarin if not specially noted.

There are two other methodological issues that should be taken into consideration in this chapter: the frequency of GM instances in spoken Chinese and the feasibility of identifying GM instances with specific words or structures in spoken Chinese. Prior to this study, there is no empirical research on interpersonal GM in Chinese. The lack of information about the real frequency of GM instances in Chinese gives rise to the difficulty of corpus selection. Chapter 6 uses a relatively small corpus for the quantitative analysis of ideational GM because this type of metaphorical expressions occurs at a high frequency in written texts. In order to determine the size of spoken

Chinese corpus to be used, a pilot study should be conducted to explore the frequency of GM instances in spoke Chinese.

A spoken Chinese corpus of 60,000 characters is collected for this purpose. Although the corpus is numerically small by today's standards of corpus linguistics, it is adequate for the pilot study of interpersonal GM. The size of the corpus is not all-important. It must follow design principles that make its material represents major varieties of naturalistic spoken Chinese. In this case, the corpus is assembled by recording spontaneous formal and informal conversation in the Chinese department of a Singapore university. It is collected between January 2010 and January 2011 as part of a research project on the grammatical characteristics of spoken Chinese. The speakers involved in the corpus are male and female native speakers of Mandarin Chinese aged between 20 and 50 years old. The corpus contains text types of daily conversation, class session, study group and staff meeting, each of which is represented by two discourses.

This small corpus is analyzed with the framework developed for interpersonal GM identification in Chapter 4. It is found that interpersonal GM instances tend to occur much less frequently than its ideational counterpart. Most categories of interpersonal GM occur fewer than five times per discourse, and some types of GM are observed only once (or not at all) in a discourse. In addition, the distribution of GM instances in the corpus is not uniform across discourses. The occurrence of GM instances may be accidentally high in a particular discourse, leading to the incorrect conclusions about the frequency of GM deployment. For example, a discourse of class session in the corpus happens to have 27 GM instances because the teacher uses interrogative clauses as examples of his teaching. Because of the low frequency and unbalanced distribution of GM instances, this chapter requires a very large corpus to examine the use of interpersonal GM in Chinese. It is worth noting that this pilot study merely provides an indication of the scope of interpersonal GM in spoken Chinese. Sections 7.4 and 7.5 investigate the distribution of GM in more detailed ways, ranging from the topic of discussion and the relation between speaker and addressee.

The feasibility of identifying GM instance in corpus with specific words and structures is another major research issue investigated in the pilot study. Section 4.6 discusses three critical lexico-grammatical phenomena for the identification of GM in Chinese. Two of these phenomena are concerned with interpersonal GM, namely Mood particle and '*shi* ... *de*' and '*you* ...' structures. The pilot study shows that they have distinctive impacts on the GM instance identification in the corpus. Mood particles increase the difficulty of identifying GM instances, while 'shi ... *de*' and '*you* ...' structures make the identification easier.

The examination of Mood particles in Section 4.6 reveals that these particles are often associated with metaphorical realizations of speech functions in Chinese. Moreover, some of these particles like *Ne* and *A/Ya* are capable of expressing different types of mood without changing the main structure of the clause. This characteristic of Mood particles determines that they cannot be used as the keywords for automatic search of GM instances in a corpus. In other words, the metaphorical expressions engendered by the use of Mood particles have to be manually identified. This is practically impossible for the analysis of a very large corpus to be conducted in the following sections. In order to solve this problem, this study assembles a relatively small corpus from the large one for manual analysis required. This point will be explained in Section 7.3 with more details.

Section 4.6 shows that grammatical structures of '*shi ... de*' and '*you ...*' are used to state the meaning of modality. They are involved in the expression of each type of modality in Chinese, namely probability, usuality, inclination and obligation. The modality meanings construed by '*shi ... de*' and '*you ...*' structures are expressed explicitly with specific words. This feature dictates that GM instances with these structures are very convenient for automatic search in a large corpus. In this sense, the special structures of '*shi ... de*' and '*you ...*' actually increase the feasibility of identifying interpersonal GM in spoken Chinese.

7.3 Corpus selection and corpus analysis

This section describes the corpus on which the analysis of interpersonal GM deployment in Chinese is based, clarifying the size of the corpus and the process of corpus collection. The corpus used in this chapter is a very large corpus of spontaneous spoken Chinese, which is composed by recordings of radio and television programs broadcasted in mainland China.

7.3.1 Selection of spoken Chinese corpus

As discussed in Chapters 4 and 5, interpersonal GM is inherently more complex than ideational GM in terms of recognition and classification. The study of interpersonal GM in Chinese is in fact a topic worthy of a book in its own right. The lack of space in this chapter precludes a comprehensive analysis of interpersonal GM in Chinese. Thus, the focus of this chapter is to reveal the overall profile of GM use in spoken Chinese and the distribution of GM across registers. For this purpose, a corpus formed by different registers of spoken discourses is required for the detailed analysis. The corpus must be large enough to contain sufficient GM instances due to the fact that interpersonal GM are not observed very frequently in spoken Chinese. In addition, it should compose of authentic examples of contemporary spoken Chinese and naturalistic conversations.

Authentic spoken language samples are always difficult to obtain although they are valuable for the linguistic studies. In the past five decades, great efforts have been made to build spoken language corpora. The most important and notable corpora developed since the 1960s include Oral Vocabulary of the Australian Worker Corpus (Schonell *et al.*., 1956), London-Lund Corpus (Svartvik, 1990), COBUILD Bank of English (Moon, 1997) and British National Corpus (Crowdy, 1993; Rundell 1995). However, these spoken corpora are ordinarily assembled for the study of English or other western languages. There have been few spoken Chinese corpora because the complexity of the language and the relatively delayed development of research in this area. Since the 1990s, some corpora have been developed in mainland China, Taiwan and the UK to collect spoken data for the study of Chinese language.

Mandarin Conversational Dialogue Corpus (MCDC) and Mandarin Topic-oriented Conversation Corpus (MTCC) are the representatives of spoken Chinese corpura developed in Taiwan. They are developed by Taiwan's Academia Sincia respectively in 1997 and 2001. Each corpus contains conversations produced by three groups of randomly selected speakers in their twenties, thirties and forties. The conversations were transcribed so that it is possible to work out syntactic structures and discourse devices used by speakers in different ages. The size of the two corpora is relatively small (120,000 characters for MCDC and 200,000 characters for MTCC).

The Lancaster Los Angeles Spoken Chinese Corpus (LLSCC) is a corpus of spoken Mandarin Chinese developed in the UK. The corpus is composed of 1,002,151 words of dialogues and monologues, both spontaneous and scripted, in 73,976 sentences and 49,670 utterance units (paragraphs). The corpus has seven sub-corpora, i.e. Conversations, Telephone Calls, Play and Movie Transcripts, TV Talk Show Transcripts, Debate Transcripts, Oral Narratives and Edited Oral Narratives.

The corpora for spoken Chinese complied in mainland China are normally large in size. The most ambitious spoken Chinese corpus under construction is Modern Spoken Chinese Corpus (MSCC), which contains about one billion Chinese characters. Broadcast Media Spoken Chinese Corpus (BMSCC) is a 100 million-character corpus developed by Media University. It is the largest spoken Chinese corpus readily available until now.

This concise review of major spoken Chinese corpora demonstrates that the resource of spoken Chinese corpus is very limited compared to that of

English. Given the low occurrence of interpersonal GM in spoken Chinese, the analysis in this chapter needs a corpus large in size. Those small corpora, such as MCDC and MTCC, are obviously not suitable for present research. The wide range of text types in LLSCC is very appropriate for the exploration of GM distribution across registers, although the corpus is still relatively small. The major limitation to LLSCC is that it has not been released to the public because of copyright restrictions. There are some other spoken Chinese corpora not mentioned above. However, these corpora are ordinarily small in size and not open to external users. Taking into account all these factors, BMSCC is the only corpus eligible for the analysis in this chapter.

BMSCC is a corpus of spoken Mandarin Chinese consisting of monologues and dialogues recorded from selected television programs broadcasted in mainland China from 2008 to 2010. The corpus comprises about 100 million Chinese characters in 15871 program episodes. The discourses in the corpus can be divided into smaller corpora according to their media form, source channels, communicative mode, discussion topic and even program host. The content of the corpus covers both read speech and spontaneous dialogues and multipart discussions. The discussion topics involved in the corpus includes news, arts, economy and society. In summary, the sub-corpora cover the major varieties of modern spoken Chinese. Such a design of corpus building thus allows me to explore distinctions between different registers of spoken Chinese with regards to interpersonal GM.

It is relatively easy to build a large corpus by recording television and radio output. However, the corpus developed in this way has its own limitation in that part of the corpus is not representative of typical conversation. For instance, some speakers in a program may prepare what they are going to say before the program is broadcast. This research is very careful in the selection of sub-corpora in BMSCC to minimize the effect of this limitation. The spoken discourses used for the analysis in this chapter are drawn from spontaneous programs broadcast in television. Moreover, only spontaneous dialogues in the corpus are selected for the analysis of GM, while read speech and multipart discussions are not included. After these selections, a corpus including 4,182 spoken Chinese discourses is utilized for the analysis in this chapter.

As discussed in Section 7.2.2, certain types of metaphorical expressions are not appropriate for automatic corpus search. This chapter thus needs a corpus which is smaller and more manageable for manual analysis. There are two methods to realize this aim: (1) using the small corpus developed for pilot study; and (2) selecting discourses from the large corpus. I adopt the second method in order to integrate the results of analyzing small and large corpora. According to the register theory of Halliday (1978), there are two considerations that should be borne in mind for the assembly of small corpus from the large one: the topic of dialogue and the relationship between speakers. This research first uses the relationship between speakers as a parameter to sample speeches from BMSCC. It is found that in some episodes speakers are equal and in other units they are unequal in social relations. Both discourses with equal and unequal social relations are selected from the large corpus. In addition, the small corpus covers the full range of discussion topics found in BMSCC, i.e. news, arts, economy and society. The detailed composition of the small corpus is shown in Table 7.1.

Topic *Relationship*	*News*	*Arts*	*Economy*	*Society*
Equal relation	5	5	5	5
Unequal relation	5	5	5	5

Table 7.1: Composition of small Corpus

Table 7.1 shows that the small corpus consists of 40 discourses, 20 involving equal relationship between speakers and 20 unequal. On the other hand, 10 discourses are collected from each area of discussion. To sum up, the analysis of GM in this chapter is based on a large corpus (hereinafter Corpus A) with 4,182 discourses and a small one (hereafter Corpus B) containing 40 transcripts of speech.

7.3.2 Corpus analysis

The detailed analysis of corpus is carried out in two steps: (1) identification of GM instances; and (2) the quantification of GM instances. The identification of GM instances is mainly implemented with the search engine on the website of BMSCC. Manual annotation of Corpus B is sometimes required to compensate the deficiency of Corpus A for the analysis of certain types of GM. The quantification of GM instances is realized by adding up the amount of each types of GM instance in the corpora. In order to conduct automatic search of GM instances, this research needs a corpus with the following three functions:

1. possibility to search for particular categories of GM instances;
2. possibility to show distributions of GM instances across different text types;
3. possibility to visualize the source text in which GM instance are located.

BMSCC has the functions of automatic keyword searching and keyword search statistic on its website. The user of the corpus may search the corpus for single Chinese character, word or phrase. The corpus allows users to search a pair of keywords at the same time. It provides different search options, enabling the user to select the area in which he wants to search for the required information. For example, a user can search the use of particular words or phrases in different radio and television programs or time periods. In addition, the corpus permits its users to read the source text in which the words or phrases are included. Moreover, a user has the option to select the linguistic unit in which his search results are displayed, i.e. in clause, paragraph or text. Finally, the results of search can be downloaded into a new file for further analysis. As a user-friendly corpus, BMCC is very suitable for the search of GM instances indicated with specific words or phrases.

The identification of interpersonal GM instances in the corpus begins with the choosing of words and structures to be used for automatic search. Following this, BMSCC is automatically processed with the search engine on its websites. The task of quantifying interpersonal GM instances directly depends on the identification of metaphorical expressions in the data. The GM instances found in the corpus are first counted according to their categories in individual sub-corpora. The GM instances in different sub-corpora are then added up in terms of category to measure the numbers of each category of interpersonal GM in the corpus. In the light of the quantifying work, I explore the distribution of each elemental GM category in the general formation of metaphorical expressions in spoken Chinese.

7.4 Overall distribution of interpersonal GM categories

This section examines how the two types of interpersonal GM, namely, metaphor of mood and metaphor of modality are distributed in Chinese. The metaphorical expressions of mood and modality are further divided into subcategories as shown in Table 7.2 (see Section 5.4 for more details). I examine the distribution of each subcategory of GM in Table 7.2 through a quantitative analysis of GM instances in the corpora selected.

7.4.1 Metaphor of Mood

Section 5.4.1 shows that the metaphor of mood in Chinese has four subcategories: (1) expressing command with interrogative Mood; (2) expressing command with declarative Mood; (3) expressing statement with

Interpersonal GM	*Subcategories*
Metaphor of Mood	1. Expressing command with interrogative Mood 2. Expressing command with declarative Mood 3. Expressing statement with interrogative Mood 4. Expressing question with declarative Mood
Metaphor of Modality	1. Metaphorical realizations of probability 2. Metaphorical realization of usuality 3. Metaphorical realizations of obligation 4. Metaphorical realizations of inclination

Table 7.2: Subcategories of interpersonal GM in Chinese

interrogative Mood; and (4) expressing question with declarative Mood. In addition, two major forms of metaphorical realization are distinguished: (1) normal form of mood expression; and (2) speech-functional formulae. The combination of the two categorizations thus results in a realization system of metaphor of mood in Chinese as shown in Figure 7.2.The detailed analysis of metaphor of mood is conducted by making reference to this realization system. The GM instances in the corpora is first identified and calculated according to their realization forms, namely normal form and

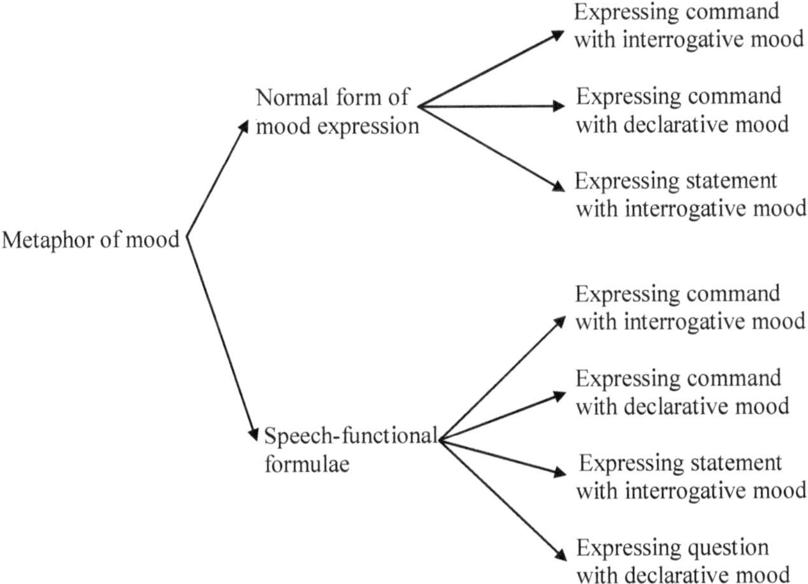

Figure 7.2: Realization system of metaphor of mood in Chinese

speech-functional formulae. The metaphorical expressions involved thus fall in two groups: (1) normal form group; and (2) speech-functional formulae group. These two groups of GM instances are then differentiated and quantified with respect to mood choices in expressing speech functions. As shown in Figure 7.2, the normal form group includes three types of speech function expressions. The speech-functional formulae are involved in all the four types of speech function expressions discussed in Section 5.4.1.

Metaphor of mood in Group 2 is appropriate for the automatic search of Corpus A because speech-functional formulae are words or structures easy to define. The metaphorical expressions in Group 1, on the other hand, must be recognized by manually analyzing a small corpus because they are usually realized with Mood particles involved in the expression of different types of mood. In other words, it is practically impossible to conduct an automatic search of Corpus A for metaphorical expressions in Group 1. I thus manually analyze Corpus B composed of 40 discourses to estimate the distribution of metaphor of mood with normal form of expression. Following this, the number of GM instances identified in Corpus B is multiplied by 10 to acquire the approximate quantity of GM instances in Corpus A. The estimated number of the three subtypes of metaphor of mood in Group 1 is shown in Table 7.3.

Metaphor of Mood realized in normal form (Group 1)	*Expressing Command with Interrogative Mood*	*Expressing Command with Declarative Mood*	*Expressing Statement with Interrogative Mood*
Estimated number	290 (29 × 10)	530 (53 × 10)	1470 (147 × 10)
Estimated Percentage (%)	12.7	23.1	64.2

Table 7.3: Numbers of metaphor of mood realized in normal form

Table 7.3 shows that the metaphorical expressions of statement occur much more frequently than those used for the purpose of realizing command. Moreover, the speech function of command is expressed more commonly with declarative Mood. The results in Table 7.3 should be considered preliminary because they are based on the analysis of a corpus small in size. However, they are adequate for describing the major trends of how metaphor of mood realized in normal form are deployed in Chinese.

The identification of metaphor of mood realized in speech-functional formulae is more straightforward because relevant expressions are concerned with words and structures easy to search in the corpus. Table 7.4 illustrates

Metaphor of mood in speech-functional formulae	*Expressing Command with Interrogative Mood*	*Expressing Command with Declarative Mood*	*Expressing Statement with Interrogative Mood*	*Expressing Question with declarative Mood*
Number	544	671	2928	352
Percentage (%)	12.1	14.9	65.1	7.9

Table 7.4: Numbers of metaphor of mood realized in speech-functional formulae

the breakdown of GM instance numbers in Corpus A across different types of metaphor of Mood.

Table 7.4 shows that the distribution of GM instances realized in speech-functional formulae is very similar to that of GM instances realized in normal form. The metaphorical expressions of Statement are by far the most common GM instances observed in the corpus. Declarative Mood is used more frequently for expressing command than interrogative Mood. In order to show the overall profile of metaphor of Mood in Chinese, the results in Tables 7.3 and 7.4 are combined in Figure 7.3.

As shown in Figure 7.2, there are three major characteristics in the distribution of metaphor of mood in Chinese:

1. The metaphor of mood in Chinese is mainly expressed in the special formula including '*haibu* ...' (yet not), '*bushi* ... *ma?*' (not is ... Mood particle) and '*Wo xiang zhidao/liaojie* ...'(I want to know/enquire ...). To be more specific, GM instances realized in

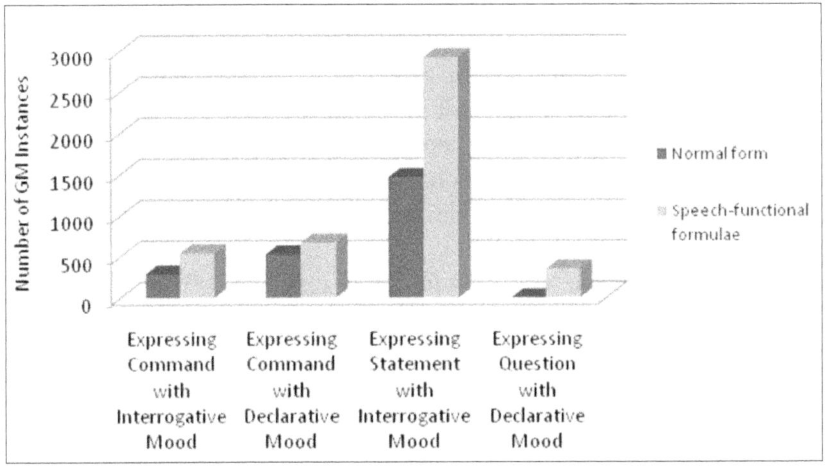

Figure 7.3: The distribution of metaphor of mood

speech-functional formulae are almost three times as many as those realized in normal form.

2. Interrogative Mood is especially common in the metaphorical realization of speech functions, accounting for half of the GM instances observed in the corpus. More specifically, interrogative Mood is used in relation to the expression of statement in the majority instances of GM.
3. The metaphorical expression of command is also prevalent in Chinese although its frequency is not as high as that of statement.

It seems that the last two characteristics of metaphor of mood in Chinese are associated with the politeness strategies described by Brown and Levinson (1987). A speaker uses an interrogative to express a statement because he or she intends to minimize face-threatening acts (FTAs). Similarly, the command metaphorically expressed by an interrogative or a declarative has the effect of maintaining face of speaker or hearer involved. This point is not discussed in detail here as it is not the main focus of this research.

7.4.2 Metaphor of Modality

As revealed in Section 5.4.2, the metaphorical realizations of modality in Chinese can be classified from two perspectives: (1) the types of modality; and (2) the grammatical methods involved in metaphorical realization. To be more specific, there are four types of modality in Chinese, i.e. probability, usuality, obligation and inclination. The grammatical methods involved in the metaphorical realization of modality meaning are projecting process, *shi ... de* structure, *you ...* structure and Mood particle. Modality type and grammatical method are combined in this section to establish a realization system of metaphor of modality in spoken Chinese, as shown in Table 7.5.

I first explore the distribution of metaphor of modality realized by projecting process. In Chinese, only probability and obligation meanings are involved in this form of realization. All the projecting processes listed in Table 7.5 are searched one by one in Corpus A. Their frequencies in the corpus are displayed in Table 7.6.

Table 7.6 shows that projecting processes realizing probability meaning are used much more frequently than those with the obligation meaning in Corpus A. In particular, metaphorical expression of probability is almost 50 times more frequent than that of obligation in the corpus. This distribution of GM instances reflects that the primary purpose of using projecting processes in spoken Chinese is to construe the meaning of probability.

Realization form *Modality*	*Projecting process*	*Special structure*
Probability	*wo xiangxin* (I believe) *wo guji* (I estimate) *wo xiang* (I think) *wo renwei* (I reckon)	*shi kending de* (is must Sub.) *you keneng* (have possibility)
Usuality		*shi changyou de* (is often Sub.)
Inclination		*shi ziyuan de* (is willing Sub.)
Obligation	*wo yaoqiu* (I require) *wo rang* (I let) *wo yunxu* (I permit)	*shi bixu de* (is necessary Sub.) *you biyao* (have necessity)

Table 7.5: Realization system of metaphor of modality in spoken Chinese

Modality	*Projecting process*	*Number of GM instances*	*Percentage (%)*	*Total*
Probability	*wo xiangxin* (I believe)	1278	13.8	9263
	wo guji (I estimate)	608	6.6	
	wo xiang (I think)	4937	53.3	
	wo renwei (I reckon)	2440	26.3	
Obligation	wo yaoqiu (I require)	47	21.8	216
	wo rang (I let)	158	73.1	
	wo yunxu (I permit)	11	5.1	
Total				9479

Table 7.6: Number of metaphor of modality realized by projecting processes

The special structures, including *'shi ... de'* and *'you ...'*, are found in the realizations of all types of modality in Chinese. Their occurrences in Corpus A are displayed in Table 7.7.

Modality	*Special structure*	*Number of GM instances*	*Total*	*Percentage (%)*
Probability	*shi kending de* (is must Sub.)	42	416	39.5
	you keneng (have possibility)	374		
Obligation	*shi bixu de* (is necessary Sub.)	70	571	54.2
	you biyao (have necessity)	501		
Usuality	*shi changyou de* (is often Sub.)	39	39	3.7
Inclination	*shi ziyuan de* (is willing Sub.)	28	28	2.6
Total			1054	100

Table 7.7: Number of metaphor of modality realized in special structures

Table 7.7 shows that metaphorical expressions realized by special structures are distributed in different ways across four types of modality. In general, the expressions with probability and obligation meanings are much more common in the corpus. Those expressing usuality and inclination meanings are obviously rare, reaching just over 7% of relevant GM instances. Unlike the unequal distribution of GM instances with the meaning of probability and obligation in Table 7.6, the deployment of these two types of GM in Table 7.7 is more balanced.

The comparison of Tables 7.6 and 7.7 reveals that GM instances realized by projecting clauses are used nine times more frequently than those expressed in the form of special structure. This distribution of grammatical methods realizing modality meaning in Corpus A shows that projecting clause is the dominant method used for the expression of metaphor of modality in Chinese. In order to demonstrate the general patterns of how metaphor of modality is distributed in Chinese, the findings in Tables 7.6 and 7.7 are integrated in Figure 7.4.

Figure 7.4 shows that two general patterns of GM deployment in Chinese emerge from the corpus analysis: (1) the distribution of interpersonal GM instances is very uneven across the four types of metaphor of modality;

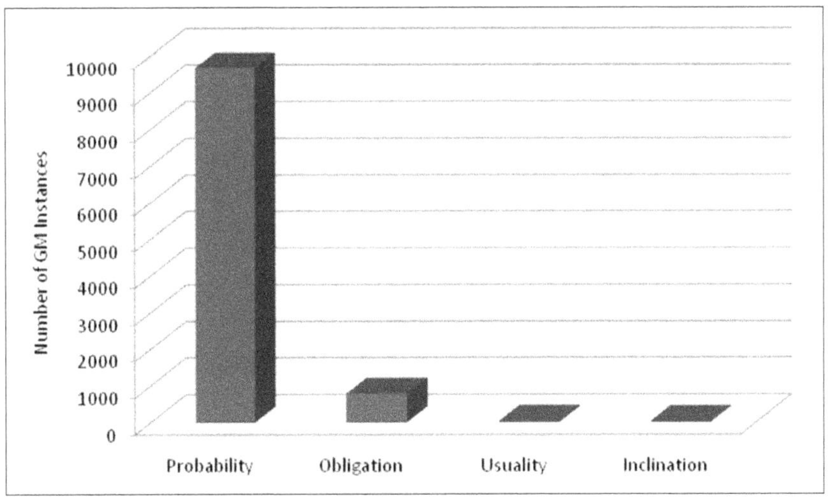

Figure 7.4: General distribution of metaphor of modality

and (2) the metaphorical expressions of probability are used much more commonly in spoken Chinese than those of any other types of modality.

I also attempt to describe the distribution of metaphor of modality observed with reference to the value of modality. According to Halliday and Matthiessen (2004: 620), one of the major variables of modality is 'the value that attached to the modal judgement: high, meidan or low'. The values of modality system in Chinese are summarized in Table 7.8 together with their metaphorical expressions. In addition, the numbers of each type of expression are included in the table to show the distribution of GM in terms of modality value.

	Probability	*Usuality*	*Obligation*	*Inclination*	*Total*
High	Certain: *wo xiangxin* (1278) *shi ...de/you* (416)	Always: *shi...de* (39)	Required: *wo yunxu* (11) *shi...de/you* (571)	Determined: *shi...de* (28)	2343 (22.3%)
Median	Probable: *wo renwei* (2440)	Usually:	Supposed: *wo yaoqiu* (48)	Keen:	2488 (23.6%)
Low	Possible: *wo guji* (608) *wo xiang* (4937)	Sometimes:	Allowed: *wo rang* (158)	Willing:	5703 (54.1%)

Table 7.8: Distribution of GM in terms of modality value

Table 7.8 shows that the metaphorical expressions with a low value of modality are highly preferred in Chinese conversations. More than half of the GM instances in the domain of modality are used to express the meanings of 'possible' and 'allowed'. Given that the proportion of the GM instances with the meaning of 'allowed' is small, the primary purpose of using metaphor of modality by Chinese speakers is to show that they are not certain about their conclusions. On the contrary, the metaphorical expressions with high and median values of modality are employed less commonly by Chinese speakers. This less preference for metaphorical expressions high in modality value explains partly the relatively low occurrence of 'shi ... *de'* and *'you ... '* structures in spoken Chinese.

7.5 Distribution of Interpersonal GM across Registers

This section compares how the two types of interpersonal GM, namely metaphor of mood and metaphor of modality are distributed across different registers. In order to describe the situation in which language is used, Halliday (1978) develops register theory and recognizes three dimensions of situation:

1. Field of discourse: what language is being used to talk about;
2. Tenor of discourse: the role relationships between the participants; and
3. Mode of discourse: the role language is playing in the interaction.

According to Eggins (2004), the variable of Field includes the topic and the interactants of discourse. The topic of discourse can be specialized or everyday, while the interactants may have specialized or common knowledge of the field. The variable of Tenor varies according to the change of status, affective involvement and contact between the participants. The variable of Mode is mainly concerned with the difference between written and spoken languages. For example, a conversation is spontaneous while a composition is planned. Given that the Mode of discourse in use has been clearly defined as spontaneous conversation in this chapter, the analysis of GM deployment across registers focuses on the effects of Field and Tenor. The contextual factors involved in the description of Field and Tenor are summarized in Table 7.9

The corpora used in this chapter are composed of conversations broadcast on television programs. The affective involvement in these programs is normally low, while the contact between speakers is occasional. The status between participants in relevant relative programs is thus the major consideration of Tenor analysis. I selected two groups of programs from Corpus A in which the status between participants is respectively equal and unequal. With respect to Field of television conversations, the factors of topic and

Field	Topic	Specialized Everyday
	Interactant	Specialized knowledge Common knowledge
Tenor	Status	Equal Unequal
	Affective involvement	High (family/friends) Low (business clients)
	Contact	Frequent Occasional

Table 7.9: Contextual factors in Field and Tenor of discourse

interactant are in fact interrelated. The experts with specialized knowledge are usually invited to participate in television programs with specialized topic. It is very rare to see ordinary people in a television program talking about a professional issue. I concentrated the analysis of Field on the topic of discussion because the automatic search option of BMSCC is restricted to the selection of topic. Taking into accout all these factors, I examine the use of interpersonal GM in different registers from two perspectives:

1. The connection between the deployment of interpersonal GM and the topic of discussion; and
2. The correlation between the deployment of GM instances and the status between speaker and hearer.

One critical methodology issue in the comparison of GM distribution across different registers is that registers are not equally represented in the corpus selected. For example, the sub-corpus for register of society consists of 1,030 texts, while the sub-corpus of arts includes only 318 discourses. I thus changed all raw frequency counts to a rate of occurrence per text to compensate the unbalance between sub-corpora of different registers. For instance, the metaphorical expressions of Probability occur 201 times in register of arts and the total number of texts in the register is 318. Thus, the rate of occurrence for this type of interpersonal GM in arts register is:

201/318 = 0.63 times per text

The corpora selected for the analysis in this study falls into four registers in terms of topic: (1) news; (2) arts; (3) economy; and (4) society. I first inspected the frequency of two types of interpersonal GM across these registers. The rate of occurrence for the four subtypes of metaphor of mood in different registers is illustrated in Table 7.10.

Metaphor of Mood / *Topics*	*Expressing Command with Interrogative Mood*	*Expressing Command with Declarative Mood*	*Expressing Statement with Interrogative Mood*	*Expressing Question with Declarative Mood*
News	0.17	0.28	1.03	0.08
Arts	0.19	0.26	1.05	0.07
Economy	0.21	0.29	1.01	0.08
Society	0.17	0.30	0.04	0.06

Table 7.10: Distribution of metaphor of mood across topics

Table 7.10 shows that the conversations with different topics are similar in using different types of metaphor of mood. In other words, the deployment of metaphor of mood in Chinese is not greatly affected by the change of conversation topic.

As discussed above, the distribution of GM instances is very uneven across different types of modality in Chinese. It is not necessary to discuss the occurrence of metaphorical expressions with the meanings of usuality and inclination since they are observed less than 40 times in the corpus. This study only calculates the rate of occurrence for GM instances with the meanings of probability and obligation, as illustrated in Table 7.11.

Metaphor of Modality / *Topics*	*Probability (9679 instances)*	*Obligation (787 instances)*	*Usuality (39 instances)*	*Inclination (28 instances)*
News	3.11	0.18	Not calculated	Not calculated
Arts	0.63	0.19	Not calculated	Not calculated
Economy	1.74	0.15	Not calculated	Not calculated
Society	4.07	0.19	Not calculated	Not calculated

Table 7.11: Distribution of metaphor of modality across topics

Table 7.11 shows that GM instances with obligation meaning are evenly distributed across registers with different topics. But the occurrence rate of metaphorical expressions with probability meaning differs dramatically in different registers. The discourses in the fields of news and society have a much higher frequency of GM deployment than those in the other two areas. It means Chinese speakers use a much larger set of GM instances to express probability when they discuss news and society. Among the four types of discourse in the corpus, news and society belong to everyday topics requiring less professional knowledge. Arts and economy are relatively more specialized topics that only a few people are qualified to discuss in depth. Those who are invited to participate in a television program covering these two topics are frequently top specialists in relevant fields. In this case, the speakers involved are very confident about their own opinions. This may be the reason why the occurrence of GM instances expressing probability meaning is low in arts and economy registers.

The examination of how GM deployment is affected by the change of social status between speaker and hearer is more complicated because the metaphorical expressions must be searched program by program. This research selects 17 programs from Corpus A in which the status between participants can be clearly defined as equal or unequal, including 2,132 spoken discourses. Considering that the number of discourses involved is smaller, only the most frequently observed GM categories are covered in this examination. The results of examination are displayed in Table 7.12.

GM / *Status*	*Metaphor of Mood*			*Metaphor of Modality*	
	Expressing Command with Interrogative Mood	*Expressing Command with Declarative Mood*	*Expressing Statement with Interrogative Mood*	*Probability*	*Obligation*
Equal (10 programs 1287 discourses)	0.10	0.24	0.83	2.01	0.15
Unequal (7 programs 845 discourses)	0.23	0.27	1.57	2.37	0.18

Table 7.12: Distribution of GM instances in relation to status

Table 7.12 shows that the most striking contrast between programs involving participants with equal and unequal status is their differential reliance on interrogative mood. The conversation participants unequal in status prefer to use more interrogatives to express the meanings of statement and command than those equal in status. In order to explore the reason for this preference on interrogative mood, I conducted a thorough analysis of 50 spoken discourses in which the status between participants is unequal. The analysis demonstrates that interrogative mood is ordinarily used by speakers lower in social status, such as program host. In other words, the reliance on interrogative mood in programs with unequal participants is largely engendered by the need of speakers low in status to show their respect to hearers with higher status. More generally, the deployment of metaphor of mood in Chinese is related to the status relationship between speaker and hearer. Table 7.12 also demonstrates that the use of two major types of metaphor of modality, i.e., probability and obligation, is not greatly affected by the status between relevant speakers and hearers.

7.6 Summary

The discussion in this chapter has been focused on the use of interpersonal GM in Chinese. Two corpora of natural spoken Chinese are analyzed to explore how interpersonal GM instances are distributed in the language and how the frequency of different types of interpersonal GM is affected by the change of dialogue topic and social relationship between speaker and addressee. Prior to the actual corpus analysis, I conducted a pilot study to determine the frequency of GM in spoken Chinese. The pilot study reveals that interpersonal GM is a relatively low frequency phenomenon in Chinese compared to ideational GM discussed. A large corpus is therefore used to conduct the empirical research on interpersonal GM. In addition, a small corpus is analyzed to compendate the dificiency of the large one.

The overall picture of interpersonal GM distribution emerging from the corpora analysis is as follows:

1. Metaphor of modality is used much more frequently than metaphor of mood in spoken Chinese;
2. The majority cases of metaphor of mood in Chinese are realized by speech-functional formulae;
3. The interrogative is the most commonly used Mood in the metaphorical expressions of various speech functions in Chinese; and
4. Metaphor of modality has a very uneven distribution in Chinese, with a particular high occurrence in the expression of probability.

It is important to recognize from these features that the use of GM in spoken Chinese has a strong preference on certain types of metaphorical expressions, such as interrogative Mood and probability.

In order to show the impact of social factors on the meaning creation in spoken Chinese, this chapter also analyzes the deployment of interpersonal GM in different registers. The detailed analysis focuses on the correlation between the deployment of GM and the register variables of Field and Tenor. It is found that the use of GM in spoken Chinese is affected by the change of conversation topic and the variation of social status between speaker and addresses. In particular, metaphor of modality is used more frequently when taking about specilized topics. Metahor of mood is used more commonly by speakers low in status.

8 Comparison of grammatical metaphor in Chinese and English

8.1 Introduction

GM exists theoretically in all human languages as a phenomenon arising from the interaction between semantics and lexicogrammar. As mentioned in Section 1.1, GM is first proposed and described in English. In order to identify and categorize GM in Chinese, the same phenomenon in English has been reviewed from time to time in the previous chapters for the purpose of reference.

This chapter compares GM in Chinese and English and interprets GM differences in the two language form the perspective of typology. The comparison in this chapter focuses on ideational GM on account of its importance in formal written varieties of English and Chinese. The focus is also related to the relatively less research on interpersonal GM in English and Chinese.

As shown in Chapters 4 to 7, the identification, categorization and deployment of metaphorical expressions are central issues in the study of GM. I first describe the typological variations in Chinese and English in terms of three variables relevant most to the lexicogrammatical realizations of semantic meanings. These variables include the order of grammatical constituents, the degree of grammatical specificity and the location of grammatical realizations. Following this, I contrastively analyze the identification, categorization and deployment of ideational GM in English and Chinese. The detailed analysis is carried out from three perspectives: (1) formal distance between congruent and metaphorical expressions; (2) subdivision of certain GM categories; and (3) the extent of using GM. The analysis shows that the differences in all these aspects of GM can be linked to the typological variations across the two languages. It is also found that the difference of GM identification, categorization and deployment in English and Chinese may be engendered by more than one typological property.

8.2 Typological differences between Chinese and English

This section is not a comprehensive survey of the typological features over which Chinese and English are distinguished. GM is the phenomenon arising from the remapping of semantic and lexicogrammatical systems of a language. I discuss only the typological variation relevant most to the lexicogrammatical construal of semantic meanings in the two languages. All the typological properties are discussed within the framework of systemic functional typology, which is mainly developed by Matthiessen (2004). In particular, they are concerned with three variables in lexicogrammatical systems of the two languages:

1. the order of grammatical constituents;
2. the degree of grammatical specificity; and
3. the location of grammatical realization.

The first aspect examines how the constituents of the clause complex, clause and group in Chinese and English are arranged in construing semantic meanings. The second explores to what extent the lexical and grammatical systems in the two languages express semantic meanings specifically. The third considers where the semantic domains in Chinese and English are located in their lexicogrammatical systems. The detailed discussion in this section focuses on these variables in Chinese, with those in English serving for comparative purpose.

8.2.1 Order of grammatical constituents

The order of grammatical constituents in clauses and groups is a major area of typological study. For instance, over half of Greenberg's (1966) universal statements are concerned with the order of grammatical constituents. It is, of course, beyond the scope of this study to give a comprehensive survey of earlier findings in the area. This section only examines the constituent orders that count for most in differentiating the structure of grammatical categories in Chinese and English. For example, only the order of Process and Circumstance is discussed because it is the key difference between English and Chinese in the structure of a clause. The scope of this section is, therefore, smaller than the traditional study of constituent order. On the other hand, the analysis here is not limited to the structures of clause and group. The formal feature of clause complexes is also taken into account to reveal the structural distance between congruent and metaphorical expressions.

In sum, this section analyzes the constituent orders which distinguish the structures of clause complexes, clauses and groups in Chinese and English.

Clause complexes are formed by clauses through two basic systems: Taxis and Logical-semantic relations. Chapter 3 reveals that the range of these systems is similar in Chinese and English. That is, the clauses in a nexus is either paratactic or hypotactic and their relationship is one of expansion and projection. However, English and Chinese adopt different grammatical forms to construe some logical relations. The most remarkable difference between the two languages is the form of hypotactic nexus. The primary clause in a Chinese hypotactic clause complex is typically preceded by the secondary one (Halliday and Matthiessen, 1999). The structure of a hypotactic clause complex in Chinese can be presented as '$\beta + \alpha$' if the primary and the secondary clauses are respectively symbolized by α and β. A hypotactic clause complex in English, by comparison, prefers to construe hypotactic sequence in the pattern of '$\alpha + \beta$'.

In the typological study of a clause, the relative ordering of subject (S), verb (V) and object (O) is referred to as the 'basic word order' in a language. The basic constituent order in English can be uncontroversially determined as SVO. Chinese basic word order is also regarded as SVO although it has been the subjection of decades of controversy (Shi and Li, 2001). Matthiessen (2004: 544) claims that the labels of S, V and O 'do not reveal the metafunctional motivation behind the sequence of elements'. He also suggests that the linear structure within the clause should be described respectively in interpersonal, textual and experiential zones. Given the focus on ideational GM in this chapter, only the experiential configuration of a clause is discussed here. The clauses in Chinese and English are constructed by a Process with its Participants and optional Circumstances. The placement of Participant and Process is similar in Chinese and English since the two languages share the basic word order of SVO. The main structural difference between Chinese and English clauses lies in the ordering of Process and Circumstance. According to Halliday and McDonald (2004), the default position of a Circumstance is immediately preceding the Process in a Chinese clause though the Circumstance expressing outcome of a Process can follow it. The Circumstance in an English clause often appears after the Process, unless it construes the meaning of degree or manner.

Halliday and Matthiessen (2004) recognize three main classes of group, namely nominal group, verbal group, adverbial group. It is the structure of nominal group that Chinese and English differ most in terms of constituent order. In systemic functional theory, a nominal group contains a Thing and other items characterizing the Thing in some way. These items in English may appear before the Thing functioning as Deictic, Numerative, Epithet and Classifier or after the Thing with the function of Qualifier. In Chinese, all kinds of modification with the meaning of deixis, numeration and classification precede the Thing of a nominal group. The modifying function in a Chinese group may be realized by nominal elements, verbal elements or embedded clauses. In other words, the modifiers in any grammatical form must precede the headword of a nominal group in Chinese. The structural difference between Chinese and English in nominal groups is of particular importance to the analysis of ideational GM. This importance is determined by the fact that the major motif of ideational GM is the general drift to thing. With this orientation of semantic shift, a large portion of sequences and figures is metaphorically realized as nominal groups. In this case, the configuration and deployment of GM are affected greatly by the constituent order in nominal groups.

The constituents of different ranks of grammatical categories are arranged according to certain principles varying from language to language. These principles determine that the same ideational semantic unit may be realized by distinct order of grammatical constituents in different languages. Depending on this description of structural features in clause complex, clause and group, the special order of grammatical constituents in Chinese is summarized as follows:

1. To construe a hypotactic sequence, the primary clause generally appears after the secondary clause of the clause complex;
2. Except for those expressing results of action, Circumstances precede the Process to be modified; and
3. The Thing in a nominal group, following all the Modifiers, always occupies the final position of the group.

Li and Thompson (1981) claim that the order of constituents with respect to Chinese verbs is primarily determined by semantic factors rather than grammatical ones. The summary of special constituent order in Chinese shows that this preference on semantic importance also affects the order of constituents in the clause complex and nominal group. From the point of view of English, Chinese has a tendency to arrange grammatical constituents in keeping with their semantic importance. In a hypotactic clause complex, the primary clause is semantically more important than the secondary one. The primary clause, therefore, occurs at the final position of the clause complex. The tendency also affects the arrangement of the major Process and its Circumstances in a Chinese clause. On account of the more important role of the major Process in a clause, it is preceded by all kinds of Circumstances except those expressing the result of the Process. The tendency to put more important constituents later is finally illustrated by the fact that the Thing in a Chinese nominal group is preceded by its modifiers. To sum up, the semantically more important constituents in different ranks of grammatical categories are generally preceded by those less crucial for the expression of semantic meanings in Chinese.

The tendency for Chinese to locate grammatical constituents in accordance with their semantic importance is a matter of degree and not absolute. However, this relatively consistent tendency across different ranks of grammatical categories in Chinese may give rise to some particular features in the structure of GM instances.

8.2.2 Degree of grammatical specificity

The same semantic domain may be manifested in different specific degrees by the lexicogrammatical systems across languages. As Halliday and Matthiessen (1999) state, linear time in Chinese is manifested through time adverbs with the meaning of 'already', 'soon', 'yesterday', etc. English, on the other hand, deploys a tense system for the manifestation of linear time. That is, the semantic domain of linear time is less manifested in Chinese than in English. More generally, Halliday and Matthiessen (1999) argue that many of the lexicalized meanings that are construed grammatically in Chinese have the characteristic of being optional. It is also stressed that 'if we look at Chinese from the point of view of English, it appears that in its lexicogrammar as a whole there is some tendency for avoiding unnecessary specificity' (Halliday and Matthiessen, 1999: 300). All these observations show that the lexicogrammatical systems in Chinese have a lower degree of specificity than those in English. This section provides a more detailed picture of the difference between Chinese and English in terms of grammatical specificity.

Before comparing the grammatical specificity in Chinese and English, it is worth noting that the term 'specificity' here has a different interpretation from the same word traditionally used in the discussion of indefiniteness of NP (see Enc, 1991 for details). The traditional 'specificity' is essentially a semantic notion though it is relevant to some syntactic phenomena. The specificity in this study is a grammatical concept used for exploring the extent to which the lexicogrammar in a language permits precision in manifesting semantic domains.

8.2.2.1 Lexical categories

At a lexical level, Chinese categories are different from those in English in their characteristic of using a general term where the more specific is rendered unnecessary by the context (Halliday and Matthiessen, 1999). This characteristic is best shown by the lexical categories of noun and preposition in Chinese. Due to the low degree of specificity of its nouns and prepositions, Chinese adopts some particular methods of accommodating these lexical categories into nominal groups and prepositional phrases. The special structures of nominal groups and prepositional phrases in turn engender the distinctive features of GM in Chinese.

A. Noun

One of the most obvious features of nouns in Chinese is that they do not change their forms for number or case. Hansen (1983) claims that the meanings of Chinese nouns appear strikingly similar to the uncountable collective and mass nouns, like 'cattle' and 'snow' in English. In addition, naming in Chinese is not grounded on the existence of abstract entities but rather on finding 'boundaries' between things. This mass nature of Chinese nouns is illustrated by the noun *shu* (book) in the following clause:

(8.1)	*Qing*	*ba*	*shu*	*di*	*gei*	*wo.*
	please	BA	book	pass	to	me

'Please pass the book to me.'

In this expression, *shu* (book) refers to a book or books which could be identified by both speaker and listener. For the readers of this clause, it becomes difficult to affirm how many books and what kind of book are concerned.

The mass nature of Chinese nouns determines that a participant in Chinese can be constructed by a single noun without any indicator of quantity or identity. In other words, the construal of the participant in Chinese is distinguished from that in English by the fact that the Thing in a Chinese participant, with or without associated quality, may stand by itself (Halliday and Matthiessen, 1999).

In order to extend a noun to a nominal group with more exact meaning, it is either specified or quantified. First, the noun can be quantified by adding a unit or a measure word before it, which is referred to as classifier by Li and Thompson (1981). These classifiers must occur with a number, like *yi* (one) and *shi* (ten), and/or a demonstrative like *zhei* (this), *na* (that) and *nei* (which), or quantifiers such as *zheng* (whole) and *mei* (every). Second, the noun in Chinese is specified by assigning qualities to it. This method is critical for the construction of taxonomy in Chinese. Taxonomies in any language are created by clarifying the relationship between a superordinate term and its hyponyms. Hyponyms in Chinese are generally constructed by differentiating a noun with the structure of 'modifier + headword', which is illustrated by Example 8.2.

(8.2) Superordinate	Hyponym	
che (vehicle)	*qi che*	(gas vehicle) 'automobile'
	huo che	(fire vehicle) 'train'
	zhan che	(fight vehicle) 'chariot'
	ma che	(horse vehicle) 'carriage'

As shown in Example 8.2, the noun *che* (vehicle) is expanded into nominal groups by adding modifiers before it. The nominal groups created are semantically the hyponyms of the superordinate term of *che* (vehicle).

B. Preposition

Prepositions in Chinese have been examined under the topic of circumstance in Section 3.2.3. It is found that many prepositions in Chinese are less specific in meaning compared to those in English. This lower specificity is closely related to the fact that prepositions in Chinese are words which can be used as verbs (Li and Thompson, 1981). These prepositions with less specific meanings in Chinese are generally used in the construal of locative circumstances. Take one of the most frequently used prepositions. *zai* for example, it is generally translated by 'in' or 'at' in English. Actually, *zai* does not express the meaning of place or time as explicitly as its English counterparts. Section 3.2.3 reveals that the prepositions like *zai* in Chinese are frequently used together with a 'facet' to construe the circumstance of Location. In this case, the preposition is extended into a prepositional phrase with the structure of 'preposition + noun + postnoun'. Halliday and Matthiessen (1999) explain that the circumstantial relation construed by this type of prepositional phrases is deconstructed into a 'relation' and a 'facet'. In other words, it is the less specific meaning of certain prepositions that gives rise to the particular circumstance with the structure of 'preposition + noun + postnoun' in Chinese.

The focus on the noun and preposition in this discussion of specificity does not mean that other lexical categories in Chinese are not concerned with this property. For instance, Matthiessen (2004: 584) stresses that 'processes are construed as very specific in Chinese in comparison with English'. This specific construal of process in Chinese in effect indicates that the verbs in Chinese are also different from those in English in terms of grammatical specificity. This difference is not explored here because the use of verb in Chinese is closely related to the phase system. In Section 8.3, the characteristic of Chinese verbs are in more detail.

8.2.2.2 Grammatical systems

Chinese and English also have different degrees of specificity in their grammatical systems. Halliday and Matthiessen (1999) claim that the grammatical systems in Chinese tend to have unmarked or neutral terms in construing meaning. They offer two situations in which the unmarked terms are chosen: (1) the systemic choice is irrelevant in the given context; and (2) the meaning is construed elsewhere in the context. In these situations, the grammatical systems in Chinese and English differ most in morphological and temporal aspects.

A. Morphological aspect

One important parameter in morphological study is the index of synthesis, which is best conceived of as a continuum (Comrie, 1989). One end of the continuum is the ideal isolating language, while the other end is represented by the ideal synthesis language. Chinese, as a language with very little morphological complexity, falls very near to the isolating pole of the continuum (Li and Thompson, 1981). By contrast, English has a system of affixing morphemes though it is located relatively far from the synthetic end of the continuum.

The lack of morphological variation in Chinese determines that many meanings signaled by morphemes in English are expressed by other means in Chinese. This difference between Chinese and English can be described from four perspectives by reference to the relevant study of Li and Thompson (1981). First, the meanings of morphological case markers in English are expressed by means of word order and prepositions. Second, the singular and plural distinction in English is realized by the words like *yixie* (some) and *xuduo* (many) in Chinese. Third, some of the morphologically marked agreements between verbs and subjects in English are indicated by word order in Chinese. Finally, English deploys particular morphemes for signaling the meaning of tense and aspect. Chinese has no morphological markers for tense though it uses aspectual morphemes of *le*, *guo, zai* and *zhe*. This point is described explicitly in the following comparison of the temporal expression in the two languages.

B. Temporal aspect

The temporal systems in Chinese are quite different from those in English. This difference is mainly shown by tense and aspect expressions which are the two most complex temporal systems in a language.

According to Comrie (1976; 1985), tense is a temporal system expressing the relationship between two points in time. Aspect, on the other hand, focuses on the internal temporal makeup of a situation. English employs mainly a tense system for the purpose of locating events in time. The construal of experience in Chinese is mainly located in time with its aspect system. In other words, the occurrence of an event is viewed from the perspectives of its own internal makeup in Chinese. As mentioned earlier, Chinese uses morphological markers to express the aspectual meaning in a clause. Li and Thompson (1981) recognize four aspectual markers in Chinese: *le*, *zai*, *zhe* and *guo*. *Le* means the action has already taken place, while *guo* denotes that an action is a past experience. Both *zhe* and *zai* imply the process is still ongoing though they are used in different locations in a Chinese clause.

In terms of grammatical specificity, particular attention needs to be paid to the fact that Chinese has expressions which do not use aspect markers at all. That is, a Chinese figure can be realized by a clause without assigning it to any category of temporal meaning. Compare the following examples taken from the study of Halliday and Matthiessen (1999: 304).

(8.3) *Wo kan zhe bao.* 'I am/was reading the newspaper'
I read Asp. (imperfective) newspaper

Wo kan le bao. 'I have/had read the newspaper'
I read Asp. (perfective) newspaper

Wo kan bao
I read newspaper
'I read newspaper.'

As Halliday and Matthiessen (1999: 304) state, 'whereas in English each process in a figure must be located somewhere in the construction of tense, in Chinese the process may simply be left as neutral, without being assigned to either category of aspect'. They also point out that the neutral aspect in Chinese is not semantically marked because it is not selecting in the perfective/imperfective system. In Chinese scientific writings where ideational GM is widely deployed, this kind of neutral expressions is used more frequently.

It is seen from the discussion above that the lexical and grammatical systems in Chinese have the ability to express meaning less specifically than those in English. I discuss the less specific property of lexical categories and grammatical systems separately. The real expressions in Chinese may be affected simultaneously by this property in the two systems. For example, the Chinese noun *che* 'vehicle' in the clause *Che lai le* 'vehicle come Asp'. is not specified lexically as a bus, a car or a horse drawn cart. Simultaneously, it is not necessary to specify the noun grammatically with a deictic such as *zhe* 'this' or *na* 'that'. Of course, this sort of expression only occurs when these lexical and grammatical specificities can be construed in a context.

8.2.3 Location of grammatical realization

Locations of the same semantic domain along the lexicogrammatical continuum vary from language to language (Halliday and Matthiessen, 1999). Similarly, the realization of a semantic domain can be located at various ranks of lexicogrammatical categories in different languages (Matthiessen, 2004). The division of labour between the logical and the experiential modes of ideational function in construing experience also differs in languages (Halliday and Matthiessen, 1999). In this section, all these differences between Chinese and English are discussed under the same heading because they are all concerned with the location of grammatical realization in different dimensions of language. The location of grammatical realization in Chinese is different from that in English in three aspects: 1) semantic domain of phase, 2) expansion of clause nucleus and 3) assignment of quality.

8.2.3.1 Semantic domain of phase

According to Halliday and Matthiessen (1999), the semantic domain of phase is located more closely to the grammatical pole of lexicogrammatical continuum in Chinese than in English. There are two types of phase in Chinese: neutral and completive. The more grammatical feature of phase in Chinese is determined by the fact that the language employs a large but closed set of postverbs to express completive meaning. According to the functions of the postverb concerned, the completive phase in Chinese is further divided into two subtypes: directional and resultative (Halliday and McDonald, 2004). The postverb in the directional subtype indicates the direction of the first, using for both concrete and abstract space. The word *jin* (enter) in the following clause is an example of this type of postverb.

(8.4) *Ta zou <u>jin</u> fangjian.*
he walk into room.
'He walks into the room.'

On the other hand, a larger set of postverb of the resultative subtype is deployed to show the result of the main verb (see Chao, 1968: 443 for detailed description). Example 8.5 illustrates the process expressed by the complex verbs with resultative meaning.

(8.5) *Ta mai <u>dao</u> le caipiao.*
he buy reach Asp lottery ticket.
'He bought a lottery ticket.'

Examples 8.4 and 8.5 show that the expression of phrase in Chinese is largely concerned with polysyllabic verbs. Depending on their meaning of phrase, the polysyllabic verbs can be classified into two types: the neutral and the completive. The neutral polysyllabic verbs in Chinese are generally used for the expression of states, realities or regular activities. The completive polysyllabic verbs, as discussed above, realized the meaning of result or direction. It is worth noting that the neutral and completive types of polysyllabic verbs are not distinguished structurally because they share the form of V+V. The widely adopted criterion for recognizing completive polysyllabic verbs is that the potential marker *de/bu* can be affixed to the main verb (see Packard, 2000 for details). For example, the verbal group *kan dao* (look arrive) has a completive meaning because it can be transferred as *kan bu dao* (look unable arrive) or *kan de dao* (look able arrive). On the contrary, the neutral verbal group *jie shao* (introduce) does not allow the insertion of *bu/de* between its verbal elements.

Halliday and McDonald (2004) propose that the main verb and the post-verb separately function as Event and Extension at a group rank though they jointly realize the function of Process in a clause. It is worth noting that the Extension in a Chinese verbal group is functionally different from the particle following the verb in an English phrasal verb, such as 'up' in 'look up'. In particular, the Extension in Chinese extends the meaning represented by the main verb in a direction or to a result. The particle in an English phrasal verb is used to make the focus on Process unmarked, functioning as Adjunct in a clause (see Halliday and Matthiessen, 2004 for detailed description). Depending on the discussion above, the neutral type of polysyllabic verb in Chinese only contains the element of Event. The completive one, on the other hand, is constructed by the elements of Event and Extension.

Unlike Chinese, English includes the meaning of completion in its verbs. For example, if the clause 'I cut a piece of string' is used, it means the string is cut in two (Halliday and Matthiessen, 1999). When the non-completed meaning in a process is construed, English uses the conative structure, such as 'try to' and 'start to', to introduce a main verb. This difference between Chinese and English in expressing completive meaning indicates the distinctive preference for construing phrase in the two languages. As Halliday and McDonald (2004: 383) summarizes, 'whereas English processes are "reussive" – that is, they assume success and mark the phase of attempt – Chinese processes are "conative": in other words, they assume attempt and mark the phase of success'.

8.2.3.2 Expansion of clause nucleus

Halliday and Matthiessen (1999) claim that the nucleus of a clause is constructed by Process and Medium. Matthiessen (2004) observes that the extent to which the clause can be expanded beyond the clause nucleus varies from language to language. Moreover, the clause nucleus is expanded 'configurationally through additional elements within the simple clause (experiential mode) or sequentially (logical mode)' (Matthiessen, 2004: 578). It is also pointed out that the clause nucleus expands in logical mode by constructing complexes either at clause rank or at group/phrase rank. The major difference between English and Chinese in expanding clause nucleus is that the expansion construed experientially in English is frequently realized logically in Chinese. In addition, this kind of logical expansion of clause nucleus is realized at group/phrase rank by using SVC in Chinese.

As mentioned in Section 4.4.1, an SVC is a sequence of verbs acting together as a single predicate. The key point is that an SVC construes a single process and occupies one functional slot in a clause. Related to this property, SVCs have just one tense, aspect, and polarity value. Another important property is that each verb in an SVC must be able to occur on its own (Aikhenvald, 2006).

The SVC in Chinese is a subject of considerable interest and controversy for several decades in relevant studies (e.g. Chao, 1968; Li and Thompson, 1981; Matthews, 2006). These studies show that SVC in Chinese is employed for construing meanings which are realized in English by a wide variety of grammatical devices such as prepositional phrases, *-ing* and infinitival complements and modal auxiliaries. In other words, the expansion through additional elements in an English clause is frequently construed as the logical sequence in a Chinese verbal group. This difference can be illustrated by the Chinese clause and its English counterpart in Example 8.6.

(8.6) *Ta yong diannao xie xin.*
he use computer write letter
'He writes letters with his computer.'

As Example 8.6 shows, the clause nucleus is expanded experientially through a prepositional phrase in English. The Process and the Circumstance of means in Chinese, by contrast, are realized logically by a SVC. In this case, both English and Chinese expand the clause nucleus circumstantially with a minor process. However, as Halliday and Matthiessen (1999) explain, the circumstantial in Chinese retains more of a 'process' flavour. This is because the Chinese equivalent of English preposition is the verb in SVC, which is capable of constructing clause by itself.

According to Halliday and McDonald (2004), the verbal group in Chinese may contain Auxiliary, Polarity, Event and Extension. The detailed structure of verbal groups in Chinese is determined by the different combinations of these components. McDonald (2004) argues that verbal groups can be classified into simple, compound and complex types which respectively include

Event, Event plus Extension and a number of verbs connected in some kind of logical relation. The discussions of phrase domain and the expansion of clause nucleus in this study show that the Event in simple verbal groups is realized by monosyllabic verbs and polysyllabic verbs with neutral phrase. The Event plus Extension in compound verbal groups is construed by polysyllabic verbs with completive meanings. Complex verb groups are constructed by SVCs which in effect have the structure of Event + Event.

8.2.3.3 Assignment of quality

Matthiessen (2004: 568–569) states that 'the assignment of qualities to a thing can be done either clausally or by means of a nominal group'. In other words, the realization of quality can be located at the grammatical ranks of clause or group. Halliday and Matthiessen (1999) observe that Chinese and English tend to locate the meaning of quality respectively at the rank of clause and group. The quality of a thing in Chinese can be realized by the Attribute in a relational clause and the Epithet in a nominal group. It is observed that Chinese has a preference for construing the quality of thing in the form of Attribute rather than Epithet. Although qualities in English can be expressed in the form of a relational clause, this is much less favored in the language. The speakers of English tend to construe the meaning of quality into a nominal group. Thus, the semantic meaning of quality is typically realized in the structure of 'Epithet + Thing' in English. Chinese, on the other hand, prefers to construe quality meaning in a structure of 'Carrier + Attribute'.

According to Halliday and McDonald (2004), the different preferences for construing quality in Chinese and English are related to the distinction of adjectives in the two languages. The Chinese and English adjectives which realize qualities can be respectively included in the class of verbal elements and the class of nominal elements. As Halliday and Matthiessen (1999: 304) points out, 'in Chinese "adjectives" are verbs, whereas in English they are a kind of noun'.

Due to the different preferences for expressing quality in Chinese and English, the same meaning is sometimes realized by different types of clause in the two languages. For instance, the English figures such as 'she has long hair' are construed ascriptively in Chinese as:

(8.7) *Ta toufa hen chang.*
she hair very be long
'As for her, the hair is very long.'

With respect to this difference between English and Chinese, Halliday and Matthiessen (1999) suggest that both languages aim to put the person rather than the part of body in thematic position. English achieves this by including the quality within the functional element of participant and relates the person and the participant with a possessive clause. Chinese does it by constructing the quality ascriptively and detaching the person as an isolated Theme.

As seen from the discussion in this section, Chinese and English show different features in the order of grammatical constituents, the degree of grammatical specificity and the location of grammatical realizations. First, Chinese is typologically different from English by ordering grammatical constituents according to their semantic importance. Meanwhile, the lexical and grammatical systems in Chinese and English have varied degrees of grammatical specificity. Finally, the grammatical realizations of phase, quality and clause nucleus expansion are also located differently in the two languages.

8.3 Differences between English and Chinese in ideational GM

As mentioned in Section 8.1, identification, categorization and deployment are the main focuses in GM studies. In keeping with these orientations of GM research, this section explores the differences of metaphorical expressions across Chinese and English in three aspects. First, I analyze the structure of metaphorical expression, which is a major consideration of GM identification. The structure of GM is analyzed by comparing a metaphorical realization with its congruent counterpart (Halliday, 1994). The comparison reveals the formal distances between congruent and metaphorical expressions in Chinese and English. According to previous studies of GM in English (Halliday, 1998; Halliday and Matthiessen, 1999) and the categorization of GM in Chinese (see Chapter 5 for more details), the two languages have the same range of GM categories in the ideational zone. These GM categories are divided further into subcategories in terms of the grammatical movements at group rank (Halliday and Matthiessen, 1999). The structural distinctions between Chinese and English at group rank determine that the subdivision of GM categories is different in the two languages. This is the second point to be discussed in this section. Finally, GM deployment is generally studied in relation to linguistic context and language development. It is possible that typological differences between languages give rise to varied degrees of GM deployment. Thus, the extent of using GM in Chinese and English is also discussed in this section.

8.3.1 Formal distance between congruent and metaphorical expressions

The review of GM categorization in Chapter 2 shows that ideational GM can be classified into three groups which respectively realize the semantic units of sequence, figure and element. In this section, the formal distances between metaphorical and congruent expressions in Chinese and English are analyzed in terms of the semantic unit they realize. I first discuss the formal distance between realizations of elements in Chinese and English by examining the structural changes arising from the semantic shifts in GM. Following this, the formal distance between realizations of figures is explored with the emphasis on the structure of nominal groups in the two languages. The realizations of sequence are compared in relation to the structure of 'favorite clause type'. Halliday and Matthiessen (2004: 656) stress that 'nominalizing is the single most powerful resource for creating grammatical metaphor'. The investigation in this section, therefore, pays particular attention to the metaphorical expressions concerned with nominalization.

8.3.1.1 Distance between realizations of elements

A figure consists of four kinds of elements: thing, quality, process and circumstance. Each of these semantic elements has its own congruent and metaphorical realizations in lexicogrammatical systems. For example, the element of process is congruently realized as a verb, while its metaphorical realization is a noun or an adjective. In other words, a semantic element is metaphorically realized by shifting a lexeme from one grammatical class to another. Thus, the formal difference between metaphorical and congruent realizations of semantic elements is determined by the structural distinction between different classes of words.

There is a set of derivational morphemes in English by which the etymons in one class can be transferred to another class. Chinese, in contrast, is characterized by a relative paucity of morphological variations for signaling the transfer of a word from one grammatical category to another. The change of word classes in Chinese is generally realized by syntactic means instead of the derivational morphemes. In this case, many words with different functions in Chinese share similar form. This typological feature of Chinese accounts for the formal similarity between many congruent and metaphorical realizations of elements in the language.

Halliday (1998) points out that the drift to thing is the main motif in ideational GM. Previous research of GM also reveals that the semantic shift to thing is the most frequent example of GM. In this case, the structural variation in nominalization is crucial for the examination of formal differences between congruent and metaphorical realizations of element. English has a battery of derivational morphemes whereby verbs, adjectives and other classes of word can be turned into nouns. The metaphorical realizations created by this means of nominalization can be clearly distinguished from their congruent counterparts.

Section 4.6.1 reveals that non-nominal elements in Chinese are metaphorically realized as nouns in two ways. First, these elements can be used as nouns without changing their structures. Second, Chinese verbs and adjectives are nominalized by adding lexemes like *xing* (property), *du* (degree) and *lü* (rate) when metaphorical realizations are constructed as technical terms in the register of science. The second method of nominalization in Chinese is similar to the nominalizing means in English. According to Kubler (1985), this method in modern Chinese in effect finds its origin in the translation of western works. The formal difference between congruent and metaphorical realizations created by this method is comparable to that in English.

However, this difference is less abrupt in Chinese than in English because the technical terms in Chinese are created by borrowing the typical structures of the everyday nominal group (Halliday and Matthiessen, 1999). Section 8.2.2.1 shows that nominal groups are generally constructed in Chinese by differentiating a noun with the structure of 'modifier + headword'. This model of constructing nominal groups is also adopted in the creation of technical terms. This point is illustrated by the following examples taken from the study of Halliday and Matthiessen (1999: 312).

(8.8)	*Pin*	*lü*	(repeat rate)	frequency
	Su	*lü*	(fast rate)	speed
	Yin	*lü*	(sound rate)	musical pitch
	Huxi	*lü*	(breathe rate)	respiration rate
	Zhouzhuan	*lü*	(turn over rate)	turnover
	Zheshe	*lü*	(refract rate)	index of refraction

The discussion above shows that the formal difference between the congruent and metaphorical realizations of element is more obvious in English than in Chinese. This shorter formal distance between realizations of element in Chinese is essentially due to the lack of morphological indicators and the less specific property of nouns in the language. The formal similarity between congruent and metaphorical realizations of elements also impacts the realizations of sequence and figure in which elements act as constituents.

8.3.1.2 Distance between realizations of figure

A figure is congruently realized as a clause, while it is realized metaphorically as a group. In the metaphorical realizations of figure, nominal groups are of particular importance for they release the energy of making meaning. As mentioned in Chapter 2, this energy pertains to the two semantic potentials for referring and expanding (Halliday, 1998). In support of this, the statistical results in Section 6.4 show that a large portion of the GM instances in Chinese occur as the constituents of nominal groups. The importance of nominal groups determines that the structural difference between clause and nominal group in the major concern of the discussion in this section.

When a figure is metaphorically reconstrued as a nominal group, the elements in a clause are most frequently transferred in two directions. The element of Process is transferred as the Thing in a nominal group, while the other elements are realized as the Modifiers and the Qualifiers of the Thing. These patterns of elemental transfer are similar in English and Chinese. However, the structural distance between the metaphorical nominal group and its agnate clause is different in the two languages. This difference of structural distance is most obviously observed by comparing the congruent and metaphorical realizations of figure with one participant. Figure 8.1 illustrates the structural distance between realizations in English and Chinese, with the shift of grammatical functions involved.

Figure 8.1 shows that the three elements in a clause are, respectively, realized as the three constituents in a nominal group. The grammatical

English:

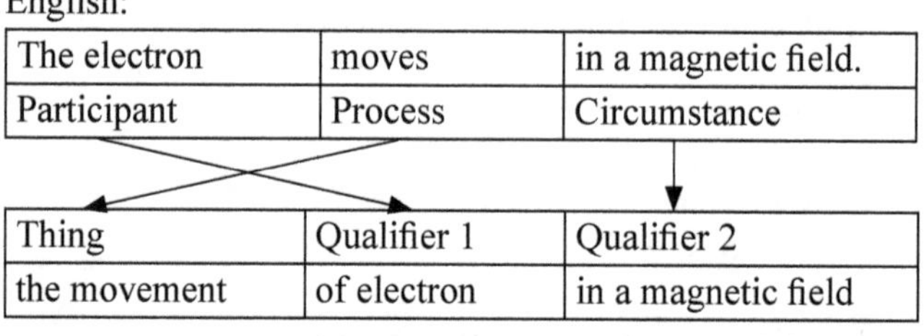

Chinese:

Dianzi electron	*zai cichang zhong* in magnetic field inside	*yundong* move
Participant	Circumstance	Process

Modifier 1	Modifier 2	Thing
dianzi electron	*zai cichang zhong de* in magnetic field inside Sub.	*yundong* movement

Figure 8.1: Structural distance between realizations of figure

constituents in the Chinese clause and nominal group are arranged in the same order. The discussion of constituent ordering in Section 8.2.1 shows that Circumstances precede the Process to be modified in Chinese clauses. Similarly, the Thing in a Chinese nominal group is preceded by its Modifiers. These typological characteristics in Chinese explain the same order of constituents in the clause and nominal group above.

It is also noted that the Process in the clause and the Thing in the nominal group are identical in form because the nominalization of verbs in Chinese is not signaled by a morphological indicator. The Participant in a clause and the Modifier in a nominal group also show formal resemblance for the same reason. With all these structural features, the Chinese clause with one participant is very similar to its metaphorical realization in the form of nominal group. By comparison, the Participant and the Circumstance in the English clause are metaphorically realized as the Qualifiers following the Thing in the nominal group. The grammatical constituents in the clause and the nominal group are also clearly distinguished by their suffixes and the use of determiner.

In the Chinese example, the only structural difference between congruent and metaphorical expressions is the subordinating particle *de* in the nominal group. In many cases, the particle *de* is not used at all. The metaphorical realization without *de* is completely similar to its congruent counterpart in structure, as shown in Example 8.9.

(8.9)	Congruent:	*Yingpan*	*gaosu*	*zhuandong.*	
		hard disk	at a high speed	run	
		'The hard disk runs at a high speed.'			
	Metaphorical:	*yingpan*	*gaosu*	*zhuandong*	(*hui daozhi* ...)
		hard disk	at a high speed	running	(will lead to ...)
		'The high speed running of hard disk			(will lead to ...).'

In sum, the structural distance between the congruent and metaphorical realizations of figure in Chinese is shorter than that in English. This shorter distance is attributable to two factors: the lack of morphological variation and the particular order of grammatical constituents in Chinese.

8.3.1.3 Distance between realizations of sequence

A sequence construed congruently as a clause complex has two forms of metaphorical realization: clause and group. The downranking movement from clause complex to clause is more important in this study due to its higher frequency of occurrence. The reconstrual of sequence as clause is always accompanied by the grammatical movement from clause to nominal group. Thus, the structural distance between clause and nominal group affects the formal difference between the congruent and metaphorical realizations of sequence.

In Chinese, the shorter formal distance between a clause and its agnate nominal group gives rise to the formal similarity between the realizations of sequences. This effect is displayed most clearly by comparing the structure of metaphorical 'favorite clause type' and its congruent clause complex. As the name suggested, this type of metaphorical clause is the most favorite choice in reconstruing clause complexes (see Section 6.4.2.1 for more details). This clause type is featured by its structure of 'nominal group + verb + nominal group'. Contrast the following Chinese expressions with their English translations.

(8.10) Congruent: *Lijü gaibian, zidan fanzhuan.*
moment change bullet overturn
'Because the moment changes, the bullet overturns.'

Metaphorical: *Lijü gaibian daozhi zidan fanzhuan.* [UP1]
moment change lead to bullet overturn
'The change of moment leads to the overturn of bullet.'

The example shows the only difference between the metaphorical clause in Chinese and its congruent clause complex is the use of verb *daozhi*. The other part of the clause is similar to the clause complex in form. This similarity is obviously attributable to the structural similarity between a clause and its nominal group in Chinese. By contrast, the metaphorical and congruent expressions in English show a larger formal distance in the above example.

When a Chinese clause complex is transferred into a clause with circumstance, this formal similarity can be observed again. This situation is represented by Example 8.11.

(8.11a) Congruent: *Wei shiyan chenggong, women zhunbei le yi xilie fangan*
To experiment succeed we design Asp. a series plan
'In order to succeed in the experiment, we designed a series of plans.'

(8.11b) Metaphorical *Wei shiyan de chenggong, women zhunbei le yi xilie fangan.*
For experiment Sub. success we design Asp. a series plan
'For the success of experiment, we designed a series of plans.' [SC2]

The example shows that the formal similarity between the congruent and metaphorical realizations arises from the transfer from the subordinate clause to the Circumstance. Since a Circumstance is in effect constructed by a preposition and a nominal group, the formal similarity is indirectly related to the short structural distance between a clause and its agnate nominal group in Chinese.

The order of grammatical constituents in Chinese also contributes to the short distance between congruent and metaphorical expressions of sequence in the language. In more detail, the principles of locating the primary clause 'backwards' and putting the Circumstance before the Process explain the similar orders of grammatical constituents in Chinese clause and clause complex. In other words, the general tendency of arranging grammatical constituents in terms of semantic importance partially accounts for the formal similarity between the congruent and metaphorical realizations of a sequence in Chinese.

The preceding discussion demonstrates that the formal distance between congruent and metaphorical expressions is shorter in Chinese than in English. This structural difference between the two languages is repeatedly observed in the realizations of element, figure and sequence. More importantly, this difference between Chinese and English is engendered by the typological variations in the two languages. At elemental level, the formal distance between realizations can be explained by appealing to the specificity degrees of morphological system in a language. The specificity of the morphological system, together with the order of grammatical constituents, also determines the formal distance between the realizations of figure. The formal distance between the realizations of sequence is typologically related to the order of grammatical constituents and the distance between a clause and its agnate nominal group. To sum up, the formal distance between congruent and metaphorical expressions is attributable to two typological parameters: the specificity of grammatical systems and the order of grammatical constituents.

8.3.2 Subdivision of GM categories

According to the discussions in Chapters 2 and 5, Chinese and English have similar categories of ideational GM. However, it is noted that the subdivisions of certain GM categories are different in the two languages. These differences are engendered by the structural distinctions of grammatical categories at the rank of group in the two languages. GM categories are concerned with semantic shifts starting from quality, process, circumstance and relator. Since the shifts starting from quality and relator are constructed similarly in English and Chinese, this section only examines the differences between the two languages in the semantic shifts starting from process and circumstance.

8.3.2.1 Shifts starting from process

According to Table 5.3, there are two ideational GM categories involved in the semantic shift starting from process: category 2 (process to thing) and category 5 (process to quality). At group rank, the element process is constructed differently in Chinese and English. These differences inevitably lead to the distinctive subdivision of GM categories 2 and 5 in the two languages. The differences between the subdivisions of these categories are shown in Table 8.1.

GM categories	*Subdivision*	
	English	*Chinese*
2. process thing	Event – Thing	Event – Thing Event + Extension – Thing
	Auxiliary (tense, modality) – Thing	Auxiliary (modality) – Thing
	Catenative – Thing	
5. process - quality	Event – Epithet/Classifier	Event – Epithet/Classifier Event + Extension - Epithet
	Auxiliary (tense, modality) – Epithet/Classifier	Auxiliary (modality) – Epithet/Classifier
	Catenative – Epithet/Classifier	

Table 8.1: Differences within GM Categories 2 and 5

As Table 8.1 illustrates, one difference between Chinese and English in the subdivision of category 2 is the absence of grammatical transfer from Catenative to Thing. This distinction attributes to the different locations of phase meaning along the lexicogrammatical continuums in Chinese and English. The relevant discussion in Section 8.2.3.1 reveals that Chinese construes phase more grammatically by employing a set of postverbs with completive meaning. Since the main verbs in Chinese generally do not imply their completion, the catenative verb is not necessary for the expression of process in the language. For instance, when the verb *jian* 'cut' is used in a Chinese clause, it only construes the phase of attempt. On the contrary, the meaning of a process in English typically includes its completion. Thus, the non-completed meaning in the language must be realized by a conative structure. In other words, the absence of the shift from Catenative to Thing in Chinese arises from the preference for assuming the attempt phase of a process in the language.

Table 8.1 also shows the difference between Chinese and English in the grammatical movement starting from their main verbs. English only has the functional shift from Event to Thing because the main verb in English construes an Event meaning. In Chinese, there are two types of movement from main verb to noun: from Event to Thing and from Event + Extension to Thing. According to the discussion in Section 8.2.3.1, the main verbs in Chinese can be expanded by a set of postverbs which function as Extension. The discussion of Chinese verbal group in Section 8.2.3.2 also shows that the meaning of Event is realized by monosyllabic verbs and polysyllabic verbs with neutral phase. The meaning of Event + Extension is only concerned with the polysyllabic verbs with completive meaning. These characteristics of Chinese verbs inevitably lead to the more complicated grammatical movement starting from main verbs in Chinese, as shown in the cells of Table 8.1. In sum, these differences between Chinese and English in the shifts starting from process arise from the different methods of phase expression in the two languages.

One further difference within category 2 involves the shift starting from Auxiliary, which is related to the less specific temporal system in Chinese. Each process in English must be located somewhere in the construction of tense, while the process in Chinese can be used without consideration of a tense system (see Section 8.2.2). The absence of a tense system in Chinese determines that the Auxiliaries in Chinese only construe the meaning of modality. Therefore, there is no grammatical transfer from Auxiliary with tense meaning to Thing in Chinese. In this case, the scope of grammatical transfer starting from Auxiliary in English is broader than that in Chinese.

All the differences between Chinese and English in GM category 2 are observed within GM category 5. These differences within category 5 also arise from the features of phase and tense expressions in the two languages. With these similarities, the subdivision of GM category 5 is not discussed in detail.

8.3.2.2 Shifts starting from circumstance

The shifts starting from circumstance include three ideational GM categories: category 3 (circumstance to thing), category 6 (circumstance to quality) and category 8 (circumstance to process). The variations between Chinese and English in subdividing these GM categories are mainly engendered by their distinctive constructions of circumstance at group rank. Given the fact that circumstances realized by adverbs are simple in structure, the comparison here focuses on those realized by prepositional phrases. According to the discussion of GM categorization in Chinese (see Section 3.2.3) and the previous research of GM in English (see Halliday and Matthiessen, 1999), the difference between these categories in Chinese and English are illustrated in Table 8.2.

GM categories	*Subdivision*	
	English	*Chinese*
3. Circumstance – Thing	Minor Process – Thing Minor Process + Participant – Thing	Minor Process –Thing Minor Process + Participant – Thing
6. Circumstance – Quality	Minor Process – Epithet/ Classifier Participant – Epithet/ Classifier Minor Process + Participant – Epithet/Classifier	Minor Process – Epithet/ Classifier Participant – Epithet/ Classifier Minor Process + Participant – Epithet/Classifier Participant + Facet - Epithet/Classifier Minor Process + Participant + Facet – Epithet/Classifier
8. Circumstance – Process	Minor Process – Process Minor Process + Participant – Process	Minor Process – Process

Table 8.2: Differences between Categories 6 and 8 in Chinese and English

Table 8.2 shows that GM category 3 involves the same grammatical movements in Chinese and English. The distinctions between the two languages in subdividing semantic shifts starting from circumstance concentrate on categories 6 and 8. These distinctions, as mentioned above, are correlated with the formal difference between Chinese and English in the structure of a prepositional phrase. Halliday (1994) recognizes the preposition and nominal group in an English prepositional phrase as Minor Process and 'indirect' Participant. That is, the prepositional phrase in English has the structure of 'Minor Process + Participant'. The prepositional phrases in Chinese have both the structures of 'Minor Process + Participant' and 'Minor Process + Participant + Facet'. This feature is directly related to the less specific property of certain Chinese prepositions, which has been discussed in Section 8.2.2.

When a Circumstance is metaphorically construed as a quality in English, the Minor Process and the Participant can be transferred individually or in combination. In other words, the shift from circumstance to quality has three subcategories in terms of the element involved. The same GM category in Chinese has more subcategories than that in English because the circumstance with Facet must be considered separately. In more detail, the

Participant and the Facet in a Chinese circumstance are always transferred together. This is because the Chinese noun involved has a mass nature and needs to be specified by the Facet. It is also noted in Table 8.2 that this type of circumstance can be metaphorically reconstrued in two forms: first, the whole prepositional phrase is interpolated into the metaphorical form; second, only the Participant and Facet are transferred. In the first case, the structure of the original circumstance is retained in the metaphorical expression, as shown in the underlined part below.

(8.12)	*Wuti*	*zai*	*zhenkong*	*zhong*	*yundong.*		
	object	in	vacuum	inside	move		
	'An object moves in vacuum.'						
	Wuti	*zai*	*zhenkong*	*zhong*	*de*	*yundong.*	[SP2]
	object	in	vacuum	inside	Sub.	movement	
	'The movement of an object in vacuum.'						

In the other case, the circumstance is adapted as Epithet by deleting *zai* (in), which is illustrated as:

(8.13)	*Wuti*	*zai*	*zhenkong*	*zhong*	*yundong.*		
	object	in	vacuum	inside	move		
	'An object moves in vacuum.'						
	zhenkong	*zhong*	*de*	*wuti*	*yundong*		[SP2]
	vacuum	inside	Sub.	object	movement		
	'the object movement in vacuum'						

These two kinds of treatment result in different forms of metaphorical expressions whose semantic meanings are different at an abstract level.

In category 8, the difference between Chinese and English is the lack of the grammatical transfer from Minor Process + Participant to Process in Chinese. In English, this type of transfer is the result of changing the Participant in circumstance to a Process, which can be exemplified by the change from 'in the box' to 'box' (Halliday and Matthiessen, 1999: 247). In contrast to English, this kind of transformation from noun to verb does not exist in modern Chinese. The different resources for transferring word classes in Chinese and English are closely related to the various specificity degrees of nouns and verbs in the two languages.

The discussion in this section illustrates that certain ideational GM categories in Chinese and English are different in their subdivisions. These differences observed are largely due to variations across the two languages in the degree of grammatical specificity and the location of grammatical realization. Particularly, the differences within categories 2 and 5 can be explained by the distinctive locations of phase domain and specificities of tense system in the two languages. The differences within categories 6 and 8 are engendered by varying specificity degrees of lexical categories in Chinese and English.

8.3.3 Extent of using GM

This section provides some insight into the differences between Chinese and English in the extent of using GM by reference to the findings in relevant studies (Ravelli, 1985; Halliday, 1998). The GM deployment in written Chinese has been examined in Chapter 6 of this study. The information of GM deployment in English is obtained from the study of Ravelli (1985).

Ravelli (1985) analyzes the use of GM in eight English texts for the purpose of exploring the relationship between mode, complexity and GM. The study identifies nine types of GM in English through transitivity analysis. Depending on this categorization, the instances of GM in each text are quantified at micro and macro levels. The quantification at micro level counts the GM instances as individual phenomenon, while the macro level quantification accounts for GM syndromes. Although the distribution of GM categories is not defined in the study, the quantity of each type of GM can be ascertained by counting GM instances in each text. Ravelli (1985) indicates the extent of using GM in a text by the proportion of total GM instances over total number of clauses. She notes that the value of counting GM at the macro level highlights those metaphorical processes which are syntagmatically interdependent. The micro level value, on the other hand, indicates the variation in GM degree across texts.

Chapter 6 investigates the use of GM in Chinese by analyzing data formed by 37 texts from scientific textbooks. GM instances in these texts are recognized according to the actually occurring metaphorical moves between semantic elements. The GM instances recognized in these texts are first quantified in terms of GM category to show the distribution of GM in Chinese. I measure the extent of using GM in each text by following the method developed by Ravelli (1985).

The extent of using GM in Chinese and English is compared by examining the findings in these studies of GM. However, the method of GM categorization adopted in Chapter 6 is different from that in Ravelli's (1985) study. Ravelli (1985: 57) classifies ideational GM into nine types by 'identifying the participants, processes and circumstances of each clause, and determining if the meaning behind the clause is realized congruently or not' (see Table 2.3). In Chapter 6, ideational GM is categorized in accordance with the thirteen types of semantic shift proposed by Halliday (1998). In this case, the comparison of GM deployment in Chinese and English only becomes possible after the findings in the studies are presented in the same framework. This study follows Halliday's (1998) methods of GM categorization in reinterpreting the findings of Ravelli (1985).

The survey of GM categorization in Chapter 2 shows that the models of Halliday (1998) and Ravelli (1985) classify the ideational GM from the same perspective of semantic shift. Ravelli's (1985) model is proposed before the systemic networks for semantics in SFL are developed. The model is inherently similar to Halliday's (1998) method of categorizing GM, although grammatical terms are used to label the semantic choices. In other words, GM categories in Ravelli's (1985) model can be converted into those recognized by Halliday (1998). This conversion is illustrated in Table 8.3.

Ravelli's (1985) Model			*Halliday's (1998) Model*		
Type	*Congruent*	*Metaphorical*	*Type*	*Congruent*	*Metaphorical*
1a-1e	verbal group	nominal group	2	process	thing
2	verbal group	adjective	5	process	quality
3a	adjective	nominal group	1	quality	thing
3b	adverb	adjective	6	circumstance	quality
3c	adverb	nominal group	3	circumstance	thing
4a	modal adverb	adjective	6	circumstance	quality
4b	adjective	nominal group	1	quality	thing
5a	conjunction	nominal group	4	relator	thing
5b	conjunction	verbal group	9	relator	process
6	prep. phrase	verbal group	8	circumstance	process
7a	nominal group	adjective	13	thing	quality
7b	nominal group	nominal group	13	thing	quality
8a	ranking clause	embedded clause			
8b	ranking clause	embedded clause			
9	prep. phrase	adjective	6	circumstance	quality

Table 8.3: Conversion of two models of GM categorization

As Table 8.3 shows, most types of GM in Ravelli's (1985) study have their equivalents in the model of Halliday (1998). Only types 8a and 8b cannot be converted because these grammatical movements are not regarded as GM by Halliday (1998). It is also noted that some types of GM in Halliday's (1998) model is not recognized in the study of Ravelli (1985). These metaphorical expressions first involve GM categories 7 and 10, which generally occur in a very low incidence. In addition, one subtype of category 13 (from Thing to Qualifier) is not treated as metaphorical expression. In this study, the findings of Ravelli (1985) are complemented by including GM instances in these categories. On the other hand, Ravelli (1985) excludes certain types of GM instances in her analysis of GM in English texts, namely, the *frozen*, the *general*, the *taxonomized* and the *technical* GM. The *frozen* and the *general* have been recognized as GM categories 12 and 11 in the framework developed by Halliday (1998). For the purpose of comparison, the *frozen* and *general* GM instances recognized by Ravelli (1985) are also taken into consideration.

The review in Chapter 2 indicates that GM is a mode-oriented resource for organizing text and a field-oriented resource for carrying reasoning and defining terms. In addition, the variable of language development is another significant factor responsible for the variation of GM deployment. For this reason, only part of the English and Chinese texts mentioned above are selected to make them comparable in terms of mode, field and ontogenetic level.

Ravelli (1985) uses four written texts produced in the written medium of book or magazine and four spoken texts transcribed from public speeches in her study. This study only uses the four written texts for the reason that all the Chinese texts in Chapter 6 are in written mode. On the other hand, the English texts used by Ravelli (1985) are writings prepared for adult readers. Chapter 6 analyzes 19 texts representing the scientific writings in university textbooks and 18 texts selected from secondary school textbooks. This study uses the Chinese texts drawn from university textbooks to avoid the possible effect of language development on GM deployment.

As mentioned above, the extent of using GM in a given text is indicated by the proportion of total instances of GM over the number of clauses in that text. To show the general extent of using GM in Chinese and English, this study measures the ratio of the total number of GM instances to the total number of the clauses in the texts involved. The results of this measure are shown in Table 8.4.

	Total number of GM instance	*Total number of clause*	*GM degree (ratio of numbers of GM instances and clauses)*
Chinese	617	434	1.42
English	271	151	1.79

Table 8.4: The general extents of using GM in Chinese and English texts

Table 8.4 shows that the Chinese texts taken from university textbooks have a lower degree of GM than those produced in English books or magazines. It is worth noting that the Chinese texts involved in this comparison are created for the purpose of science teaching. The English texts, on the other hand, are scientific writings for general readers. This study compares the GM deployment in these texts since there has been no quantitative research of GM deployment in English scientific textbooks However, it is reasonable to predict that the difference between Chinese and English texts in GM degree will be greater if more scientific English texts are involved in the comparison. In other words, the result in Table 8.4 implies that the extent of using GM in Chinese is smaller than that in English.

In order to explain the difference between Chinese and English in GM degree, this study compares the deployment of various GM categories in the texts involved. The extent of using a GM category is illustrated by the ratio of GM instances in the category to the total number of clauses. The results of calculation are presented in Table 8.5, given correct to two decimal places.

GM categories	*Chinese texts (434 clauses)*		*English texts (151 clauses)*	
	GM Number	*GM/clause*	*GM Number*	*GM/clause*
1. quality – thing	22	0.05	29	0.19
2. process – thing	205	0.47	112	0.74
3. cir. – thing	12	0.03	9	0.06
4. relator – thing	6	0.01	2	0.01
5. process – quality	62	0.12	17	0.11
6. cir. – quality	119	0.20	49	0.32
7. relator – quality	11	0.02	3	0.02
8. cir. – process	8	0.02	1	0.01
9. relator – process	20	0.04	3	0.02
10. relator – cir.	20	0.04	5	0.03
11. + thing	12	0.03	3	0.02
12. + verb	15	0.05	5	0.03
13. thing – quality	105	0.27	33	0.22
Total	617	1.42	271	1.79

Table 8.5: The extents of using various types of GM in Chinese and English

Table 8.5 shows that Chinese and English texts differ most in the deployment of GM categories 1 and 2. The semantic shift from quality to thing (category 1) in English texts occurs about three times as frequently as that in Chinese texts. The GM instances in GM category 2 (from process to thing) are also used much more frequently in Chinese texts than they are in English texts. In sum, the quantitative differences in categories 1 and 2 across the two languages account for the varied extents of using GM in Chinese and English.

These deployment differences of GM categories are interrelated with the typological distinctions between Chinese and English. The different occurrences of category 1 (from quality to thing) are concerned with the different preferences for construing quality in Chinese and English. Section 8.2.3.3 presents that Chinese tends to assign quality to a thing with the Attribute in an ascriptive clause rather than the Epithet in a nominal group. The GM category 1 in Chinese is thus mainly concerned with the shift from Attribute to Thing. In addition, 'If the quality is to be construed in a nominal group in Chinese, there is a tendency for it first to be constructed into a figure and then deconstructed again in a form of rankshift' (Halliday and Matthiessen, 1999: 305). For example, the Chinese clause '*Nage ren hen pang*' (that man very fat) is normally transferred as the nominal group '*hen pang de ren*' (very fat Sub. man) which means 'a man who is very fat' (Halliday and Matthiessen, 1999). In other words, the Attribute in a Chinese ascriptive clause is less frequently reconstrued as Thing. This characteristic of GM in Chinese is also supported by the quantification of two transferring patterns of ascriptive clause in Section 6.4.1. To sum up, the particular features of quality assignment in Chinese determine that the occurrence of GM category 1 (from quality to thing) is much lower in Chinese than in English.

With respect to the difference in the deployment of category 2, it is related to the structural distinctions of verbal groups in the two languages. The discussions of phase and clause nucleus expansion in section 8.2.3 reveal that there are three types of verbal group in Chinese. Their main constituents and the functional roles of these constituents are described in Table 8.6.

Verbal group	*Constituent*	*Function*
Simple	Monosyllabic verbs and polysyllabic verbs with neutral phase	Event
Compound	Polysyllabic verbs with completive phase	Event + Extension
Complex	Monosyllabic or polysyllabic verbs jointed in logical relation (SVCs)	Event + Event

Table 8.6: Main constituents of verbal groups in Chinese

The discussion of GM category 2 in Section 8.3.2 shows that only the simple and compound verbal groups are involved in the metaphorical realizations of process. The process in the form of SVC cannot be construed metaphorically as a thing. This is mainly because SVCs in Chinese express the logical meaning at group rank (see Section 8.2.3.2). In this case, it is very difficult to transfer two or more than two Events in a complex verbal group into a Thing.

Additionally, Chinese has a tendency to reconstrue the process realized by compound verbal group as Epithet instead of Thing. This tendency is attributable to the difficulty of transferring the functions of Event and

Extension into one Thing. In the following transfer from congruent clause to metaphorical group, the tendency is illustrated by the functional change of verbal group *mai dao* (buy reach).

(8.14) Congruent:	*Ta*	*mai*	*dao*	*le*	*caipiao.*
	he	buy	reach	Asp.	lottery ticket.
	Participant	Process			Participant

'He bought a lottery ticket.'

Metaphorical:	*Ta*	*mai*	*dao*	*de*	*caipiao*
	he	buy	reach	Sub.	lottery ticket
	Epithet	Epithet			Thing

'The lottery ticket he bought'

This is of course not to say that every process realized by a compound verbal group is reworded as quality in constructing GM. The completive verbs in Chinese are divided into the subtypes of directional and resultative, each of which can be further divided according to various criteria. The processes realized by various subcategories of completive verb have different preferences when they are metaphorically construed. The detailed transfer of each subcategory of completive verb in Chinese is not explored due of space constraints.

In the case of simple verbal group, only the proceses realized in the form of polysyllabic verbs can be metaphorically construed as things. For example, the neutral verb *reai* (love) functions as a Thing in the following metaphorical expression.

(8.15) Congruent:	*Wo*	*reai*	*wo*	*de*	*zuguo.*
	I	love	I	Sub.	motherland
	Participant	Process	Participant		

'I love my motherland.'

Metaphorical:	*Wo*	*dui*	*zugou*	*de*	*reai.*
	I	to	motherland	Sub.	love
	Epithet		Epithet		Thing

'My love to motherland'

To summarize, the metaphorical thing in Chinese is mainly realized by the polysyllabic verbs with neutral meanings and certain subcategories of polysyllabic verbs with completive meanings. In other words, the scope of verbs which can be transferred into nouns is relatively smaller in Chinese than in English. This is the inherent reason for the less deployment of GM category 2 in Chinese. The explanation above shows that the varying extents of using GM categories 1 and 2 in Chinese and English are engendered by their different locations of grammatical realizations. In this case, the typological features in Chinese and English also account for the different extents of GM deployment in the two languages.

So far, this section has contrastively analyzed ideational GM in Chinese and English from three points of view. The findings of the analysis can be summarized as follows:

1. Compared to English, Chinese has a shorter formal distance between congruent and metaphorical expressions;
2. Chinese and English are similar in their range of GM categories, but the subdivisions of certain types of GM are different in the two languages; and
3. The general extent of using ideational GM is smaller in Chinese than in English.

More importantly, these differences arise from the typological variations across the two languages. Figure 8.2 summarizes the relations between the typological features and the GM differences discussed in Sections 8.2 and 8.3.

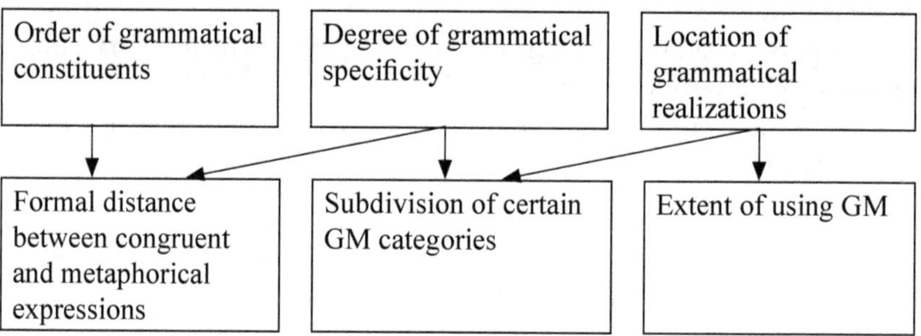

Figure 8.2: Relations between typological features and GM differences

8.4 Summary

The discussion in this chapter centers on three points: the typological features in Chinese and English, the differences between the two languages in ideational GM and the typological interpretation of these GM differences. In order to provide a detailed interpretation of GM differences, the chapter examines the typological variations between Chinese and English from three perspectives. First, the two languages are compared in terms of the order of grammatical constituents in various ranks. The comparison shows that Chinese has a tendency to locate grammatical constituents according to their semantic importance. Second, the two languages are contrastively analyzed from the perspective of grammatical specificity. It is found that many lexical categories and grammatical systems in Chinese have a lower degree of grammatical specificity than those in English. Finally, this chapter examines the location of grammatical realizations to show how the semantic domains of phase, clause nucleus expansion and quality are construed differently in the two languages.

On the basis of the analysis of typological features, the GM differences and their inherent reasons are explored together in this chapter. The exploration of GM differences shows that Chinese and English are different in three aspects of GM, namely structure, categorization and deployment. In terms of GM structure, the two languages are distinguished by the formal distance between congruent and metaphorical expressions. More precisely, the formal distances between the congruent and metaphorical realizations of sequence, figure and element are shorter in Chinese than in English. The distinctions of GM categorization across the two languages concentrate on the subdivision of semantic shifts starting from process and circumstance. Within these GM categories, the metaphorical expressions in Chinese have a more complicated subdivision than those in English. The differences of GM deployment in Chinese and English are investigated by comparing the findings of relevant GM research. It is found that extent of GM use in Chinese is lower than that in English.

The GM differences are inherently engendered by the typological features in Chinese and English. In particular, the differences of GM structure pertain to the order of grammatical constituents and the degree of grammatical specificity. The distinctions of GM categorization are connected with the degree of grammatical specificity and the location of grammatical realizations. The difference of GM deployment is only relevant to the location of grammatical realizations. More generally, the discussion in this chapter shows that the potential of extending meaning through metaphorical expressions varies from language to language. This potential is closely related to the particular typological features of a language.

9 Conclusions and future directions

9.1 Introduction

This chapter brings together the issues discussed in the preceding chapters, summarizing the significant findings of this book. The chapter also discusses the possible implications of the findings and suggests the directions for future research. As explained in Chapter 1, this book is mainly concerned with three research objectives: (1) to provide new insights into GM by analyzing the phenomenon in a language other than English; (2) to explore how GM is recognized, classified and deployed in Chinese; and (3) to show the differences between English and Chinese in GM and the inherent reasons for these differences.

For these purposes, this book conducts a comprehensive research on GM in Chinese which has two methodological features. First, the present research is based on a systemic functional description of the semantic and lexicogrammatical systems in Chinese. This research method ensures that the phenomenon of GM is investigated in the linguistic environment of Chinese. This book thus prevents the possibility of imposing the GM characteristics in English on the GM in Chinese. Second, this book integrates the theoretical analysis and the empirical investigation. Thus, it provides a comprehensive view of the characteristics of GM in Chinese. The main findings and future directions to be summarized are closely related to the research objectives and the methodological features of this study.

9.2 Conclusions

The main body of this book is divided into several chapters which present different findings. Corresponding to the three research objectives, these findings can be outlined from three perspectives: the general theory of GM, the features of GM in Chinese, and the GM differences between Chinese and English.

9.2.1 General theory of GM

This study is undertaken based on the general theory of GM which is applicable to every human language. Conversely, some important findings in the study enrich the general theory of GM. The first theoretical finding of this study comes from the survey of the previous GM research in Chapter 2. The survey shows that GM studies are concerned with four areas, i.e. the exploration of the nature of GM, the categorization of GM, the semogenic research of GM and the contextual research of GM. The exploration of the nature of GM involves the identification of GM, while the semogenic and contextual studies of GM are concerned with the deployment of GM. This study thus claims that the identification, the categorization and the deployment of GM are the three main issues to be considered in GM research. In fact, this study investigates GM in Chinese from these three points of view. Chapters 4 and 5 clarify the identifying and classifying issues of GM in Chinese from a theoretical perspective, while Chapters 6 and 7 explore the GM deployment in Chinese based on an analysis of 'real' texts. The finding of three main issues of GM research points out the directions for further studies in the same field. It is suggested that the research of GM in other languages could be conducted by focusing on how the phenomenon is identified, categorized and deployed.

The literature review in Chapter 2, together with the reexamination of the nature of GM in Chapter 4, illustrates that there are three motifs of GM. They are the realignment between semantics and lexicogrammar, the reliance of GM on transgrammatical semantic domains and the expansion of meaning potential. Among them, the realignment between semantics and lexicogrammar is the main motif and serves as the key criterion for GM identification. In addition, GM relies on the transgrammatical semantic domains and gives rise to the expansion of the meaning potential in a language.

This study shows that the three motifs are features shared by both ideational GM and interpersonal GM. This means that the metaphorical expressions in ideational and interpersonal zones have a common theoretical foundation. This finding provides a theoretical support for the claim that ideational GM and interpersonal GM are the different aspects of the same phenomenon (Halliday and Matthiessen, 2004). In other words, the metaphorical realizations of ideational and interpersonal meanings can be identified according to the same criterion despite the obvious distinctions between them.

Depending on the three motifs of GM, this book describes the remapping relationship between semantics and lexicogrammar in Chinese by examining transgrammatical semantic domains. The metaphorical move is made possible in a language because the transgrammatical semantic domains engender continuity across different ranks of grammatical categories. In other words, transgrammatical semantic domains are the precondition for GM in a language. One finding of this study is thus that the phenomenon of GM can be identified by examining the transgrammatical semantic domains in a language. This finding shows that the examination of transgrammatical domains is a practical and reliable method of GM identification.

In order to investigate the relationship between GM deployment in Chinese and its external environment, this study statistically examines the extent of GM use in text groups different in context of culture and situation and level of language development. I first compare the GM degree in two groups of texts respectively belonging to report and explanation genres. The comparison shows that the extent of GM deployment in the explanation genre is greater than that in report genres. Following this, I compare the extent of GM use in two groups of texts representing the scientific writing in university and secondary school textbooks. The comparison reveals that the extent of GM deployment in the university textbooks is greater than that in the secondary school textbooks. Finally, I examine the use of GM in discourses differ in the register variables of Field and Tenor, demonstrating that the choice of metaphorical expressions is closely related to the role relation between speakers and the topic of conversation. These findings indicate that GM deployment in Chinese is affected by social context and language development.

These findings are valuable with respect to the general theory of GM because they fill the gaps of previous GM studies. The overview of contextual research of GM shows that the relationship between GM and genre has not been investigated in depth. The analysis of GM deployment in different genres thus enhances the contextual understanding of GM. The literature review in Chapter 2 also shows that the developmental period from adolescence to adult were not covered in previous research on the correlation between GM deployment and language development. The comparison of GM deployment in different levels of writing sheds light on the use of GM in this period of language development. The finding of this comparison, together with the observations in other ontogenetic GM research, suggests that GM is a lexicogrammatical resource which is increasingly used in the process of individual language development.

9.2.2 GM in Chinese

This study explores GM in Chinese in accordance with the three main themes of identification, categorization and deployment. Thus, the conclusions concerned with GM in Chinese can be divided into three parts. In terms of identification, an important contribution in this study is the establishment of a complete framework for recognizing GM instances in both ideational and interpersonal metafunctions in Chinese. The framework describes the congruent and metaphorical realizations of semantic units in Chinese by clarifying the grammatical variations involved. In particular, the metaphorical expression of ideational meanings can be recognized by referring to the grammatical variations occurred in downranking movements and the shifts of semantic elements. The instances of interpersonal GM, on the other hand, can be identified by investigating the grammatical variations involved in metaphorical realizations of speech function and modality.

The identification of GM in Chinese is characterized by three lexicogrammatical phenomena in the language. First, the recognition of ideational GM is closely related to the phenomenon of transcategorization. Chinese is featured by its lack of morphological indicators for different word classes. That is, the Chinese words with different grammatical functions are frequently similar in form. This feature determines that the recognition of GM instances is not as clear as that for English. Second, the use of Mood particle in Chinese leads to the particular features of metaphorical realizations of speech functions. One Chinese clause could be used for the expression of different speech functions by adding different particles to its end. Third, the employment of the structures of *shi ... de* and *you ...* distinguishes the metaphorical realizations of modality in Chinese. These structures are in fact a special type of relational clause which extends other types of clauses. However, they are less isolated and cover a broader range of meanings compared to the relational processes used for GM in English.

There are two important findings with respect to the GM categorization in Chinese. The first is that ideational GM and interpersonal GM in Chinese must be classified according to different principles. The literature review shows that ideational GM is characterized by two kinds of grammatical movements: the downranking movement of grammatical categories and the shift between functional elements. This study describes in detail various categories and subcategories of GM in Chinese by referring to these grammatical movements. It is found that there are 13 categories of ideational GM in Chinese which correspond to the 13 shifts between semantic elements. The categorization of interpersonal GM is more complex than that of ideational GM mainly because interpersonal GM does not have a clear pattern of grammatical movement. In this case, this study classifies interpersonal GM in relation to the different types of modality and speech functions in Chinese.

The second finding in the categorization of GM in Chinese is that the subdivision of GM categories is greatly affected by the typological features of the language. In particular, the recognition of ideational GM subcategories is based on the typological structures of various groups or phrases in Chinese. For instance, the structural features of different types of verbal groups in Chinese determine that the GM categories concerned (Categories 2 and 5) must be subdivided by considering the transfers of Auxiliary, Event and Event + Extension.

The identification and categorization of GM in Chinese are interrelated although they are discussed separately in Chapters 4 and 5. The categorization of GM is based on the detailed description of metaphorical realizations, while the correct recognition of each type of metaphorical expressions is guided by the classification of GM. The identification and categorization of GM in Chinese enrich the description and understanding of GM in previous research. More importantly, the metaphorical realizations of various semantic meanings and the GM categories and subcategories presented in this study form a theoretical foundation for further study of GM in Chinese.

This book analyzes a corpus formed by 37 texts to show how ideational GM is deployed in Chinese. By investigating how frequently different categories of GM instances are used, this study obtains a quantitative profile of ideational GM in Chinese. The profile reveals that the 13 GM categories in Chinese show a polarization in term of incidence. Four GM categories are quantitatively predominant in the general deployment of metaphorical expressions in Chinese, while the other nine categories are strikingly low in frequency. The profile also demonstrates that the deployment of GM in Chinese is featured by a preference for *thinginess*, as illustrated by following three points. First, the semantic shift from process to thing is the most pervasive GM category in Chinese. Second, about 38% of the GM instances in Chinese present in the form of nominalization. Third, most GM instances in Chinese occur in the metaphorical construal of figure as a nominal group. All these findings are compatible with what has been found in previous research of GM in English (Ravelli, 1985). This preference for *thinginess* in GM correlates with the fact that the primary motif of ideational GM is the drift towards *thing* (Halliday and Matthiessen, 1999). Considering that things are the most easily taxonomized semantic element, it could be predicted that the preference for *thinginess* is the common feature of GM in any language.

The quantitative profile also illustrates the special features of ideational GM deployment in Chinese. The most salient points are the unexpected low frequency of semantic shift from quality to thing and the high occurrence of semantic shift ending as quality. According to the discussion in Section 6.4, these two points can be explained by the preference for one pattern of ascriptive figure reconstrual and the lack of postmodifier in Chinese. More generally, this study shows that the characteristics of ideational GM distribution in Chinese are engendered by the typological properties of the language.

The investigation of GM syndromes extends and complements the findings in the quantification of GM categories. The observation of ideational GM instances in data demonstrates that most of them occur in the form of clusters. In addition, these GM clusters are identified as seven GM syndromes in Chinese, which center around particular GM categories. These findings support Halliday's (1998) claim that GM tends to occur in syndromes which are driven by controlling types of GM. The quantification of GM syndromes in data reveals the following features of GM deployment in Chinese. First, more than half of the ideational GM instances in data are driven by the GM categories occurring in a low frequency. This finding indicates that the contribution of a GM category to the construction of Chinese texts is not simply determined by its quantity. Second, a larger part of ideational GM instances in the data are involved in the manifestation of logical relations in the forms of clause or nominal group. This observation suggests that the need to encapsulate logical relations in texts acts as an important driving force for metaphorical expressions in Chinese. Third, the higher rank GM syndromes in the data overrun the lower rank ones in terms of the contribution to the general formation of metaphorical expressions. Therefore, the reasoning function is a more important driving force in constructing Chinese texts compared with the taxonomizing function.

Apart from these findings in the exploration of ideational GM distribution, this study quantifies different categories of interpersonal GM instance in a large spoken Chinese corpus. Through the quantification, the study provides information about how different types of interpersonal GM are employed in the negotiation of meaning. It is found that there are systematic patterns of the use of two types of interpersaonl GM, namely metaphor of mood and metaphor of modality. These patterns are complex with each subcategory of interpersonal GM being distributed in accordance with its register variables of Field and Tenor. In particular, the distribution of metaphor of modality is determined by the topic and setting of a spoken discourse. The use of metaphor of mood, on the other hand, is closely related to the social relations between speaker and addressee.

The overall allocation of interpersonal GM in Chinese also emerges from the corpus analysis in Chapter 7. The use of some types of interpersoanl GM in Chinese is found to correlate with the change of modality value. The GM instances with a high value of modality are used less frequently in conversation, while those low in modality value occur with a much higher frequency. This correlation is attributable to the distinction between different types of interpersoanl GM in terms of politeness class. In addition, some features of interpersonal GM deployment in Chinese are engendered by the use of structures of *shi ... de* and *you ...* and Mood particles in the language.

In sum, this study shows that GM deployment in Chinese is not random but determined jointly by the general tendency of GM construction and the particular typological properties of the language. It is worth noting that the analysis of GM deployment in Chinese is based on the identifying and categorizing work of GM in Chinese. In this sense, the analysis of GM deployment is a practical application of the findings in GM identification and categorization.

9.2.3 GM differences between Chinese and English

This book explores the differences between Chinese and English in ideational GM and interprets these differences from a typological perspective. The exploration of GM differences shows that Chinese and English are different in all the three aspects of GM, namely identification, categorization and deployment. In terms of GM identification, the two languages are distinguished by the formal distance between congruent and metaphorical expressions of ideational meanings. More specifically, the formal distances between congruent and metaphorical realizations of sequences, figures and elements are shorter in Chinese than in English. This finding shows that the GM in ideational zone are more accessible to readers of Chinese. However, this shorter distance between realizations increases the difficulty of recognizing the GM instances in Chinese.

The distinctions of ideational GM categorization across the two languages concentrate on the subdivision of semantic shifts starting from process and circumstance. Within these GM categories, GM in Chinese have a more complicated subdivision than those in English. This finding confirms that the subdivision of GM categories is impacted by the structural features of grammatical categories in a language. The differences between Chinese and English in GM deployment are investigated by comparing the findings of previous GM research (Ravelli, 1985). It is found that Chinese has a lower degree of GM deployment than English. This outcome of comparison shows that GM is a lexicogrammatical resource with different extents of deployment in different languages.

Furthermore, this book has shown that the GM differences between Chinese and English are inherently engendered by the typological features of the two languages. The typological features have been described in terms of three variables: (1) the order of grammatical constituents; (2) the degree of grammatical specificity; and (3) the location of grammatical realizations. The GM differences between Chinese and English are attributable to one or more than one typological variable. Specifically, the differences of GM structure are concerned with the order of grammatical constituents and the degree of grammatical specificity. The distinctions of GM categorization can be explained in relation to the degree of grammatical specificity and the location of grammatical realizations. The difference of GM deployment only involves the location of grammatical realizations. These findings suggest that the potential of extending meaning through GM is closely related to the particular typological features of a language. Rather, these findings contribute to the general theory of GM by illustrating that the particular features of GM in a language must be investigated with the consideration of the typological features of the language.

9.3 Future directions

In addition to the findings presented above, this book has its theoretical importance and practical applications in other linguistic fields. Theoretically, the comparison of GM in different languages, especially well-researched languages like English and Chinese, benefits the study of the nature of human language. For instance, this book illustrates the distinctions between Chinese and English in creating and deploying GM. These distinctions provide a window for viewing the essential features of GM across languages. The more insightful understating of GM will in turn facilitate our study of human language because the concept of GM is critical for the comprehension of many linguistic phenomena.

This corpus based study of GM in Chinese also provides quantitative evidence for confirming or refuting the arguments previously advanced in GM research. Halliday and Matthiessen (1999) have the impression that range of types of GM in Chinese is similar to that in English, although they do not conduct a systemic study of GM in the language. This hypothesis is confirmed by the fact that all the 13 types of GM in English are also observed in the data of this study. Halliday and Matthiessen (1999) also propose that 'the scope of GM in technical and other formal written varieties of modern Chinese is about the same as it is in English'. This prediction can be testified based on the results of this study and the research of GM in English (Ravelli 1985).

With respect to practical application, the findings in GM comparison in English and Chinese contribute to the translation between the two languages. As an important method to extend meaning potential in a language, GM is critical for the understanding of both source language and target language. Thus, the successful translation between Chinese and English is partially determined by the correct understanding of GM in the two languages. The role played by GM in meaning expression also accounts for its importance in the teaching of language. The findings in Chapter 8 illustrate the areas to be considered in reducing the difficulty of English speakers in Chinese learning.

The relationship between Theme and GM in Chinese is not explored in this book. Both Theme and GM are key roles in organizing texts and constructing ideational experience. The exploration of the relationship between GM and particular types of Theme, especially the Theme created by thematic bracketing (see Section 3.3.3 for details) and the unmarked Theme would be of great interest. In order to undertake such an exploration, the data collected in this study could be analyzed again in terms of Theme. The relationship between different types of GM and Theme can be defined by quantitatively examining their coincidences. An investigation of the inherent reason for these coincidences will give a more complete picture of the texture and structure in Chinese writings.

The data analysis in Chapter 6 shows that the deployment of GM in Chinese varies in different genres of writing. However, this study focuses on the two general genres of report and explanation. Further studies may be directed to a more comprehensive investigation of the effect of genre on GM deployment, involving a greater number of genres. The data used in this book has to be expanded to include texts from other disciplines for this purpose.

This book presents a first attempt to characterize GM in Chinese on the basis of theoretical analysis and empirical research. However, it is worth noting that there are limitations to the findings. These limitations are related to the fact that both the description of Chinese from a SFL perspective and the research on GM in Chinese are at a preliminary stage. The findings summarized above should be regarded as suggestive more than conclusive for future research in the same field.

References

Anderson, J. M. (1968) Ergative and nominative in English. *Journal of Linguistics* 4 (1): 1–32.

Aikhenvald, A. Y. (2006) Serial verbal construction in typological perspective. In A. Y. Aikhenvald and R.M.W. Dixon (eds) *Serial Verb Constructions: A Cross-linguistic Typology*, 1–67. Oxford: Oxford University Press.

Austin, J. L. (1975) *How to Do Things with Words*. Oxford: Clarendon Press.

Banks, D. (2003) The evolution of grammatical metaphor in scientific writing. In A. Vandenbergen, M. Taverniers and L. Ravelli (eds) *Grammatical Metaphor: Views from Systemic Functional Linguistics*, 127–147. Amsterdam: John Benjamins.

Brown, P. and Levinson, S. C. (1987) *Politeness: Some Universals in Language Usage*. Cambridge: Cambridge University Press.

Chafe, Wallace, L. (1982) Integration and involvement in speaking, writing and oral literature. In D. Tannen (ed.) *Spoken and Written Language: Exploring Orality and Literacy*. Norwood, NJ: Ablex Publishing Corporation.

Chao, Y. (1968) *A Grammar of Spoken Chinese*. Berkeley and Los Angeles, CA: University of California Press.

Chen, Y. P. (2001) *The Use of Grammatical Metaphor by EFL Learners and Their Language Proficiency*. Ph.D. Thesis. National University of Singapore.

Chu, Chauncey C. (1983) *A Reference Grammar of Mandarin Chinese for English Speaker*. New York: Peter Lang

Comrie, B. (1976) *Aspect. Cambridge Textbooks in Linguistics*. Cambridge: Cambridge University Press.

Comrie, B. (1985) *Tense. Cambridge Textbooks in Linguistics*. Cambridge: Cambridge University Press.

Comrie, B. (1989) *Language Universals and Linguistic Typology*. Chicago, IL: University of Chicago Press.

Crowdy, S. (1993) Spoken corpus design. *Literary and Linguistic Computering* 8 (2): 259–265.

Derewianka, B. (1995) *Language Development in the Transition from Childhood to Adolescence: The role of grammatical metaphor*. Ph.D. thesis. Macquarie University

Devito, J. A. (1966) Psychogrammatical factors in oral and written discourse. In S. Eggins (ed.) (1994) *An Introduction to Systemic Functional Linguistics*. New York: Continuum.

Drieman, G. H. J. (1962) Differences between written and spoken languages: an exploratory study. *Acta Psychologica* 20: 36–57, 78–100.

Enc, M. (1991) The semantics of specificity. *Linguistic Inquiry* 22 (1): 1–25.

Eggins, S. (1994) *An Introduction to Systemic Functional Linguistics*. London: Pinter.

Eggins, S. and Slade, D. (1994) *Analyzing Casual Conversation*. London: Continuum.

Fan, W. F. (1999) The cohesive function of grammatical metaphor in the form of nominalization. *Foreign Language Research* 1999 (1): 8–12.

Fang, Y., McDonald, E. and Cheng, M. S. (1995) On theme in Chinese: From clause to discourse. In R. Hasan and P. H. Fries (eds) *On Subject and Theme: A Discourse Functional Perspective,* 235–274. Amsterdam: John Benjamins.

Faraday, M. (1838) Experimental researches in electricity – Thirteenth Series. *Philosophical Transactions of the Royal Society* 128: 125–168.

Fillmore, C. (1968) The case for case. In E. Bach, and R. Harms (eds) *Universals in Linguistic Theory,* 1–90. New York: Holt, Rinehart.

Gamow, G. and Cleveland, J. M. (1976) *Physics: Foundations and Frontiers*. Englewood Cliffs, NJ: Prentice-Hall, Inc.

Greenberg, J. (1966) Some universals of grammar with particular reference to the order of meaningful elements. In J. Greenberg (ed.) *Universals of Language,* 73–113. Cambridge, MA: MIT Press.

Halliday, M. A. K. (1956) Grammatical categories in modern Chinese. In G. R. Kress (ed.) *Halliday: System and Function in Language,* 36–51. Oxford: Oxford University Press.

Halliday, M. A. K. (1975) *Learning How to Mean: Explorations in the Development of Language.* London: Edward Arnold.

Halliday, M. A. K. (1978) *Language as Social Semiotic: The Social Interpretation of Language and Meaning.* London: Edward Arnold.

Halliday, M. A. K. (1984a) Grammatical Metaphor in English and Chinese. In B. Hong (ed.) *New Papers on Chinese Language Use*. Canberra: Australian National University.

Halliday, M. A. K. (1984b) Language as code and language as behaviour: A systemic-functional interpretation of the nature and ontogenesis of dialogue. In R. P. Fawcett, M. A. K. Halliday, S. M. Lamb and A. Makkai (eds) *The Semiotics of Culture and Language,* 3–36. London: Frances Pinter.

Halliday, M. A. K. (1985a) *An Introduction to Functional Grammar.* London: Edward Arnold.

Halliday, M. A. K. (1985b) *Spoken and Written Language*. Geelong Victoria: Deakin University Press.

Halliday, M. A. K. (1988) On the language of physical science. In M. Ghadessy (ed.) *Registers of Written English,* 162–177. London: Pinter Publishers.

Halliday, M. A. K. (1993) Some grammatical problems in scientific English. In: M. A. K. Halliday, and J. R. Martin (eds) *Writing Science: Literacy and Discursive Power,* 69–85. London: Falmer

Halliday, M. A. K. (1994) *An Introduction to Functional Grammar.* London: Edward Arnold.

Halliday, M. A. K. (1998) Things and relations: Regrammaticising experience as technical knowledge. In J. R. Martin and R. Veel (eds) *Reading Science: Critical and Functional Perspectives on Discourses of Science,* 185–236. London: Routledge.

Halliday, M. A. K. (1999) Language and knowledge: The ‘Unpacking’ of text. In D. Allison, L. Wee, Z. M. Bao and S. A. Abraham (eds) *Text in Education and Society,* 157–177. Singapore: Singapore University Press

Halliday, M. A. K. (2003) On language and linguistics. In J. Webster (ed.) *Collected Works of M. A. K. Halliday.* Vol. 4. London: Continuum.

Halliday, M. A. K. and Matthiessen, C. M. I. M. (1999) *Construing Experience through Meaning: A Language-based Approach to Cognition.* London: Cassell.

Halliday, M. A. K. and Matthiessen, C. M. I. M. (2004) *An Introduction to Functional Grammar*. London: Edward Arnold.

Halliday, M. A. K. and McDonald, E. (2004) Metafunctional profile of the grammar of Chinese. In A. Caffarel, J. R. Martin and C. M. I. M. Matthiessen *Language Typology: A Functional Perspective,* 305–396. Amsterdam: John Benjamins.

Hansen, C. (1983) *Language and Logic in Ancient China*. Ann Arbor, MI: The University of Michigan Press

Hu, Z. L. (2004) *Metaphor and Cognition*. Beijing: Peking University Press

Jones, J. (1991) Grammatical metaphor and technicality in academic writing: An exploration of ESL and NS student texts. In F. Christie (ed.) *Literacy in Social Processes: Papers from the Inaugural Australian Systemic Functional Linguistics Conference,* 178-198. Darwin: Centre for Studies of Language in Education Northern Territory University.

Kress, G. (1989) History and language: Towards a social account of linguistic change. *Journal of Pragmatics* 13 (3): 445–466.

Kroll, Barbara. (1977) Combining ideas in written and spoken English. Discourse across time and space, ed. by E. O. Keenan and T. L. Bennett. Southern California Occasional Papers in Linguistics 5: 69–108.

Leech, G. (1991) The state of art in the corpus linguistics. In K. Aijmer and B. Altenberg (eds) *English Corpus Linguistics*, 8–29. London: Longman.

Kubler, C. C. (1985) *A Study of Europeanized Grammar in Modern Written Chinese.* Taipei: Student Book Co. Ltd.

Li, C. and Thompson, S. A. (1981) *Mandarin Chinese: A Functional Reference Grammar.* Berkeley, CA: University of California Press.

Liu, Y. H. and Pan, W. Y. (2004) *A Practical Grammar of Modern Chinese*. Beijing: Commercial Press.

Long, R. J. (1981) *Transitivity in Chinese*. M.A. Thesis. Fisher Library: University of Sydney.

Lü, S. X. (1982) *Zhongguo Wenfa Yaolüe* (An Outline of Chinese Grammars). Shanghai: Commercial Press.

Lyons, J. (1977) *Semantics.* Cambridge: Cambridge University Press.

Martin, J. R. (1992) *English Text: System and Structure.* Amsterdam: John Benjamins.

Martin, J. R. (1993a) Life as a noun: Arresting the universe in science and humanities. In M. A. K. Halliday and J. R. Martin (eds) *Writing Science: Literacy and Discursive Power*, 221–267. London: Falmer.

Martin, J.R. (1993b) Literacy in science: Learning to handle text as technology. In M.A.K. Halliday and J.R. Martin (eds) *Writing Science: Literacy and Discursive Power*, 166–220. London: Falmer.

Martin, J. R., Matthiessen C. M. I. M. and Painter C. (1997) *Working with Functional Grammar*. London: Edward Arnold.

Matthews, S. (2006) On serial verb constructions in Chinese. In A. Y. Aikhenvald and R. M. W. Dixon (eds) *Serial Verb Constructions: A Cross-linguistic Typology,* 69–87. Oxford: Oxford University Press.

Matthiessen, C. M. I. M. (2004) Descriptive motifs and generalizations. In A. Caffarel, J. R. Martin and C. M. I. M. Matthiessen (eds) *Language Typology: A Functional Perspective,* 537–663. Amsterdam: John Benjamins.

McDonald, E. (1992) Outline of a functional grammar of Chinese for Teaching purposes. *Language Sciences* 14 (4): 435–458.

McDonald, E. (2004) Verb and clause in Chinese discourse: Issues of constituency and functionality. *Journal of Chinese Linguistics* 32 (2): 200–247.

Melrose, R. (2003) 'Having things both ways': Grammatical Metaphor in a systemic-functional model of language. In A.-M. Simon-Vandenbergen, M. Taverniers and L. J. Ravelli (eds) *Grammatical Metaphor: Views from Systemic Functional Linguistics,* 417–442. Amsterdam: John Benjamins.

Moon, R. (1997) Vocabulary connections: Multi-word items in English. In N. Schmitt and M. J. McCarthy (eds) *Second Language Vocabulary: Description, Acquisition and Pedagogy,* 40–63. Cambridge University Press.

Newton, I. (1704) *Opticks, or a Treatise of the Reflections Refractions Inflections and Colours of Light*, New York: Dover Publications 1952 (London, G. Bell and Sons, 1931; based on the Fourth Edition, London 1730; originally published 1704).

O'Donnell, R. C. (1974) Syntactic differences between speech and writing. *American Speech* 49 (1/2): 102–110.

O'Halloran, K. L. (2005) *Mathematical Discourse: Language, Symbolism, and Visual Images.* London: Continuum.

Ouyang, X. (1986) *The clause complex in Chinese*. MA Thesis. Fisher Library: University of Sydney

Packard, J. L. (2000) *The Morphology of Chinese: A Linguistic and Cognitive Approach.* Cambridge: Cambridge University Press.

Painter, C. (2003) The use of a metaphorical mode of meaning in early language development. In A.-M. Simon-Vandenbergen, M. Taverniers and L. J. Ravelli (eds) *Grammatical Metaphor: Views from Systemic Functional Linguistics,* 151–168. Amsterdam: John Benjamins.

Palmer, F. R. (1994) *Grammatical Roles and Relation.* Cambridge: Cambridge University Press.

Palmer, F. R. (2001) *Mood and Modality.* Cambridge: Cambridge University Press.

Ravelli, L. (1985) *Metaphor, Mode and Complexity: An Exploration of Co-varying Patterns.* BA Dissertation. University of Sydney.

Ravelli, L. (2003) Integrating theory and practice in an understanding of Grammatical Metaphor. In A.-M. Simon-Vandenbergen, M. Taverniers and L. J. Ravelli (eds) *Grammatical Metaphor: Views from Systemic Functional Linguistics,* 37–65. Amsterdam: John Benjamins.

Rundell, M. (1995) The BNC: A spoken corpus. *Modern English Teacher* 4 (2): 13–15.

Sacks, H., Schegloff, E. and Jefferson, G. (1974) A simplest systematics for the organization of turntaking for conversation. *Language* 50 (4): 696–735.

Saussure, F. de (1959/1966) *Course in General Linguistics* (C. Bally and A. Sechehaye, eds). New York: McGraw-Hill.

Schonell, F., Meddleton, I., Shaw, B., Routh, M., Popham, D., Gill, G., Mackrell, G. and Stephens, C. (1956) *A Study of the Oral Vocabulary of Adults*. Brisbane: University of London Press.

Shi, Y. and Li. C. (2001) *A History of Grammaticalization in Chinese: Motivations and Mechanisms of Evolution of Chinese Morpho-syntax.* Beijing: Beijing University Press.

Shum, S. (2003) *The Functions of Language and the Teaching of Chinese*. Hong Kong: Hong Kong University Press.

Svartvik, J. (1990) *The London-Lund Corpus of Spoken English: Description and Research*. Lund: Lund University Press.

Tam, M. (1979) *A Grammatical Description of Transitivity in Mandarin Chinese with Special Reference to Correspondences with English Based on a Study of Texts in Translation*. PhD Thesis. University of London.

Taverniers, M. (2003) Grammatical Metaphor in SFL. In A.-M. Simon-Vandenbergen, M. Taverniers and L. J. Ravelli (eds) *Grammatical Metaphor: Views from Systemic Functional Linguistics*, 5–33. Amsterdam: John Benjamins.

Thompson, G. (1996) *Introducing Functional Grammar.* London: Edward Arnold.

Thibault, P. J. (1991) Grammar, technocracy and the noun: Technocratic values and cognitive linguistics. In E. Ventola (ed.) *Functional and Systemic Linguistics: Approaches and Uses*, 281–305. Berlin: Mouton de Gruyter.

Torr. J. and Simpson A. (2003) The emergence of grammatical metaphor: Literacy-oriented expressions in the everyday speech of young children. In A.-M. Simon-Vandenbergen, M. Taverniers and L. J. Ravelli (eds) *Grammatical Metaphor: Views from Systemic Functional Linguistics*, 169–183. Amsterdam: Benjamins.

Tsang, C. L. (1981) *A Semantic Study of Modal Auxiliary Verbs in Chinese*. PhD Thesis. Stanford University.

Tsao, F. U. (1979) *A Functional Study of Topic in Chinese: First Step Towards Discourse Analysis.* Taipei: Student Book Co.

Tsao, F. U. (1990) *Sentence and Clause Structure in Chinese: A Functional Perspective.* Taipei: Student Book Co.

Tsung, T. H. (1986) *Circumstantial Elements in Chinese*. MA Thesis. Fisher Library: University of Sydney.

Veel, R. (1997) Learning how to mean – scientifically speaking: Apprenticeship into scientific discourse in the secondary school. In F. Christie and J. R. Martin (eds) *Genre and Institutions: Social Processes in the Workplace and School*. New York: Cassell.

Wang, L. (1956) *Zhongguo Xiandai Yufa (Modern Chinese Grammar)*. Shanghai: Commercial Press.

Zhou, X. K. (1997) *Material and Relational Transitivity in Chinese*. Ph.D. Thesis. University of Melbourne.

Zhu, D. X. (1982) *Yufa Jiangyi*. (lectures notes on grammar.) Beijing: Commercial Press.

Zhu, Y. S. (1996) Modality and Modulation in Chinese. In M. Berry, C. Bulter and R. Fawcett (eds) *Meaning and Form: Systemic Functional Interpretations*. Norwood, NJ: Ablex Publishing Corporation.

Index

www.ingramcontent.com/pod-product-compliance
Lightning Source LLC
LaVergne TN
LVHW021126110826
R19582500001B/R195825PG844660LVX00006B/9
* 9 7 8 1 7 8 1 7 9 1 0 2 8 *